DEATH OF THE LIBERAL CLASS

Also by Chris Hedges

War Is a Force That Gives Us Meaning (2002)

What Every Person Should Know About War (2003)

Losing Moses on the Freeway (2005)

American Fascists (2007)

I Don't Believe in Atheists (2008)

Collateral Damage (2008)

Empire of Illusion (2009)

Death of the Liberal Class

CHRIS HEDGES

NATION
BOOKS
New York

Nation Books
New York
www.nationbooks.org
Copyright © 2010 by Chris Hedges
Published by Nation Books, A Member of the Perseus Books Group
116 East 16th Street, 8th Floor
New York, NY 10003

Nation Books is a co-publishing venture of the Nation Institute and the
Perseus Books Group

Books published by Nation Books are available at special discounts for bulk
purchases in the United States by corporations, institutions, and other
organizations. For more information, please contact the Special Markets
Department at the Perseus Books Group, 2300 Chestnut Street, Suite 200,
Philadelphia, PA 19103, or call (800) 810-4145, extension 5000, or e-mail
special.markets@perseusbooks.com.

Editorial production by the Book Factory.

Library of Congress Cataloging-in-Publication Data
Hedges, Chris.
Death of the liberal class / Chris Hedges.
p. cm.
Includes bibliographical references and index.
ISBN 978-1-56858-644-1 (alk. paper)
1. Liberalism—United States. 2. Political culture—United States. I. Hedges,
Chris. Title.
JC574.2.U6H43 2010
320.510973—dc22
2010032916

10 9 8 7 6 5 4 3 2 1

For Eunice,
Tv mihi cvrarvm reqvies, tv nocte vel atra lvmen,
et in solis tv mihi tvrba locis.

At any given moment there is an orthodoxy, a body of ideas which it is assumed that all right-thinking people will accept without question. It is not exactly forbidden to say this, that or the other, but it is "not done" to say it, just as in mid-Victorian times it was "not done" to mention trousers in the presence of a lady. Anyone who challenges the prevailing orthodoxy finds himself silenced with surprising effectiveness. A genuinely unfashionable opinion is almost never given a fair hearing, either in the popular press or in the highbrow periodicals.

—GEORGE ORWELL, *"Freedom of the Press"*[1]

Contents

I
Resistance 1

II
Permanent War 19

III
Dismantling the Liberal Class 59

IV
Politics as Spectacle 109

V
Liberal Defectors 141

VI
Rebellion 193

Notes 219

Acknowledgments 227

Bibliography 229

Index 235

I / Resistance

To allow the market mechanism to be sole director of the fate of human beings and their natural environment, indeed, even of the amount and use of purchasing power, would result in the demolition of society. For the alleged commodity "labor power" cannot be shoved about, used indiscriminately, or even left unused, without affecting the human individual who happens to be the bearer of this peculiar commodity. In disposing of a man's labor power the system would, incidentally, dispose of the physical, psychological, and moral entity of "man" attached to the tag. Robbed of the protective covering of cultural institutions, human beings would perish from the effects of social exposure; they would die as the victims of acute social dislocation through vice, perversion, crime, and starvation. Nature would be reduced to its elements, neighborhoods and landscapes defiled, rivers polluted, military safety jeopardized, the power to produce food and raw material destroyed.

—KARL POLANYI, *The Great Transformation*[1]

ERNEST LOGAN BELL, an unemployed twenty-five-year-old Marine Corps veteran, walks along Route 12 in Upstate New York. A large American flag is strapped to the side of his green backpack. There is a light drizzle and he is wearing a green Army poncho. Short, muscular, and affable, with his brown hair in a close military crop, Bell tells me when I stop my car that he is on a six-day, ninety-mile, self-styled "Liberty Walk" from Binghamton to Utica. He plans to mount a quixotic campaign to challenge Democratic incumbent Rep.

Michael Arcuri in the 24th Congressional District as the Republican candidate. Bell has camped out along the road for three nights and stayed in cheap motels the other nights. He opposes the health-care bill recently passed by the Democratic-majority Congress, calls for an end to the wars in Iraq and Afghanistan, advocates the abolishment of the Federal Reserve, is against the Federal Government's Wall Street bailouts, and wants to see immediate government relief for workers, including himself, trapped in prolonged unemployment. He carries a handwritten sign: "End the Fed," echoing the title of a book by U.S. Representative Ron Paul he keeps in his backpack, along with a copy of *U.S. Constitution for Dummies* by Michael Arnheim. He says he plans to deliver Paul's book to Arcuri's office in Utica.

"I just walked through the town of Norwich," he says as a car passes and the driver honks in support, "and there is a strong Tea Party movement there":

> The Tea Party movement, for the most part, is just a bunch of disgruntled Americans. They know something is wrong and they are ready to be engaged. A lot of the people in my area who are in the Tea Party are Democrats. People are confused. They are shell-shocked. They don't know what to think. But acting like these problems started January 20 [the date of the presidential inauguration] is absurd. To single out the current president and not the presidents before him is not productive for trying to figure out what is going on.[2]

Bell, who lives in Lansing, New York, is the new face of resistance. He is young, at home in the culture of the military, deeply suspicious of the Federal Government, dismissive of the liberal class, unable to find work, and angry. He swings between right-wing and left-wing populism, expressing admiration for both Paul and U.S. Representative Dennis Kucinich, as well as the Tea Party movement. He started out as a supporter of John McCain in the last presidential election but soured on the Arizona senator and the Republican Party's ties to Wall Street. He ended up not voting in that election. He has raised about $1,000 from neighbors and friends for his own campaign. Adept at martial arts, he made it to the semifinals of the 2010 Army National Guard Combative Championship at Fort Benning in Georgia, where, in his last bout, he suffered a broken nose, bruised his opponent's ribs and thighs, and lost in a split decision.

"I am truly terrified when I think about our future," he says:

I believe all signs point to a real systemic economic collapse in the near future, maybe even before the midterm elections. I believe this is why many incumbents are stepping down. They seem to know what is coming and of course the rats are jumping ship and taking their pensions with them. There will be nothing the government or the Fed can do to slow the pain, no more tricks in the bag. I assure you it's going to hurt everyone, except of course, the corporate and banking elite. I say let the empire collapse; sometimes we must die to be reborn. The political system as it stands offers little hope for influencing real change or social justice. I propose we attempt to reverse this coup d'état by attempting a coup of our own. First, we must try to retake the traditional means of control, power and discourse by restoring integrity to our sold-out democratic election system. Unfortunately, this will probably do little good but it is a worthy effort. It is our patriotic duty to resist tyranny. We must break these chains of oppression and restore our government to principles based on liberty and justice for all. I am not confident that standing outside buildings with signs is going to provide any fundamental power shifts, as power is not often transferred without a struggle. Inalienable rights are not a courtesy of the Federal Government. We must stand in the streets and refuse to be silenced. We must reject corporate-controlled politics and focus on rebuilding a localized political structure and society. A revolution is the only alternative to complete surrender and defeat. Cold, hard suffering and pain will be the only hope for a real revolution, and this is all but guaranteed. At this point protest must be transformed into acts of defiance. We must be bold.

Bell grew up in Oakwood, a small town in East Texas between Dallas and Houston. His father struggled with alcoholism and is now in recovery. His parents, who frequently fought, separated, and reunited, divorced when Bell was thirteen. His mother was left to raise Bell, along with his younger brother (currently in the Army's 82nd Airborne Division) and his younger sister in a one-bedroom apartment. There was little money, and his mother worked sporadically at odd jobs. There were eighteen people in his high-school graduating class. With few jobs in Oakwood, Bell, along with several of his classmates, joined the military.

"My father worked two jobs to support us; he suffered from the disease of alcoholism but is a good guy and tried to be supportive father," Bell says:

> My mom had her own set of problems. She is now living in a one-room shack. She had breast cancer four years ago and has no insurance and is living in poverty. I know the system is not working. She lives at the little house, a one-bedroom cabin on her mother's land, where me and my brother lived off and on when my parents were arguing. We lived in several different houses and apartments with both my mom and dad. I left home when I was seventeen, drifting between friends' houses, then moved back to Oakwood, where I finished high school, living with my grandparents, who had a profound effect on my life and values. My life was inconsistent, chaotic, and working-class. I believe this environment helped develop my character and perspective. I have to give credit where it's due. My dad tried.

"You couldn't stay in Oakwood, Texas, and have a job," he adds.

Bell moved to upstate New York two years ago after leaving the Marine Corps to be near Shianne, his three-year-old daughter. He and the girl's mother are separated. Bell found work as a carpenter with a traveling construction crew. He earned $14.50 an hour and could sometimes make as much as $800 a week. Then the financial meltdown knocked the wind out of the local economy.

"Everybody in my apartment building has had their hours cut, are unemployed, or have taken minimum-wage jobs," he says. "I was laid off last year. I try to find work as an independent carpenter. I don't have health insurance."

The dearth of work, which left him attempting to survive at times on $600 a month, saw him enlist last year in the New York National Guard, even though it means almost certain deployment to Afghanistan. The enticement of a $20,000 signing bonus was too lucrative to pass up. The National Guard unit he joined recently returned from a tour in Afghanistan.

"We are training to go back to Afghanistan," he says. "The fact that they are still using Army National Guard, state-level troops, to police the streets of Afghanistan is not good. These units are really overstretched. We do not get the benefits. We don't get health insurance like active-duty military. But the guard gets deployed just as much. Some of these guys have been on three and four tours.

"I got out of the Marine Corps and went back to Texas for ten months and was involved in the John McCain campaign," he says:

I really got disillusioned with the neoconservatism. I had never been involved in politics. The idea that we needed all these troops all around the world "defending freedom," as they called it, when we were actually engaged in nation-building and supporting special interests that drive these wars, was something I began to understand. As far as foreign and economic policy, I could see there was no difference between the two main political parties. There is a false left/right paradigm which diverts the working class from the real reasons for their hardships.

"The winters [in New York State] are really hard," Bell says:

There are less jobs and the heating costs are high. I pay about $200 a month for electric and gas. I live really cheaply. I don't have cable. I don't go out or spend money that is not necessary. It is a struggle. But at least I have not had to devote forty hours a week to a minimum-wage job that does not pay me a living wage. People here are really hurting. The real underemployment rate must be at least twenty percent. A lot of people are working part-time jobs when they want full-time jobs. There are many people like me, independent contractors and small business owners, who can't file for unemployment insurance. Unemployment [coverage] is not available to me because I worked as a 1099, a self-employed contractor, even when I worked for the construction company.

"People are scared," he says. "They want to live their lives, raise their children, and be happy. This is not possible. They don't know if they can make their next mortgage payment. They see their standard of living going down."

Bell says he and those around him are being pushed off the edge. He says he fears the social and political repercussions.

"I hope there is a populist revolution," he says:

> We have to take the corporate bailouts and the money we are sending overseas and use that money in our communities. If this does not happen there will be more anger and eventually violence. When people lose everything they start to lose it. When you can't find a job, even though you look repeatedly, it leads to things like random shootings and suicides. We will see acts of domestic terrorism. The state will erode more of our civil liberties to control mass protests. We are seeing some student protests, but we will see these on a wider scale. I hope the protests will be constructive. I hope people will not resort to extreme measures. But people will do what they have to do to survive. This may mean things like food riots. The political establishment better work very fast to take the pressure off.

Anger and a sense of betrayal: these are what Ernest Logan Bell and tens of millions of other disenfranchised workers express. These emotions spring from the failure of the liberal class over the past three decades to protect the minimal interests of the working and middle class as corporations dismantled the democratic state, decimated the manufacturing sector, looted the U.S. Treasury, waged imperial wars that can neither be afforded nor won, and gutted the basic laws that protected the interests of ordinary citizens. Yet the liberal class continues to speak in the prim and obsolete language of policies and issues. It refuses to defy the corporate assault. A virulent right wing, for this reason, captures and expresses the legitimate rage articulated by the disenfranchised. And the liberal class has become obsolete even as it clings to its positions of privilege within liberal institutions.

Classical liberalism was formulated largely as a response to the dissolution of feudalism and church authoritarianism. It argued for noninterference or independence under the rule of law. It incorporates a few aspects of ancient Athenian philosophy as expressed by Pericles and the Sophists, but was a philosophical system that marked a radical rupture with both Aristotelian thought and medieval theology. Classical liberalism has, the philosopher John Gray writes,

> four principle features, or perspectives, which give it a recognizable identity: it is individualist, in that it asserts the moral primacy of the person against any collectivity; egalitarian, in that it confers on all human beings the same basic moral status; universalist, affirming the moral unity of the species; and meliorist, in that it asserts the open-ended improvability, by use of critical reason, of human life.[3]

Thomas Hobbes (1588–1679), John Locke (1632–1704), and Baruch Spinoza (1632–1677) laid the foundations for classical liberalism. The work of these theorists was expanded in the eighteenth century by the Scottish moral philosophers, the French *philosophes,* and the early architects of American democracy. The philosopher John Stuart Mill (1806–1873) redefined liberalism in the nineteenth century to call for the redistribution of wealth and the promotion of the welfare state.

The liberal era, which flourished in the later part of the nineteenth century and the early years of the twentieth, was characterized by the growth of mass movements and social reforms that addressed working conditions in factories, the organizing of labor unions, women's rights, universal education, housing for the poor, public health campaigns, and socialism. This liberal era effectively ended with World War I. The war, which shattered liberal optimism about the inevitability of human progress, also consolidated state and corporate control over economic, political, cultural, and social affairs. It created mass culture, fostered through the consumer society the cult of the self, led the nation into an era of permanent war, and used fear and mass propaganda to cow citizens and silence independent and radical voices within the liberal class. Franklin Delano Roosevelt's New Deal, put in place only when the capitalist system collapsed, was the final political gasp of classical liberalism in the United States. The New Deal reforms, however, were systematically dismantled in the years after World War II, often with the assistance of the liberal class.

A mutant outgrowth of the liberal class, one that embraced a fervent anticommunism and saw national security as the highest priority, emerged after World War I in the United States. It was characterized by a deep pessimism about human nature and found its ideological roots in moral philosophers such as the Christian realist Reinhold Niebuhr, although Niebuhr was frequently misinterpreted and oversimplified by those seeking to justify political passivity and imperial adventurism. This brand of liberalism, fearful of being seen as soft on communism, struggled to find its place in contemporary culture as its stated value systems became increasingly at odds with increased state control, the disempowerment of workers, and the growth of a massive military-industrial complex. By the time Cold War liberalism shifted into a liberal embrace of globalization, imperial expansion, and unfettered capitalism, the ideals that were part of classical liberalism no longer characterized the liberal class.

What endures is not the fact of democratic liberalism but the myth of it. The myth is used by corporate power elites and their apologists to justify the subjugation and manipulation of other nations in the name of national self-interest and democratic values. Political theorists such as Samuel Huntington wrote about the carcass of democratic liberalism as if it was a vibrant philosophical, political, and social force that could be exported abroad, often by force, to those they deem less civilized. The liberal class, cornered and weak, engaged in the politically safe game of attacking the barbarism of communism—and, later, Islamic militancy—rather than attempting to fight the mounting injustices and structural abuses of the corporate state.

The anemic liberal class continues to assert, despite ample evidence to the contrary, that human freedom and equality can be achieved through the charade of electoral politics and constitutional reform. It refuses to acknowledge the corporate domination of traditional democratic channels for ensuring broad participatory power. Law has become, perhaps, the last idealistic refuge of the liberal class. Liberals, while despairing of legislative bodies and the lack of genuine debate in political campaigns, retain a naïve faith in law as an effective vehicle for reform. They retain this faith despite a manipulation of the legal system by corporate power that is as flagrant as the corporate manipulation of electoral politics and legislative deliberation. Laws passed by Congress, for example, deregulated the economy and turned it over to speculators. Laws permitted the pillaging of the U.S. Treasury on behalf of Wall Street. Laws have suspended vital civil liberties including habeas corpus and permit the president to authorize the assassination of U.S. citizens deemed complicit in terror. The Supreme Court, overturning legal precedent, ended the recount in the 2000 Florida presidential election and anointed George W. Bush as president.

"A decayed and frightened liberalism," as C. Wright Mills put it, was disarmed by "the insecure and ruthless fury of political gangsters." The liberal class, found it was more prudent to engage in empty moral posturing than confront the power elite. "It is much safer to celebrate civil liberties than to defend them, and it is much safer to defend them as a formal right than use them in a politically effective way. Even those who would most willingly subvert these liberties, usually do so in their very name," Mills wrote. "It is easier still to defend someone else's right to have used them years ago than to have something yourself to say *now* and to say it now forcibly. The defense of civil liberties—even of their practice a decade ago—has become the major concern of many liberal and once leftward scholars. All of which is a safe way of diverting intellectual effort from the sphere of political reflection and demand."[4]

In a traditional democracy, the liberal class functions as a safety valve. It makes piecemeal and incremental reform possible. It offers hope for change and proposes gradual steps toward greater equality. It endows the state and the mechanisms of power with virtue. It also serves as an attack dog that discredits radical social movements, making the liberal class a useful component within the power elite.

But the assault by the corporate state on the democratic state has claimed the liberal class as one of its victims. Corporate power forgot that the liberal class, when it functions, gives legitimacy to the power elite. And reducing the liberal class to courtiers or mandarins, who have nothing to offer but empty rhetoric, shuts off this safety valve and forces discontent to find other outlets that often end in violence.

The inability of the liberal class to acknowledge that corporations have wrested power from the hands of citizens, that the Constitution and its guarantees of personal liberty have become irrelevant, and that the phrase *consent of the governed* is meaningless, has left it speaking and acting in ways that no longer correspond to reality. It has lent its voice to hollow acts of political theater, and the pretense that democratic debate and choice continue to exist.

The liberal class refuses to recognize the obvious because it does not want to lose its comfortable and often well-paid perch. Churches and universities—in elite schools such as Princeton, professors can earn $180,000 a year—enjoy tax-exempt status as long as they refrain from overt political critiques. Labor leaders make lavish salaries and are considered junior partners within corporate capitalism as long as they do not speak in the language of class struggle. Politicians, like generals, are loyal to the demands of the corporate state in power and retire to become millionaires as lobbyists or corporate managers. Artists who use their talents to foster the myths and illusions that bombard our society live comfortably in the Hollywood Hills.

The media, the church, the university, the Democratic Party, the arts, and labor unions—the pillars of the liberal class—have been bought off with corporate money and promises of scraps tossed to them by the narrow circles of power. Journalists, who prize access to the powerful more than they prize truth, report lies and propaganda to propel us into a war in Iraq. Many of these same journalists assured us it was prudent to entrust our life savings to a financial system run by speculators and thieves. Those life savings were gutted. The media, catering to corporate advertisers and sponsors, at the same time renders invisible whole sections of the population whose misery, poverty, and grievances should be the principle focus of journalism.

In the name of tolerance—a word the Rev. Dr. Martin Luther King Jr., never used—the liberal church and the synagogue refuse to denounce Christian heretics who acculturate the Christian religion with the worst aspects of consumerism, nationalism, greed, imperial hubris, violence, and bigotry. These institutions accept globalization and unfettered capitalism as natural law. Liberal religious institutions, which should concern themselves with justice, embrace a cloying personal piety expressed in a how-is-it-with-me kind of spirituality and small, self-righteous acts of publicly conspicuous charity. Years spent in seminary or rabbinical schools, years devoted to the study of ethics, justice, and morality, prove useless when it comes time to stand up to corporate forces that usurp religious and moral language for financial and political gain.

Universities no longer train students to think critically, to examine and critique systems of power and cultural and political assumptions, to ask the broad questions of meaning and morality once sustained by the humanities. These institutions have transformed themselves into vocational schools. They have become breeding grounds for systems managers trained to serve the corporate state. In a Faustian bargain with corporate power, many of these universities have swelled their endowments and the budgets of many of their departments with billions in corporate and government dollars. College presidents, paid enormous salaries as if they were the heads of corporations, are judged almost solely on their ability to raise money. In return, these universities, like the media and religious institutions, not only remain silent about corporate power but also condemn as "political" all within their walls who question corporate malfeasance and the excesses of unfettered capitalism.

Unions, organizations formerly steeped in the doctrine of class struggle and filled with members who sought broad social and political rights for the working class, have been transformed into domesticated negotiators with the capitalist class. Cars rolling off the Ford plants in Michigan were said to be made by UAW Ford. But where unions still exist, they have been reduced to simple bartering tools, if that. The social demands of unions in the early twentieth century that gave the working class weekends off, the right to strike, the eight-hour workday, and Social Security, have been abandoned. Universities, especially in political science and economics departments, parrot the discredited ideology of unregulated capitalism and have no new ideas. The arts, just as hungry as the media or the academy for corporate money and sponsorship, refuse to address the social and economic disparities that create suffering for tens of millions of citizens. Commercial artists peddle the mythical narrative, one propagated by corporations, self-help gurus, Oprah and the Christian Right, that if we dig deep enough within ourselves, focus on happiness, find our inner strength, or believe in miracles, we can have everything we desire.

Such magical thinking, a staple of the entertainment industry, blinds citizens to corporate structures that have made it impossible for families to lift themselves out of poverty or live with dignity. But perhaps the worst offender within the liberal class is the Democratic Party.

The party consciously sold out the working class for corporate money. Bill Clinton, who argued that labor had nowhere else to go, in 1994 passed the North American Free Trade Agreement (NAFTA), which betrayed the working class. He went on to destroy welfare and in 1999 ripped down the firewalls between commercial and investment banks to turn the banking system over to speculators. Barack Obama, who raised more than $600 million to run for president, most of it from corporations, has served corporate interests as assiduously as his party. He has continued the looting of the U.S. Treasury by corporations, refused to help the millions of Americans who have lost their homes because of bank repossessions or foreclosures, and has failed to address the misery of our permanent class of unemployed.

Populations will endure the repression of tyrants, as long as these rulers continue to manage and wield power effectively. But human history has demonstrated that once those in positions of power become redundant and impotent, yet insist on retaining the trappings and privileges of power, their subject populations will brutally discard them. Such a fate awaits the liberal class, which insists on clinging to its positions of privilege while at the same time refusing to play its traditional role within the democratic state. The liberal class has become a useless and despised appendage of corporate power. And as corporate power pollutes and poisons the ecosystem and propels us into a world where there will be only masters and serfs, the liberal class, which serves no purpose in the new configuration, is being abandoned and discarded. The death of the liberal class means there is no check to a corporate apparatus designed to enrich a tiny elite and plunder the nation. An ineffectual liberal class means there is no hope, however remote, of a correction or a reversal. It ensures that the frustration and anger among the working and middle classes will find expression outside the confines of democratic institutions and the civilities of a liberal democracy.

In killing off the liberal class, the corporate state, in its zealous pursuit of profit, has killed off its most integral and important partner. The liberal class once ensured that restive citizens could settle for moderate reforms. The corporate state, by shutting down reform mechanisms, has created a closed system defined by polarization, gridlock, and political theater. It has removed the veneer of virtue and goodness provided by the liberal class. The collapse of past constitutional states, whether in Weimar Germany or the former Yugoslavia, was also presaged by the death of the liberal class. The loss of the liberal class creates a power vacuum filled by speculators, war profiteers, gangsters, and killers, often led by charismatic demagogues. It opens the door to totalitarian movements that rise to prominence by ridiculing and taunting the liberal class and the values it claims to champion. The promises of these totalitarian movements are fantastic and unrealistic, but their critiques of the liberal class are grounded in truth.

Liberals have also historically discredited radicals within American society who have defied corporate capitalism and continued to speak the language of class warfare. The fate of the liberal class is tragic. It has been annihilated by the corporate state it supported, while it willingly silenced radical thinkers and iconoclasts who could have rescued it. By refusing to question the utopian promises of unfettered capitalism and globalization, and by condemning those who did, the liberal class severed itself from the roots of creative and bold thought, from the only forces that could have prevented it from being subsumed completely by the power elite. It was at once betrayed and betrayed itself.

The death of the liberal class means a new and terrifying political configuration. It permits the corporate state to demolish, without impediment, the last vestiges of protection put into place by the liberal class. Employees in public-sector unions—one of the last havens from the onslaught of the corporate state—are denounced for holding "Cadillac health plans" and generous retirement benefits. Teachers' unions in California and New Jersey are attacked by corporate pundits and politicians who portray teachers as parasites thriving at taxpayer expense. The establishment of charter schools will help hasten the extinction of these unions. The increasing restrictions imposed on public-sector employees, despite their ostensible union protection, are draconian and illustrate the corporate state's final attack on unionized workers. In turn, labor organizations (for the diminishing number of workers who still have unions) facilitate the disempowerment and impoverishment of workers. In April 2009, teachers at the Renaissance Charter School in Jackson Heights, New York, saw lawmakers cut their budgets by some $600,000 a year. Union representatives not only were powerless to halt the ruling, but also failed to warn the teachers about it. A contract passed in the West Contra Costa Unified School District in Richmond, California, in December 2009 summarily increased class sizes, froze teachers' wages, and cut health-care benefits. The concessions were accepted by the United Teachers of Richmond, even though teachers in the district voted overwhelmingly for a strike, which the union refused to call.

The liberal class cannot reform itself. It does not hold within its ranks the rebels and iconoclasts with the moral or physical courage to defy the corporate state and power elite. The corporate forces that sustain the media, unions, universities, religious institutions, the arts, and the Democratic Party oversaw the removal of all who challenged the corporatism and unfettered capitalism. By the 1980s, political philosophers, such as Sheldon Wolin, who attacked the rise of the corporate state, were no longer printed in publications such as the *New York Review of Books* or the *New York Times*. Radical clerics, such as Father Daniel Berrigan, spent the later part of their careers harassed by church authorities. Economists, such as Michael Hudson, who attacked the financial bubble and system of casino capitalism, had difficulty finding academic employment. Those left in these institutions lack the vision and fortitude to challenge dominant free-market ideologies. They have no ideological alternatives, even as the Democratic Party openly betrays every principle the liberal class claims to espouse: nonprofit health care; an end to our permanent war economy; high-quality, affordable public education; a return of civil liberties; jobs and welfare for the working class.

Since the presidency of Ronald Reagan, the corporate state has put the liberal class on a death march. Liberals did not protest the stripping away of the country's manufacturing base, the dismantling of regulatory agencies, and the destruction of social service programs. Liberals did not decry speculators, who in the seventeenth century would have been hanged, as they hijacked the economy. Liberals retreated into atrophied institutions. They busied themselves with the boutique activism of political correctness. The liberal class was eventually forced in this death march to turn itself inside out, championing positions it previously condemned. That it did so with almost no protest exposed its moral bankruptcy.

"The left once dismissed the market as exploitative," Russell Jacoby writes. "It now honors the market as rational and humane. The left once disdained mass culture as exploitative; now it celebrates it as rebellious. The left once honored independent intellectuals as courageous; now it sneers at them as elitist. The left once rejected pluralism as superficial; now it worships it as profound. We are witnessing not simply a defeat of the left, but its conversion and perhaps inversion."[5]

The greatest sin of the liberal class, throughout the twentieth century and into the early part of this century, has been its enthusiastic collusion with the power elite to silence, ban, and blacklist rebels, iconoclasts, communists, socialists, anarchists, radical union leaders, and pacifists who once could have given Ernest Logan Bell, as well as others in the working class, the words and ideas with which to battle back against the abuses of the corporate state. The repeated "anti-Red" purges of the twentieth-century United States, during and after both World Wars, and continuously from the 1950s until the fall of the Berlin Wall in 1989, were carried out in the name of anticommunism, but in reality proved to be devastating blows to popular social movements. The old communists in the American labor movement spoke in the language of class struggle. They understood that Wall Street, along with corporations such as BP, is the enemy. They offered a broad social vision that allowed even the non-communist left to employ a vocabulary that made sense of the destructive impulses of capitalism. But once the Communist Party, along with other radical movements, was eradicated as a social and political force in the 1940s and 1950s, once the liberal class took government-imposed loyalty oaths and collaborated in the hunts for phantom communist agents, the country was robbed of the ability to make sense of the struggle with the corporate state. The liberal class became fearful, timid, and ineffectual. It lost its voice. It became part of the corporate structure it should have been dismantling. It created an ideological vacuum on the left and ceded the language of rebellion to the far right.

Capitalism was once viewed by workers as a system to be fought. But capitalism is no longer challenged. Capitalist bosses, men such as Warren Buffett, George Soros, and Donald Trump, are treated as sages, celebrities and populists. The liberal class functions as their cheerleaders. Such misguided loyalty, illustrated by environmental groups that refuse to excoriate the Obama White House over the ecological catastrophe in the Gulf of Mexico, ignores the fact that the divide in America is not between Republican and Democrat. It is a divide between the corporate state and the citizen. It is a divide between capitalists and workers. And, for all the failings of the communists, they got it.

Fear is a potent weapon in the hands of the power elite. The fear of communism, like the fear of Islamic terrorism, was used to suspend civil liberties, including freedom of speech, habeas corpus, and the right to organize—values the liberal class claims to support. In the name of anticommunism, the capitalist class, terrified of the numerous labor strikes following World War II, rammed through the Taft-Hartley Act in 1947, culminating with a congressional override of President Harry Truman's veto. It was the most destructive legislative blow to the working class until NAFTA. It was fear that in 2001 allowed the state to push through the Patriot Act, practice extraordinary rendition, and establish offshore penal colonies where we torture detainees stripped of their rights. Fear led us to embrace the endless wars in the Middle East. Fear allowed us to stand meekly by as Wall Street helped itself to billions of taxpayer dollars. The timidity of the liberal class leaves it especially prone to manipulation.

The organs of mass propaganda used by the power elite to make us afraid employ the talents of artists and intellectuals who come from the liberal class. The robber barons of the late nineteenth century turned to police, goons, vigilantes, and thugs to beat up the opposition. The work of justifying corporate power is now carried out by the college-educated elite, drawn from the liberal class, who manufacture mass propaganda. The role of the liberal class in creating these sophisticated systems of manipulation has given liberals a financial stake in corporate dominance. It is from the liberal class that we get the jingles, advertising, brands, and mass-produced entertainment that keep us trapped in cultural and political illusions. And the complicity of the liberal class, cemented by the corporate salaries the members of that class earn, has sapped intellectual and moral independence. It is one of the great ironies of corporate control that the corporate state needs the abilities of intellectuals to maintain power, yet outside of this role it refuses to permit intellectuals to think or function independently.

As Irving Howe pointed out in his 1954 essay "This Age of Conformity," the "idea of the intellectual vocation, the idea of a life dedicated to values that cannot possibly be realized by a commercial civilization, has gradually lost its allure. And, it is this, rather than the abandonment of a particular program, which constitutes our rout."[6] The belief that capitalism is the unassailable engine of human progress, Howe wrote, "is trumpeted through every medium of communication: official propaganda, institutional advertising and scholarly writings of people who, until a few years ago, were its major opponents."

"The truly powerless people are those intellectuals—the new realists—who attach themselves to the seats of power, where they surrender their freedom of expression without gaining any significance as political figures," Howe wrote. "For it is crucial to the history of the American intellectuals in the past few decades—as well as to the relationship between 'wealth' and 'intellect'—that whenever they become absorbed into the accredited institutions of society they not only lose their traditional rebelliousness but to one extent or another *they cease to function as intellectuals*" [italics in original]. [7]

Hope will come with the return of the language of class conflict and rebellion, language that has been purged from the lexicon of the liberal class. This does not mean we have to agree with Karl Marx, who advocated violence and whose worship of the state as a utopian mechanism led to another form of working class enslavement, but we have to learn again to speak in the vocabulary Marx employed. We have to grasp, as Marx and Adam Smith did, that corporations are not concerned with the common good. They exploit, pollute, impoverish, repress, kill, and lie to make money. They throw poor families out of homes, let the uninsured die, wage useless wars to make profits, poison and pollute the ecosystem, slash social assistance programs, gut public education, trash the global economy, plunder the U.S. Treasury and crush all popular movements that seek justice for working men and women. They worship money and power. And, as Marx knew, unfettered capitalism is a revolutionary force that consumes greater and greater numbers of human lives until it finally consumes itself. The dead zone in the Gulf of Mexico is the perfect metaphor for the corporate state. It is part of the same nightmare experienced in postindustrial pockets, in the old mill towns of New England and the abandoned steel mills in Ohio. It is a nightmare that Iraqis, Pakistanis, and Afghans, mourning their dead, live each day.

In the late nineteenth century, Fyodor Dostoyevsky saw Russia's useless liberal class, which he satirized and excoriated, as presaging a period of blood and terror. In novels such as *Demons*, he wrote that the impotence and disconnection of the liberal class, the failure of liberals to defend the ideals they espoused, led to an age of moral nihilism. In *Notes from Underground* he portrayed the sterile, defeated dreamers of the liberal class, those who hold up high ideals but do nothing to defend them. The main character in *Notes from Underground* carries the bankrupt ideas of liberalism to their logical extreme. He eschews passion and moral purpose. He is rational. He accommodates a corrupt and dying power structure in the name of liberal ideals. The hypocrisy of the Underground Man dooms imperial Russia as it now dooms the American empire. It is the fatal disconnect between belief and action.

"I never even managed to become anything: neither wicked nor good, neither a scoundrel nor an honest man, neither a hero nor an insect," the Underground Man writes. "And now I am living out my life in my corner, taunting myself with the spiteful and utterly futile consolation that it is even impossible for an intelligent man seriously to become anything, and only fools become something. Yes, sir, an intelligent man of the nineteenth century must be and is morally obliged to be primarily a characterless being; and a man of character, an active figure—primarily a limited being."[8]

II / Permanent War

One of the most pathetic aspects of human history is that every civilization expresses itself most pretentiously, compounds its partial and universal values most convincingly, and claims immortality for its finite existence at the very moment when the decay which leads to death has already begun.

—REINHOLD NIEBUHR, *Beyond Tragedy*[1]

SINCE THE END of World War I, the United States has devoted staggering resources and money to battling real and imagined enemies. It turned the engines of the state over to a massive war and security apparatus. These battles, which have created an Orwellian state illusion of permanent war, neutered all opposition to corporate power and the tepid reforms of the liberal class. The liberal class, fearful of being branded as soft or unpatriotic in the Cold War, willingly joined the state's campaign to crush popular and radical movements in the name of national security. Permanent war is the most effective mechanism used by the power elite to stifle reform and muzzle dissent. A state of war demands greater secrecy, constant vigilance and suspicion. It generates distrust and fear, especially in culture and art, often reducing it to silence or nationalist cant. It degrades and corrupts education and the media. It wrecks the economy. It nullifies public opinion. And it forces liberal institutions to sacrifice their beliefs for a holy crusade, a kind of surrogate religion, whether it is against the Hun, the Bolshevik, the fascist, the communist, or the Islamic terrorist. The liberal class in a state of permanent war is rendered impotent.

Dwight Macdonald warned of the ideology of permanent war in his 1946 essay *The Root Is Man*. He despaired of an effective counterweight to the power of the corporate state as long as a state of permanent war continued to exist. The liberal class, like the Marxist cadre from which Macdonald had defected in favor of anarchism, had, he wrote, mistakenly placed its hopes for human progress in the state. This was a huge error. The state, once the repository of hope for the liberal class and many progressives, devoured its children in America as well as in the Soviet Union. And the magic elixir, the potent opiate that rendered a population passive and willing to be stripped of power, was a state of permanent war.

The political uses of the ideology of perpetual war eluded the theorists behind the nineteenth- and early twentieth-century reform and social movements, including Karl Marx. The reformists limited their focus to internal class struggle and, as Macdonald noted, never worked out "an adequate theory of the political significance of war." Until that gap is filled, Macdonald warned, "modern socialism will continue to have a somewhat academic flavor."[2]

The collapse of liberalism, whether in imperial Russia, the Austro-Hungarian Empire, Weimar Germany, the former Yugoslavia, or the United States, was intimately tied to the rise of a culture of permanent war. Within such a culture, exploitation and violence, even against citizens, are justified to protect the nation. The chant for war comes in a variety of slogans, languages, and ideologies. It can manifest itself in fascist salutes, communist show trials, campaigns of ethnic cleansing, or Christian crusades. It is all the same. It is a crude, terrifying state repression by the power elite and the mediocrities in the liberal class who serve them, in the name of national security.

It was a decline into permanent war, not Islam, that killed the liberal, democratic movements in the Arab world, movements that held great promise in the early part of the twentieth century in countries such as Egypt, Syria, Lebanon, and Iran. The same prolonged state of permanent war killed the liberal classes in Israel and the United States. Permanent war, which reduces all to speaking in the simplified language of nationalism, is a disease. It strips citizens of rights. It reduces all communication to patriotic cant. It empowers those who profit from the state in the name of war. And it corrodes and diminishes democratic debate and institutions.

"War," Randolph Bourne remarked, "is the health of the state."

U.S. military spending, which consumes half of all discretionary spending, has had a profound social and political cost. Bridges and levees collapse. Schools decay. Domestic manufacturing declines. Trillions in debt threaten the viability of the currency and the economy. The poor, the mentally ill, the sick, and the unemployed are abandoned. Human suffering is the price for victory, which is never finally defined or attainable.

The corporations that profit from permanent war need us to be afraid. Fear stops us from objecting to government spending on a bloated military. Fear means we will not ask unpleasant questions of those in power. Fear permits the government to operate in secret. Fear means we are willing to give up our rights and liberties for promises of security. The imposition of fear ensures that the corporations that wrecked the country cannot be challenged. Fear keeps us penned in like livestock.

Dick Cheney and George W. Bush may be palpably evil while Obama is merely weak, but to those who seek to keep us in a state of permanent war, such distinctions do not matter. They get what they want. The liberal class, like Dostoyevsky's Underground Man, can no longer influence a society in a state of permanent war and retreats into its sheltered enclaves, where its members can continue to worship themselves. The corridors of liberal institutions are filled with Underground men and women. They decry the social chaos for which they bear responsibility, but do nothing. They nurse an internal bitterness and mounting distaste for the wider society. And, because of their self-righteousness, elitism, and hypocrisy, they are despised.

The institutional church, when it does speak, mutters pious non-statements. It seeks to protect its vision of itself as a moral voice and yet avoids genuine confrontations with the power elite. It speaks in a language filled with moral platitudes. We can hear such language in a letter written March 25, 2003, by Archbishop Edwin F. O'Brien, head of the Archdiocese for the Military Services, telling his priests that Catholic soldiers could morally fight in the second Iraq war: "Given the complexity of factors involved, many of which understandably remain confidential, it is altogether appropriate for members of our armed forces to presume the integrity of our leadership and its judgments, and therefore to carry out their military duties in good conscience." The

U.S. Conference of Catholic Bishops told believers that Iraqi president Saddam Hussein was a menace, and that reasonable people could disagree about the necessity of using force to overthrow him. It assured those who supported the war that God would not object. B'nai B'rith supported a congressional resolution to authorize the 2003 attack on Iraq. The Union of American Hebrew Congregations, which represents Reform Judaism, agreed it would back unilateral action, as long as Congress approved and the president sought support from other nations. In a typical bromide, the National Council of Churches, which represents thirty-six different faith groups, urged President George W. Bush to "do all possible" to avoid war with Iraq and to stop "demonizing adversaries or enemies" with good-versus-evil rhetoric, but, like the other liberal religious institutions, did not condemn the war.

A Gallup Poll in 2006 found that "the more frequently an American attends church, the less likely he or she is to say the war was a mistake." Given that Jesus was a pacifist, and given that all of us who graduated from seminary rigorously studied just war doctrine, a doctrine flagrantly violated by the invasion of Iraq, this is startling.

The attraction of the right wing, and the war-makers, is that they appear to have the courage of their convictions. When someone like Sarah Palin posts a map with crosshairs centering on Democratic districts, when she favors a slogan such as "Don't Retreat, Instead—RELOAD!," there are desperate people listening who are cleaning their weapons. When Christian fascists stand in the pulpits of megachurches and denounce Obama as the Antichrist, there are believers who listen. When during a 2010 House debate on the pending health-care bill, Republican lawmaker Randy Neugebauer shouts, "Baby killer!" at Michigan Democrat Bart Stupak, violent extremists nod their heads, seeing the mission of saving the unborn as a sacred duty. These zealots have little left to lose. We made sure of that. And the violence they inflict is an expression of the economic and institutional violence they endure.

These movements are not yet full-blown fascist movements. They do not openly call for the extermination of ethnic or religious groups. They do not openly advocate violence. But, as I was told by Fritz Stern, a scholar of fascism and a refugee from Nazi Germany, "In Germany there was a yearning for fascism before fascism was invented." This is the yearning that we now see, and it is dangerous. Stern, who sees similarities between the deterioration of the U.S. political system and the fall of Weimar Germany, warned against "a historic process in which resentment against a disenchanted secular world found deliverance in the ecstatic escape of unreason." Societies that do not reincorporate the unemployed and the poor into the economy, giving them jobs and relief from crippling debt, become subject to the hysterical mass quest for ecstatic deliverance in unreason. The nascent racism and violence leaping up around the edges of U.S. society could become a full-blown conflagration. Attempts by the liberal class to create a more civil society, to respect difference, will be rejected by a betrayed populace along with the liberal class itself.

"One thing that is very likely to happen is that the gains made in the past forty years by black and brown Americans, and by homosexuals, will be wiped out," the philosopher Richard Rorty warned in his book *Achieving Our Country*:

> Jocular contempt for women will come back into fashion. The words "nigger" and "kike" will once again be heard in the workplace. All the sadism that the academic Left has tried to make unacceptable to its students will come flooding back. All the resentment which badly educated Americans feel about having their manners dictated to them by college graduates will find an outlet.[3]

The hatred for radical Islam will transform itself into a hatred for Muslims. The hatred for undocumented workers in states such as Arizona will become a hatred for Mexicans and Central Americans. The hatred for those not defined as American patriots by a largely white mass movement will become a hatred for African Americans. The hatred for liberals will morph into a hatred for all democratic institutions, from universities and government agencies to cultural institutions and the media. In their continued impotence and cowardice, members of the liberal class will see themselves, and the values they support, swept aside.

The liberal class refused to resist the devolution of the U.S. democratic system into what Sheldon Wolin calls a system of inverted totalitarianism. Inverted totalitarianism, Wolin writes, represents "the political coming of age of corporate power and the political demobilization of the citizenry." Inverted totalitarianism differs from classical forms of totalitarianism, which revolve around a demagogue or charismatic leader. It finds its expression in the anonymity of the corporate state. The corporate forces behind inverted totalitarianism do not, as classical totalitarian movements do, replace decaying structures with new, revolutionary structures. They do not import new symbols and iconography. They do not offer a radical alternative. Corporate power purports, in inverted totalitarianism, to honor electoral politics, freedom, and the Constitution. But these corporate forces so corrupt and manipulate power as to make democracy impossible.

Inverted totalitarianism is not conceptualized as an ideology or objectified in public policy. It is furthered by "power-holders and citizens who often seem unaware of the deeper consequences of their actions or inactions," Wolin writes. But it is as dangerous as classical forms of totalitarianism. In a system of inverted totalitarianism, it is not necessary to rewrite the Constitution, as fascist and communist regimes would. It is enough to exploit legitimate power by means of judicial and legislative interpretation. This exploitation ensures that the courts, populated by justices selected and ratified by members of the corporate culture, rule that huge corporate campaign contributions are protected speech under the First Amendment. It ensures that heavily financed and organized lobbying by large corporations is interpreted as an application of the people's right to petition the government. Corporations are treated by the state as persons, as the increasingly conservative U.S. Supreme Court has more and more frequently ruled, except in those cases where the "persons" agree to a "settlement." Those within corporations who commit crimes can avoid going to prison by paying large sums of money to the government without "admitting any wrongdoing," according to this twisted judicial reasoning. There is a word for this: corruption.

Corporations have thirty-five thousand lobbyists in Washington and thousands more in state capitals that dole out corporate money to shape and write legislation. They use their political action committees to solicit employees and shareholders for donations to fund pliable candidates. The financial sector, for example, spent more than $5 billion on political campaigns, influence peddling, and lobbying during the past decade, which resulted in sweeping deregulation, the gouging of consumers, our global financial meltdown, and the subsequent looting of the U.S. Treasury. The Pharmaceutical Research and Manufacturers of America spent $26 million in 2009, and drug companies such as Pfizer, Amgen, and Eli Lilly kicked in tens of millions more to buy off the two parties. The so-called health-care reform bill will force citizens to buy a predatory and defective product, while taxpayers provide health-related corporations with hundreds of billions of dollars in subsidies. The oil and gas industry, the coal industry, defense contractors, and telecommunications companies have thwarted the drive for sustainable energy and orchestrated the steady erosion of regulatory control and civil liberties. Politicians do corporate bidding and give lip service to burning political and economic issues. The liberal class is used as a prop to keep the fiction of the democratic state alive. The Constitution, Wolin writes, is "conscripted to serve as power's apprentice rather than its conscience."

There is no national institution left that can accurately be described as democratic. Citizens, rather than authentically participating in power, are have only virtual opinions, in what Charlotte Twight calls "participatory fascism." They are reduced to expressing themselves on issues that are meaningless, voting on *American Idol* or in polls conducted by the power elite. The citizens of Rome, stripped of political power, are allowed to vote to spare or kill a gladiator in the arena, a similar form of hollow public choice.

"Inverted totalitarianism reverses things," Wolin writes:

> It is politics all of the time but a politics largely untempered by the political. Party squabbles are occasionally on public display, and there is a frantic and continuous politics among factions of the party, interest groups, competing corporate powers, and rival media concerns. And there is, of course, the culminating moment of national elections when the attention of the nation is required to make a choice of personalities rather than a choice between alternatives. What is absent is the political, the commitment to finding where the common good lies amidst the welter of well-financed, highly organized,

single-minded interests rabidly seeking governmental favors and overwhelming the practices of representative government and public administration by a sea of cash.

Hollywood, the news industry, and television—all corporate-controlled—have become instruments of inverted totalitarianism, as I illustrated in my book *Empire of Illusion*. They saturate the airwaves with manufactured controversy, whether it is the Tiger Woods sex scandal or the dispute between NBC late-night talk-show hosts Jay Leno and Conan O'Brien or the extramarital affair of John Edwards. We confuse knowledge with our potted responses to these non-events. And the draconian internal control employed by the U.S. Department of Homeland Security, the military, and the police, coupled with the censorship, witting or unwitting, practiced by the corporate media, does for inverted totalitarianism what thugs and bonfires of prohibited books did in previous totalitarian regimes.

Liberals, socialists, trade unionists, independent journalists, and intellectuals, many of whom were once important voices in our society, have been banished or muzzled by corporate control throughout academia, culture, the media, and government. "It seems a replay of historical experience that the bias displayed by today's media should be aimed consistently at the shredded remains of liberalism," Wolin writes:

> Recall that an element common to most twentieth-century totalitarianism, whether Fascist or Stalinist, was hostility toward the left. In the United States, the left is assumed to consist solely of liberals, occasionally of "the left wing of the Democratic Party," never of democrats.

The uniformity of opinion molded by the media is reinforced through the skillfully orchestrated mass emotions of nationalism and patriotism, which paint all dissidents as "soft" or "unpatriotic." The "patriotic" citizen, plagued by fear of job losses and possible terrorist attacks, unfailingly supports widespread surveillance and the militarized state. There is no questioning of the $1 trillion spent each year on defense. Military and intelligence agencies are held above government, as if somehow they are not part of the government. The most powerful instruments of state control effectively have no public oversight. We, as imperial citizens, are taught to be contemptuous of government bureaucracy, yet we stand like sheep before Homeland Security agents in airports and are mute when Congress permits our private correspondence and conversations to be monitored and archived. We endure more state control than at any time in U.S. history.

And yet the civic, patriotic, and political language we use to describe ourselves remains unchanged. We pay fealty to the same national symbols and iconography. We find our collective identity in the same national myths. We continue to deify the founding fathers. But the America we celebrate is an illusion. It does not exist.

The liberal class has aided and abetted this decline. Liberals, who claim to support the working class, vote for candidates who glibly defend NAFTA and increased globalization. Liberals, who claim to want an end to the wars in Iraq and Afghanistan, continue to back a party that funds and expands these wars. Liberals, who say they are the champions of basic civil liberties, do not challenge politicians who take these liberties from them.

Obama lies as cravenly, if not as crudely, as George W. Bush. He promised that the transfer of $12.8 trillion in taxpayer money to Wall Street would open up credit and lending to the average consumer following the financial crisis. It did not. The Federal Deposit Insurance Corporation (FDIC) admitted that banks have reduced lending at the sharpest rate since 1942. As a senator, Obama promised he would filibuster amendments to the Foreign Intelligence Surveillance Act (FISA), which retroactively made legal the wiretapping and monitoring of millions of American citizens without warrant; instead, he supported passage of that legislation. He told us he would withdraw American troops from Iraq, close the Guantánamo Bay detention camp, end torture, restore civil liberties such as habeas corpus, pass a health-care bill with a robust public option, and create new jobs. Some troops have been withdrawn, slowly and piecemeal, from Iraq, but other than this too-little-too-late process, almost none of his promises has been kept.

He shoved a health-care bill down our throats that will mean ever-rising co-pays, deductibles, and premiums and leave most of the seriously ill bankrupt and unable to afford medical care. Obama, after promising meaningful environmental reform, did nothing to halt the collapse of the 2009 Copenhagen Climate Conference, a decision that ended perhaps our final chance to save the planet from the catastrophic effects of climate change. He empowers Israel's brutal apartheid regime. He has expanded the war in Afghanistan and Pakistan, where hundreds of civilians, including entire families, have been slaughtered by sophisticated weaponry such as drones and the AGM-144 Hellfire missile, which sucks the air out of its victims' lungs. He is delivering war and death to Yemen, Somalia, and, perhaps soon, he will bring it to Iran. Obama is part of the political stagecraft that trades in perceptions of power rather than real power.

The illegal wars and occupations, the largest transference of wealth upward in U.S. history, the deregulation that resulted in the environmental disaster in the Gulf of Mexico, and the egregious assault on civil liberties—begun under George W. Bush—raise only a flicker of protest from the liberal class. Liberals, unlike the right wing, are emotionally disabled. They appear not to feel. They do not recognize the legitimate anger of those who have been dispossessed. They retreat instead into the dead talk of policy and analysis. The Tea Party protesters, the myopic supporters of Sarah Palin, the veterans signing up for Oath Keepers, and myriad groups of armed patriots have brought into their ranks legions of dispossessed workers, angry libertarians, John Birchers, and many others who, until now, were never politically active.

The three-thousand-word suicide note left by Joe Stack, who flew his Piper Dakota into an Internal Revenue Service office in Austin, Texas, on February 18, 2010, murdering an IRS worker and injuring thirteen others, two seriously, expressed the frustration of tens of millions of workers over the treachery of global corporations and a liberal class that abandoned them.[4]

Stack, in his note, remembered that when he was an eighteen- or nineteen-year-old student living in Harrisburg, Pennsylvania, he occupied an apartment next to an elderly widow. The woman had been married to a steel worker, who, Stack wrote, "had worked all his life in the steel mills of central Pennsylvania with promises from big business and the union that, for his thirty years of service, he would have a pension and medical care to look forward to in his retirement." But the worker got nothing "because the incompetent mill management and corrupt union (not to mention the government) raided their pension funds and stole their retirement." The widow survived on Social Security.

"In retrospect, the situation was laughable because here I was living on peanut butter and bread (or Ritz crackers when I could afford to splurge) for months at a time," he wrote:

> When I got to know this poor figure and heard her story I felt worse for her plight than for my own (I, after all, thought I had everything in front of me). I was genuinely appalled at one point, as we exchanged stories and commiserated with each other over our situations, when she in her grandmotherly fashion tried to convince me that I would be "healthier" eating cat food (like her) rather than trying to get all my substance from peanut butter and bread. I couldn't quite go there, but the impression was made. I decided that I didn't trust big business to take care of me, and that I would take responsibility for my own future and myself.

Stack's life, like Ernest Logan Bell's, soon made clear that the corporate government served its own interests at the expense of the citizen. And the liberal class and its institutions, including labor unions, the media, and the Democratic Party, would not defend them.

"Why is it that a handful of thugs and plunderers can commit unthinkable atrocities (and in the case of the GM executives, for scores of years) and when it's time for their gravy train to crash under the weight of their gluttony and overwhelming stupidity, the force of the full federal government has no difficulty coming to their aid within days if not hours?" Stack wrote:

> Yet at the same time, the joke we call the American medical system, including the drug and insurance companies, are murdering tens of thousands of people a year and stealing from the corpses and victims they cripple, and this country's leaders don't see this as important as bailing out a few of their vile, rich cronies. Yet, the political "representatives" (thieves, liars, and self-serving scumbags is far more accurate) have endless time to sit around for year after year and debate the state of the "terrible health care problem." It's clear they see no

crisis as long as the dead people don't get in the way of their corporate profits rolling in.

And justice? You've got to be kidding!

"How can any rational individual explain that white elephant conundrum in the middle of our tax system and, indeed, our entire legal system?" the note went on:

> Here we have a system that is, by far, too complicated for the brightest of the master scholars to understand. Yet, it mercilessly "holds accountable" its victims, claiming that they're responsible for fully complying with laws not even the experts understand. The law "requires" a signature on the bottom of a tax filing; yet no one can say truthfully that they understand what they are signing; if that's not "duress" th[e]n what is. If this is not the measure of a totalitarian regime, nothing is."

This letter is a coherent and lucid expression of views and concerns, many of them legitimate, shared by millions of sane, struggling citizens. All of them feel betrayed, as they should, by both the government and the liberal class.

American workers are not the only workers who have been betrayed by the new global economy. Nor are they alone in their anger, as illustrated by strikes and protests in countries such as Greece and China. Sociologist Ching Kwan Lee's study of Chinese labor, *Against the Law: Labor Protests in China's Rustbelt and Sunbelt*, shows that workers in these regions of China experience bitterness and a sense of betrayal very similar to those expressed by Stack.

Lee writes about workers in the northeast province of Liaoning, which, like the rust belt in states such as Ohio, has been abandoned by the Chinese government for the southeast. Liaoning has "declined into a wasteland of bankruptcy and a hotbed of working-class protest by its many unemployed workers and pensioners. Unpaid pensions and wages, defaults on medical subsidies, and inadequate collective consumption are the main grievances triggering labor unrest in Liaoning."[5]

In the southern province of Guangdong, China's export-oriented industry is booming. The province in 2000 accounted for forty-two percent of all China's exports, 90 percent of which came from eight cities in the Pearl River Delta. The area attracts many of China's eighty to one hundred million migrant workers. But here Lee found "satanic mills" that run "at such a nerve-racking pace that workers' physical limits and bodily strength are put to the test on a daily basis."[6] Workers can put in fourteen- to sixteen-hour days with no rest day during the month until payday. In these factories it is "normal" to work four hundred hours or more a month, especially for those in the garment industry. Working conditions are in open defiance of official labor laws, which mandate a forty-hour work week and a maximum of thirty-six hours of overtime per month as well as a day off each week. But labor laws are rarely enforced in China. Most workers, Lee found, endure unpaid wages, illegal deductions, and substandard wage rates. They are often physically abused at work and do not receive compensation if they are injured on the job. Every year a dozen or more workers die from overwork in the city of Shenzhen alone. In Lee's words, the working conditions "go beyond the Marxist notions of exploitation and alienation."[7] A survey published in 2003 by the official China News Agency, cited in Lee's book, found that three in four migrant workers have trouble collecting their pay. Each year scores of workers threaten to commit suicide, Lee writes, by jumping off high-rises or setting themselves on fire over unpaid wages. "If getting paid for one's labor is a fundamental feature of capitalist employment relations, strictly speaking many Chinese workers are not yet laborers," Lee writes.[8]

Workers in China, according to Lee, feel deeply betrayed by a state that espoused Maoist collectivism rather than liberal democratic principles. But the sense of betrayal, and the expressions of rage and bitterness, by workers in China and the United States are very similar. Workers in China have been used and discarded, in much the same way as workers in other global industrial centers, from Michigan to India to Vietnam to South Korea. There are, Lee estimates, some thirty million "excess workers" in China who are effectively but not officially unemployed.[9] Lee found that many of the workers "broke down in tears in the course of our conversation, while others could barely contain their indignation and anger." She noted that "a sense of being victimized by injustice was widely shared in the local communities."[10] Lee sees a looming crisis in China that will mirror the crisis in the United States and in other parts of the world where corporations have been permitted to ruthlessly exploit workers and move to new locations once wages begin to rise or workers become organized. The fury Joe Stack expressed against corporate abuse of the working class is a fury that, Lee warns, is reverberating around the globe in a multiplicity of tongues.

India, along with China and other emergent economies, has experienced the same desperation. An estimated 182,936 Indian farmers committed suicide between 1997 and 2007. Nearly two-thirds of these suicides occurred in five of India's twenty-eight states. Those who took their lives, the Indian journalist Palagummi Sainath has written, were primarily farmers who fell deeply in debt.[11] Debt in Indian peasant households doubled in the first decade of India's neoliberal "economic reforms," from twenty-six percent of farm households to 48.6 percent, Sainath found. The farmers who killed themselves largely grew cash crops for export, such as cotton, coffee, sugarcane, groundnut, pepper, and vanilla. The switch from subsistence farming to cash crops, pushed on farmers by corporations, eventually led to higher cultivation costs, higher loans, and unsustainable debts, leaving farmers at the mercy of global commodity markets. Seed prices, controlled by corporate seed companies such as Monsanto, skyrocketed. And farmers, finally, could not cope. Many simply walked away from their land.[12]

"There's much excited talk these days about a great global shift of power, with speculation about whether, or when, China might displace the U.S. as the dominant global power, along with India, which, if it happened, would mean that the global system would be returning to something like what it was before the European conquests," said Noam Chomsky, speaking at the Left Forum at Pace University in New York:

And indeed their recent GDP growth has been spectacular. But there's a lot more to say about it. So if you take a look at the U.N. human development index, basic measure of the health of the society, it turns out that India retains its place near the bottom. It's now 134th, slightly above Cambodia, below Laos and Tajikistan. Actually, it's dropped since the reforms began. China ranks ninety-second, a bit above Jordan, below the Dominican Republic and Iran. By comparison, Cuba, which has been under harsh U.S. attack for fifty years, is ranked fifty-second. It's the highest in Central America and the Caribbean, barely below the richest societies in South America. India and China also suffer from extremely high inequality, so well over a billion of their inhabitants fall far lower in the scale. Furthermore, an accurate accounting would go beyond conventional measures to include serious costs that China and India can't ignore for long: ecological, resource depletion, many others.[13]

Front-page speculations about a global shift of power "disregard a crucial factor that's familiar to all of us: nations divorced from the internal distribution of power are not the real actors in international affairs," Chomsky said:

That truism was brought to public attention by that incorrigible radical Adam Smith, who recognized that the principal architects of power in England were the owners of the society—in his day, the merchants and manufacturers—and they made sure that policy would attend scrupulously to their interests, however grievous the impact on the people of England and, of course, much worse, the victims of what he called "the savage injustice of the Europeans" abroad. British crimes in India were the main concern of an old-fashioned conservative with moral values.

Chomsky said that there is indeed a global shift on power, "though not the one that occupies center stage":

It's a shift from the global work force to transnational capital, and it's been sharply escalating during the neoliberal years. The cost is substantial, including the Joe Stacks of the U.S., starving peasants in India, and millions of protesting workers in China, where the labor share in income is declining even more rapidly than in most of the world.

Chomsky is one of the few intellectuals who challenges the structure and inequity of corporate capitalism and our state of permanent war. Perhaps America's greatest intellectual, Chomsky is deeply reviled by the liberal class. His massive body of work, which includes nearly one hundred books, has for decades deflated and exposed the lies of the power elite, the myths they perpetrate, and the complicity of the liberal class. Chomsky has done this despite being largely blacklisted by the commercial media and turned into a pariah by the academy. He combines moral autonomy with rigorous scholarship, a remarkable grasp of detail, and a searing intellect. He curtly dismisses our two-party system as a mirage orchestrated by the corporate state, excoriates the liberal class for being toadies, and describes the drivel of the commercial media as a form of "brainwashing." And as our nation's most prescient critic of unregulated capitalism, globalization, and the poison of empire, he enters his eighty-first year warning us that we have little time left to save our anemic democracy and our ecosystem.

"It is very similar to late Weimar Germany," Chomsky said when I spoke with him.[14] "The parallels are striking. There was also tremendous disillusionment with the parliamentary system. The most striking fact about Weimar was not that the Nazis managed to destroy the Social Democrats and the Communists but that the traditional parties, the Conservative and Liberal Parties, were hated and disappeared. It left a vacuum which the Nazis very cleverly and intelligently managed to take over.

"The United States is extremely lucky that no honest, charismatic figure has arisen," Chomsky went on:

> Every charismatic figure is such an obvious crook that he destroys himself, like [Joseph] McCarthy or [Richard] Nixon or the evangelist preachers. If somebody comes along who is charismatic and honest, this country is in real trouble because of the frustration, disillusionment, the justified anger, and the absence of any coherent response. What are people supposed to think if someone says, "I have got an answer, we have an enemy"? There it was the Jews. Here it will be the illegal immigrants and the blacks. We will be told that white males are a persecuted minority. We will be told we have to defend ourselves and the honor of the nation. Military force will be exalted. People will be beaten up. This could become an overwhelming force. And if it happens it will be more dangerous than Germany. The

United States is the world power. Germany was powerful but had more powerful antagonists. I don't think all this is very far away. If the polls are accurate it is not the Republicans but the right-wing Republicans, the crazed Republicans, who will sweep the [November 2010] election.

"I have never seen anything like this in my lifetime," Chomsky added.

I am old enough to remember the 1930s. My whole family was unemployed. There were far more desperate conditions than today. But it was hopeful. People had hope. The CIO [Congress of Industrial Organizations] was organizing. No one wants to say it anymore, but the Communist Party was the spearhead for labor and civil-rights organizing. Even things like giving my unemployed seamstress aunt a week in the country. It was a life. There is nothing like that now. The mood of the country is frightening. The level of anger, frustration, and hatred of institutions is not organized in a constructive way. It is going off into self-destructive fantasies.

"I listen to talk radio," Chomsky said. "I don't want to hear Rush Limbaugh. I want to hear the people calling in. They are like Joe Stack. 'What is happening to me? I have done all the right things. I am a God-fearing Christian. I work hard for my family. I have a gun. I believe in the values of the country, and my life is collapsing.' "

In works such as *On Power and Ideology and Manufacturing Consent*, Chomsky has, more than any other American intellectual, charted the downward spiral of the American political and economic system. He reminds us that genuine intellectual inquiry is always subversive. It challenges cultural and political assumptions. It critiques structures. It is relentlessly self-critical. It implodes the self-indulgent myths and stereotypes we use to aggrandize ourselves and ignore our complicity in acts of violence and oppression. And genuine inquiry always makes the powerful, as well as their liberal apologists, deeply uncomfortable.

Chomsky reserves his fiercest venom for members of the liberal class who serve as a smoke screen for the cruelty of unchecked capitalism and imperial war. He has consistently exposed their moral and intellectual posturing as a fraud. And this is why Chomsky is hated, and perhaps feared, more among liberals than among the right wing he also excoriates. When Christopher Hitchens decided to become a windup doll for the Bush administration after 9/11, one of the first things he did was write a vicious article attacking Chomsky. Hitchens, unlike most of the right-wing elites he served, knew which intellectual in America mattered.

"I don't bother writing about Fox News," Chomsky said:

> It is too easy. What I talk about are the liberal intellectuals, the ones who portray themselves and perceive themselves as challenging power, as courageous, as standing up for truth and justice. They are basically the guardians of the faith. They set the limits. They tell us how far we can go. They say, 'Look how courageous I am.' But do not go one millimeter beyond that. At least for the educated sectors, they are the most dangerous in supporting power.

Because he steps outside of the clichéd demarcations of intellectual left and right, equally eschewing all ideologies, Chomsky has been crucial to American discourse for decades, from his work on the Vietnam War to his criticisms of the Obama administration. He stubbornly maintains his position as an iconoclast, one who distrusts power in any form. And he is one of the few voices that speak to the reality of war, the disastrous effects of imperial power, and the fact that, rather than promoting virtue or waging war based on good intentions, the permanent war economy is consuming and destroying innocent lives at home and abroad.

"Most intellectuals have a self-understanding of themselves as the conscience of humanity," said the Middle East scholar Norman Finkelstein, a former student of Chomsky's:

> They revel in and admire someone like Václav Havel. Chomsky is contemptuous of Havel. Chomsky embraces the Julien Benda view of the world. There are two sets of principles. They are the principles of power and privilege and the principles of truth and justice. If you pursue truth and justice, it will always mean a diminution of power and privilege. If you pursue power and privilege it will always be at the expense of truth and justice. Benda says that the credo of any true intellectual has to be, as Christ said, "My kingdom is not of this

world." Chomsky exposes the pretenses of those who claim to be the bearers of truth and justice. He shows that in fact these intellectuals are the bearers of power and privilege and all the evil that attends it.[15]

"I try to encourage people to think for themselves, to question standard assumptions," Chomsky said when asked about his goals:

Don't take assumptions for granted. Begin by taking a skeptical attitude toward anything that is conventional wisdom. Make it justify itself. It usually can't. Be willing to ask questions about what is taken for granted. Try to think things through for yourself. There is plenty of information. You have got to learn how to judge, evaluate, and compare it with other things. You have to take some things on trust or you can't survive. But if there is something significant and important, don't take it on trust. As soon as you read anything that is anonymous, you should immediately distrust it. If you read in the newspapers that Iran is defying the international community, ask, "Who is the international community?" India is opposed to sanctions. China is opposed to sanctions. Brazil is opposed to sanctions. The Non-Aligned Movement is vigorously opposed to sanctions and has been for years. Who is the international community? It is Washington and anyone who happens to agree with it. You can figure that out, but you have to do work. It is the same on issue after issue.

Chomsky's courage to speak on behalf of those whose suffering is minimized or ignored in mass culture, such as the Palestinians, is an example for anyone searching for models of the moral life. Perhaps even more than his scholarship, his example of moral independence sustains all those who defy the cant of the crowd, and that of the liberal class, to speak the truth.

The role of the liberal class in defending the purportedly good intentions of the power elite was on public display in 1985, when *Foreign Affairs* published a tenth-anniversary retrospective on the Vietnam War. The liberals in the magazine, writers such as David Fromkin and James Chace, argued that the military intervention in Vietnam was "predicated on the view that the United States has a duty to look beyond its purely national interests," and that, pursuant to its "global responsibilities," the United States must "serve the interests of mankind." In moral terms, in other words, the intent of the military intervention was good. It was correct to oppose "communist aggression" by the Vietnamese. But the war, these liberals argued, was ultimately wrong because it was impractical, because "our side was likely to lose." The liberal class critiqued the war on practical but not moral grounds. They were countered by the militarists who argued that with more resolve the North Vietnamese could have been defeated on the battlefield. The virtues of the nation, even in an act of war, are sacrosanct. The liberal class cannot question these virtues and remain within the circles of the power elite.[16]

The same scenario was played out in the wars in Iraq and Afghanistan. David Remnick, the editor of the *New Yorker*, and Bill Keller, a columnist for the *New York Times* and later the paper's executive editor, along with Michael Ignatieff, the former director of the Carr Center for Human Rights Policy at Harvard and current head of the Labor Party in Canada, joined Leon Wieseltier, along with academics such as Jean Bethke Elshtain of the University of Chicago Divinity School, Michael Walzer of the Institute for Advanced Study in Princeton, and Anne-Marie Slaughter at Princeton's Woodrow Wilson School of Public and International Affairs, to become self-described "reluctant hawks." The *New Republic*'s Peter Beinart, joining the calls for war by the liberal class, wrote a book called *The Good Fight: Why Liberals— and Only Liberals—Can Win the War on Terror and Make America Great Again.*

At the start of the war, Slaughter, then dean of the Woodrow Wilson School and president of the American Society of International Law (as of this writing, she is now director of Policy Planning for the U.S. Department of State), wrote in *Foreign Affairs* that "the world cannot afford to look the other way when faced with the prospect, as in Iraq, of a brutal ruler acquiring nuclear weapons or other weapons of mass destruction":

> Addressing this danger requires a different strategy, one that maximizes the chances of early and effective collective action. In this regard, and in comparison to the changes that are taking place in the area of intervention for the purposes of humanitarian protection,

the biggest problem with the Bush preemption strategy may be that it does not go far enough.[17]

Ignatieff told the *Guardian* newspaper at the start of the war:

> I still think that Bush is right when he says Iraq would be better off if Saddam were disarmed and, if necessary, replaced by force. . . . Ideology cannot help us here. In the weeks and years ahead, the choices are not about who we are or what company we should keep nor even about what we think America is or should be. They are about what risks are worth running, when our safety depends on the answer, and when the freedom of 25 million people hangs in the balance.[18]

Ignatieff, defending the invasion on National Public Radio's *Fresh Air with Terry Gross* in March 2003, laid out the classic arguments of the liberal class. He insisted that war was a humanitarian action, that he supported the war with a heavy heart, but that there was no other option. This humanitarian and moral coloring to war, the insistence that the motives of the war-makers is virtuous, is the primary function of the liberal class, the reason the power elite tolerates its existence.

The liberal class played the same function during the war in Vietnam. War becomes a necessary evil. The rhetoric of the liberal class, however, mocks the brutal reality of war. Most liberals, including Ignatieff, have never been in combat. Their children rarely serve in the military. They neither know nor understand the destructive power of modern weaponry or the propensity on the part of armed combatants, whose fear and paranoia are raised to a fever pitch, to shoot any person, armed or unarmed, or obliterate whole villages in air strikes, if they feel threatened. Ignatieff's assertion at the time that "the only real chance that Iraq has to become a decent society is through American force of arms" is, when juxtaposed with the reality of industrial warfare, little different from the cruder propaganda disseminated by the Bush White House.[19] He and the liberal class joined the Bush administration in carrying out a project that under international law was illegal and resulted in the deaths of hundreds of thousands of Iraqis, far more than had ever been slaughtered by Saddam Hussein, and thousands more Afghani and Pakistani civilians. The wars in the Middle East have also driven several million Iraqis, Pakistanis, and Afghanis into squalid displacement and refugee camps. War and violence, as instruments of virtue, are a contradiction in terms. But you can't fully grasp this unless you have been in combat, and combat is something the liberal class has been able to hand off to the working class since World War II.

The solitary voices of dissent that condemned the war at its inception were attacked as fiercely by the liberal class as by the right wing. When documentary filmmaker Michael Moore accepted the Oscar for his film *Bowling for Columbine* on March 23, 2003, he used the occasion to denounce the war, which had begun a few days earlier, as well as the legitimacy of the Bush presidency.

"We live in a fictitious time," Moore, dressed in an ill-fitting tuxedo, told an increasingly hostile audience:

> We live in a time when we have fictitious election results that elect a fictitious president. We live in a time where we have a man sending us to war for fictitious reasons, whether it is the fiction of duct tape or Orange Alerts. We are against this war, Mr. Bush. Shame on you, Mr. Bush! Shame on you![20]

Moore was booed and jeered. He told me he skipped the afterparties and spent the night alone in his hotel room, flipping through channels on which commentators, which included liberal pundits such as Al Franken and Keith Olbermann, unleashed vicious denunciations against him. Moore had crossed the parameters drawn by the power elite. Liberals, in denouncing him, fulfilled their political role. They discredited Moore because he did not obey the rules. And they did it with enthusiasm. Moore was portrayed as a "far-left" radical who needed to be escorted off the premises.

"American liberal intellectuals take special pride in their 'toughmindedness,' in their success in casting aside the illusions and myths of the old left, for these same 'tough' new liberals reproduce some of that old left's worst characteristics," Tony Judt wrote in the *London Review of Books*:

> They may see themselves as having migrated to the opposite shore; but they display precisely the same mixture of dogmatic faith and cultural provincialism, not to mention the exuberant enthusiasm for

violent political transformation at other people's expense, that marked their fellow-traveling predecessors across the Cold War ideological divide. The value of such persons to ambitious, radical regimes is an old story. Indeed, intellectual camp followers of this kind were first identified by Lenin himself, who coined the term that still describes them best. Today, America's liberal armchair warriors are the "useful idiots" of the War on Terror.[21]

I traveled to Washington in May 2010 to join U.S. Representative Dennis Kucinich for a public teach-in on the wars. Kucinich used the Capitol Hill event to denounce the request by Obama for an additional $33 billion for the war in Afghanistan. The Ohio Democrat had introduced House Concurrent Resolution 248, with sixteen co-sponsors, which would have required the House of Representatives to debate whether to continue the Afghanistan war. Kucinich, to his credit, was, along with Ron Paul, one of only two members of the House to publicly condemn the Obama administration's authorization to assassinate Anwar al-Awlaki, a U.S. citizen and cleric living in Yemen, over alleged links to a failed Christmas airline bombing in Detroit. Kucinich also invited investigative journalist Jeremy Scahill, writer David Swanson, retired army colonel Ann Wright, and Iraq war veteran Josh Stieber.

The gathering, held in the Rayburn Building, was a sober reminder of the insignificance of the left. No other Congress members were present, and only a smattering of young staff members attended. Most of the audience of about seventy were peace activists who, as is usual at such events, were joined by a motley collection of conspiracy theorists who insisted that 9/11 was an inside job, or that Senator Paul Wellstone, who died in a 2002 plane crash, had been assassinated. Scahill provided a litany of statistics that illustrated how corporations have taken over our internal security and intelligence apparatus. They not only run our economy and manage our systems of communication. They not only own the two major political parties. They have built a private military. And they have become unassailable.

Scahill, who has done most of the groundbreaking investigative reporting on the conduct of private contractors in Iraq, including that of the security firm Blackwater (renamed, after a firestorm of bad publicity and public outrage at its methods, Xe), laid out that afternoon how the management of the wars in Iraq and Afghanistan was steadily transferred by the Pentagon to unaccountable private contractors. He lamented the lack of support in Congress for a bill put forward by Representative Jan Schakowsky of Illinois. House Resolution 4102, known as the *Stop Outsourcing Security (SOS) Act*, would "responsibly phase out the use of private security contractors for functions that should be reserved for U.S. military forces and government personnel."

"It is one of the sober realities of the time we are living in that you can put forward a bill that says something as simple as 'we should not outsource national security functions to private contractors' and you only get twenty members of Congress to support the bill," Scahill said:

> The unfortunate reality is that Representative Schakowsky knows that the war industry is bipartisan. They give on both sides. For a while there, it seemed *contractor* was the new *Israel*. You could not find a member of Congress to speak out against them because so many members of Congress are beholden to corporate funding to keep their House or Senate seats. I also think Obama's election has wiped that out, as it has with many things, because the White House will dispatch emissaries to read the riot act to members of Congress who don't toe the party line.[22]

The privatization of government functions has at once empowered corporate dominance and weakened the traditional role of government. There are eighteen military and civilian intelligence agencies, and seventy percent of their combined budgets is outsourced to corporations, who use the experience and expertise gained on these projects to provide similar services to other corporations, as well as foreign governments. The Pentagon has privatized sixty-nine percent of its workforce. Scahill pointed out the overwhelming privatization of the Afghanistan war effort. As of this writing, there are 104,000 Department of Defense contractors and sixty-eight thousand troops, almost 1.5 corporate employees for every member of the military. The State Department in Afghanistan has hired an additional fourteen thousand private contractors.

"Within a matter of months, and certainly within a year, the United States will have upwards of 220,000 to 250,000 U.S. government-funded personnel occupying Afghanistan, a far cry from the 70,000 U.S. soldiers that those Americans who pay attention understand the United States has in Afghanistan," Scahill said. "This is a country where the president's national security adviser, General James Jones, said there are less than one hundred al-Qaida operatives who have no ability to strike at the United States. That was the stated rationale and reasoning for being in Afghanistan. It was to hunt down those responsible for 9/11."

Josh Stieber spoke at the end of the event. Stieber was deployed with the army to Iraq from February 2007 to April 2008. He was in Bravo Company 2–16 Infantry, which was involved in the July 2007 Apache helicopter attack on Iraqi civilians depicted on a controversial video released in April 2010 by WikiLeaks, an organization that publishes anonymous submissions of and commentary on sensitive government and corporate documents. Stieber, who left the army as a conscientious objector, has issued a public apology to the Iraqi people.

"This was not by any means the exception," he said of the video, which showed helicopter pilots nonchalantly gunning down civilians, including a Reuters photographer and children, in a Baghdad street:

It is inevitable given the situation we were going through. We were going through a lot of combat at the time. A roadside bomb would go off or a sniper would fire a shot, and you had no idea where it was coming from. There was a constant paranoia, a constant being on edge. If you put people in a situation like that where there are plenty of civilians, that kind of thing was going to happen and did happen and will continue to happen as long as our nation does not challenge these things. Now that this video has become public, it is our responsibility as a people and a country to recognize that this is what war looks like on a day-to-day basis.[23]

The voices of sanity, the voices of reason, of those who have a moral core, those like Kucinich or Scahill or Stieber, have little chance now to be heard. The liberal class, which failed to grasp the dark intentions of the corporate state and its servants in the Democratic Party, bears some responsibility.

Support for war has allied the liberals with venal warlords in Afghanistan who are as opposed to the rights of women and basic democratic freedoms, and as heavily involved in opium trafficking, as the Taliban. The supposed moral lines between the liberal class and our adversaries are fictional. The uplifting narratives used to justify the war in Afghanistan are pathetic attempts by the liberal class to redeem acts of senseless brutality. War cannot be waged to instill any virtue, including democracy or the liberation of women. War always empowers those who have a penchant for violence and access to weapons. War turns the moral order upside down and abolishes all discussions of human rights. War banishes the just and the decent to the margins of society. The power of modern weapons means inevitable civilian deaths or "collateral damage." An aerial drone is our version of an improvised explosive device. An iron fragmentation bomb is our answer to a suicide bomb. A burst from a belt-fed light machine gun causes the same terror and bloodshed among civilians no matter who pulls the trigger.

"We need to tear the mask off of the fundamentalist warlords who after the tragedy of 9/11 replaced the Taliban," Malalai Joya, who was expelled from the Afghan parliament for denouncing government corruption and the Western occupation, told me[24]:

> They used the mask of democracy to take power. They continue this deception. These warlords are mentally the same as the Taliban. The only change is physical. These warlords during the civil war in Afghanistan from 1992 to 1996 killed sixty-five thousand innocent people. They have committed human rights violations, like the Taliban, against women and many others.

"We believe that this is not war on terror," she said:

> This is war on innocent civilians. Look at the massacres carried out by NATO forces in Afghanistan. Look what they did in May in the Farah Province, where more than 150 civilians were killed, most of them women and children. They used white phosphorus and cluster

bombs. There were two hundred civilians on ninth of September killed in the Kunduz Province, again most of them women and children. . . . The United States and NATO eight years ago occupied my country under the banner of woman's rights and democracy. But they have only pushed us from the frying pan into the fire. They put into power men who are photocopies of the Taliban.

Over the past ten years of occupation, Afghanistan's boom in the opium trade, used to produce heroin, has funneled hundreds of millions of dollars to the Taliban, al-Qaida, local warlords, criminal gangs, kidnappers, private armies, drug traffickers, and many of the senior figures in the government of President Hamid Karzai. The *New York Times* reported that Ahmed Wali Karzai, brother of President Karzai, was collecting money from the CIA although he is a major player in the illegal opium business. Afghanistan produces ninety-two percent of the world's opium in a trade worth some $65 billion, the United Nations estimates. This opium feeds some fifteen million addicts worldwide and kills around one hundred thousand people annually. These fatalities should be added to the lists of war dead.

Antonio Maria Costa, executive director of the United Nations Office on Drugs and Crime (UNODC), has said that the drug trade has permitted the Taliban to thrive and expand despite the presence of NATO troops: "The Taliban's direct involvement in the opium trade allows them to fund a war machine that is becoming technologically more complex and increasingly widespread."[25]

The UNODC estimates the Taliban earned $90 million to $160 million a year from taxing the production and smuggling of opium and heroin between 2005 and 2009, as much as double the amount it earned annually while it was in power nearly a decade ago. And Costa described the Afghanistan-Pakistan border as "the world's largest free-trade zone in anything and everything that is illicit," an area blighted by drugs, weapons, and illegal immigration. The "perfect storm of drugs and terrorism" may be on the move along drug trafficking routes through Central Asia, he warned. Opium profits are being pumped into militant groups in Central Asia, and "a big part of the region could be engulfed in large-scale terrorism, endangering its massive energy resources."

"Afghanistan, after eight years of occupation, has become a world center for drugs," Joya told me:

> The drug lords are the only ones with power. How can you expect these people to stop the planting of opium and halt the drug trade? How is it that the Taliban, when they were in power, destroyed the opium production, and a superpower not only cannot destroy the opium production but allows it to increase? And while all this goes on, those who support the war talk to you about women's rights. We do not have human rights now in most provinces. It is as easy to kill a woman in my country as it is to kill a bird. In some big cities like Kabul, some women have access to jobs and education, but in most of the country the situation for women is hell. Rape, kidnapping, and domestic violence are increasing. These fundamentalists during the so-called free elections made a misogynist law against Shia women in Afghanistan. This law has even been signed by Hamid Karzai. All these crimes are happening under the name of democracy.

Thousands of Afghan civilians have died from insurgent and foreign military violence. And American and NATO forces are responsible for almost *half* the civilian deaths in Afghanistan. Tens of thousands of Afghan civilians have also died from displacement, starvation, disease, exposure, lack of medical treatment, crime, and lawlessness resulting from the war.

Joya said that NATO, by choosing sides in a battle between two corrupt and brutal opponents, has lost all legitimacy in the country, an opinion echoed by a high-level U.S. diplomat in Afghanistan, Matthew Hoh, who resigned in protest over the war. Hoh wrote in his resignation letter that Karzai's government is filled with "glaring corruption and unabashed graft." Karzai, he wrote, is a president "whose confidants and chief advisers comprise drug lords and war crimes villains who mock our own rule of law and counter-narcotics effort."[26]

Joya was skeptical about the fate of the touted billions in international aid to Afghanistan:

> Where do you think the $36 billion of money poured into the country by the international community have gone? This money went

into the pockets of the drug lords and the warlords. There are 18 million people in Afghanistan who live on less than $2 a day while these warlords get rich. The Taliban and warlords together contribute to this fascism while the occupation forces are bombing and killing innocent civilians. When we do not have security, how can we even talk about human rights or women's rights?

"Many Afghanis side with the Taliban," Joya said.

They do not support the Taliban, but they are fed up with these warlords and this injustice, and they go with the Taliban to take revenge. I do not agree with them, but I understand them. Most of my people are against the Taliban and the warlords, which is why millions did not take part in this tragic drama of an election.

Joya, who changes houses in Kabul frequently because of death threats, decried the support for the Karzai administration:

The U.S. wastes taxpayers' money and the blood of their soldiers by supporting such a Mafia-corrupt system of Hamid Karzai. They chained my country to the center of drugs. If Obama was really honest he would support the democratic-minded people of my country. We have a lot [of those people]. But he does not support the democratic-minded people of my country. He is going to start war in Pakistan by attacking in the border area of Pakistan. More civilians have been killed in the Obama period than even during the criminal Bush.

"My people are sandwiched between two powerful enemies," she lamented:

The occupation forces from the sky bomb and kill innocent civilians. On the ground, Taliban and these warlords deliver fascism. As NATO kills more civilians, the resistance to the foreign troops increases. If the U.S. government and NATO do not leave voluntarily, my people will give to them the same lesson they gave to Russia and to the English who three times tried to occupy Afghanistan. It is easier for us to fight against one enemy rather than two.

Success in Afghanistan depends on the ability to create an indigenous army that will battle the Taliban, provide security and stability for Afghan civilians, and remain loyal to the puppet Karzai government. A similar task eluded the Red Army, although the Soviets spent a decade attempting to pacify the country. It eluded the British a century earlier. And the United States, too, will fail.

U.S. military advisers who work with the Afghan National Army, or ANA, speak of poorly trained and unmotivated Afghan soldiers with little stomach for military discipline and even less for fighting. The advisers describe many ANA units as filled with brigands who terrorize local populations, engaging in extortion, intimidation, rape, theft, and open collusion with the Taliban. They contend that the ANA is riddled with Taliban sympathizers. And when U.S. and ANA soldiers fight together against Taliban insurgents, the U.S, advisers say the ANA soldiers prove to be fickle and unreliable combatants.

Military commanders in Afghanistan, rather than pump out statistics about enemy body counts, measure progress by the size of the ANA. The bigger the ANA, the better we are supposedly doing. The pressure on trainers to increase ANA numbers means that training and vetting of incoming Afghan recruits are nearly nonexistent.

The process of induction for Afghan soldiers begins at the Kabul Military Training Center. American instructors routinely complain of shortages of school supplies such as whiteboards, markers, and paper. They often have to go to markets and pay for these supplies on their own or do without. Instructors are pressured to pass all recruits, and they graduate many who have been absent for a third to half the training time. Most are inducted into the ANA without having mastered rudimentary military skills.

"I served the first half of my tour at the Kabul Military Training Center (KMTC), where I was part of a small team working closely with the ANA to set up the country's first officer basic course for newly commissioned Afghan lieutenants," a U.S. Army first lieutenant told me. He asked not to be identified by name. "During the second half of my tour, I left Kabul's military schoolhouse and was reassigned to an embedded tactical training team, or ETT team, to help stand up a new Afghan logistics battalion in Herat.

"Afghan soldiers leave the KMTC grossly unqualified," said this lieutenant, who remains on active duty. "American mentors do what they can to try and fix these problems, but their efforts are blocked by pressure from higher, both in Afghan and American chains of command, to pump out as many soldiers as fast as possible."

Afghan soldiers are sent from the KMTC directly to active-duty ANA units. The units always have American trainers, known as a "mentoring team," attached to them. The rapid increase in ANA soldiers has outstripped the ability of the American military to provide trained mentoring teams. The teams, normally composed of members of the Army Special Forces, are now formed by groups of American soldiers, plucked more or less at random, from units all over Afghanistan.

"This is how my entire team was selected during the middle of my tour: a random group of people from all over Kabul—air force, navy, army, active-duty, and national guard—pulled from their previous assignments, thrown together and expected to do a job that none of us were trained in any meaningful way to do," the officer said:

> We are expected, by virtue of time in grade, and membership in the U.S. military, to be able to train a foreign force in military operations, an extremely irresponsible policy that is ethnocentric at its core and which assumes some sort of natural superiority in which an untrained American soldier has everything to teach the Afghans, but nothing to learn.

"You're lucky enough if you had any mentorship training at all, something the army provides in a limited capacity at premobilization training at Fort Riley, [Kansas], but having none is the norm," he said. "Soldiers who receive their premobilization training at Fort Bragg [North Carolina] learn absolutely nothing about mentoring foreign forces aside from being given a booklet on the subject, and yet soldiers who go through Bragg before being shipped to Afghanistan are just as likely to be assigned to mentoring teams as anyone else."

The differences between the Afghan military structure and the U.S. military structure are substantial. The ANA handles logistics differently. Its rank structure is not the same. Its administration uses different military terms. It rarely works with the aid of computers or basic technology. The cultural divide leaves most trainers, who do not speak Dari, struggling to figure out how things work in the ANA.

"The majority of my time spent as a mentor involved trying to understand what the Afghans were doing and how they were expected to do it, and only then could I even begin to advise anyone on the problems they were facing," this officer said. "In other words, American military advisers aren't immediately helpful to Afghans. There is a major learning curve involved that is sometimes never overcome. Some advisers play a pivotal role, but many have little or no effect as mentors."

The real purpose of American advisers assigned to ANA units, however, is not ultimately to train Afghans but rather to function as liaisons between Afghani units and American firepower and logistics. The ANA is unable to integrate ground units with artillery and air support. It has no functioning supply system. It depends on the U.S. military to do basic tasks. The United States even pays the bulk of ANA salaries.

"In the unit I was helping to mentor, orders for mission-essential equipment, such as five-ton trucks, went unfilled for months, and winter clothes came late due to national shortages," the officer told me. "Many soldiers in the unit had to make do for the first few weeks of Afghanistan's winter without jackets or other cold-weather items."

But what disturbs advisers most is the widespread corruption within the ANA, which has enraged and alienated local Afghans and proved a potent recruiting tool for the Taliban.

"In the Afghan logistics battalion I was embedded with, the commander himself was extorting a local shopkeeper, and his staff routinely stole from the local store," the adviser said:

In Kabul, on one humanitarian aid mission I was on, we handed out school supplies to children, and in an attempt to lend validity to the ANA we had them [ANA members] distribute the supplies. As it turns out, we received intelligence reports that that very same group of ANA had been extorting money from the villagers under threat of violence. In essence, we teamed up with well-known criminals and local thugs to distribute aid in the very village they had been terrorizing, and that was the face of American charity.

We currently spend some $4 billion a month on Afghanistan. But we are unable to pay for whiteboards and markers for instructors. Afghan soldiers lack winter jackets. Kabul is still in ruins. Unemployment is estimated at about forty percent. And Afghanistan is one of the most food-insecure countries on the planet.

What are we doing? Where is this money going?

Look to the civilian contractors. These contractors dominate the lucrative jobs in Afghanistan. The American military, along with the ANA, is considered a poor relation. And war, after all, is primarily a business.

"When I arrived in the theater, one of the things I was shocked to see was how many civilians were there," the U.S. officer said:

> Americans and foreign nationals from Eastern Europe and Southeast Asia were holding jobs in great numbers in Kabul. There are a ton of corporations in Afghanistan performing labor that was once exclusively in the realm of the military. If you're a [military] cook, someone from Kellogg Brown & Root[now KBR] has taken your spot. If you're a logistician or military adviser, someone from MPRI, Military Professional Resources Inc., will probably take over your job soon. If you're a technician or a mechanic, there are civilians from Harris Corp[oration] and other companies there who are taking over more and more of your responsibilities.

This officer deployed to Afghanistan with about one hundred military advisers and mentors, he says. But when they arrived, they encountered an unpleasant surprise:

> [N]early half our unit had to be reassigned because their jobs had been taken over by civilians from MPRI. It seems that even in a war zone, soldiers are at risk of losing their jobs to outsourcing. And if you're a reservist, the situation is even more unfortunate. You are torn from your life to serve a yearlong tour of duty away from your civilian job, your friends, and family, only to end up in Afghanistan with nothing to do because your military duty was passed on to a civilian contractor. Eventually you are thrown onto a mentoring

team somewhere, or some [other] responsibility is created for you. It becomes evident that the corporate presence in Afghanistan has a direct effect on combat operations.

What was once done by the military, concerned with tactical and strategic advancement, is now done by war profiteers, concerned solely with profit. The aims of the military and the contractors are in conflict. Any scaling down of the war or withdrawal means a loss of business for corporations. But expansion of the war, as many veterans will attest, is making the situation only more precarious.

"American and Afghan soldiers are putting their lives at risk, Afghan civilians are dying, and yet there's this underlying system in place that gains more from keeping all of them in harm's way rather than taking them out of it," the officer complained. "If we bring peace and stability to Afghanistan, we may profit morally, we might make gains for humanity, but moral profits and human gains do not contribute to the bottom line. Peace and profit are ultimately contradictory forces at work in Afghanistan."

We hear of the wells dug, the schools built, the roads paved and the food distributed in Afghan villages by the occupation forces—and almost nothing about the huge profits made by contractors. It is estimated that only ten percent of the money poured into Afghanistan is used to ameliorate the suffering of Afghan civilians. The remainder is swallowed by contractors who siphon the money out of Afghanistan and into foreign bank accounts. This misguided allocation of funds is compounded in Afghanistan because the highest-paying jobs for Afghans go to those who can act as interpreters for the American military and foreign contractors. The best-educated Afghans are enticed away from Afghan institutions that desperately need their skills and education.

"It is this system that has broken the logistics of Afghanistan," the officer said:

It is this system of waste and private profit from public funds that keeps Kabul in ruins. It is this system that manages to feed Westerners all across the country steak and lobster once a week while an estimated 8.4 million Afghans—the entire population of New York City, the Five Boroughs—suffer from chronic food insecurity and starvation every day. When you go to Bagram Air Base, or Camp Phoenix, or Camp Eggers, it's clear to see that the problem does not lie in getting supplies into the country. The question becomes who gets them. And we wonder why there's an insurgency.

The problem in Afghanistan is not ultimately a military problem. It is a political and social problem. The real threat to stability in Afghanistan is not the Taliban, but widespread hunger and food shortages, crippling poverty, rape, corruption, and a staggering rate of unemployment that mounts as foreign companies take jobs away from the local workers and businesses. The corruption and abuse by the Karzai government and the ANA, along with the presence of foreign contractors, are the central impediments to peace. The more we empower these forces, the worse the war will become. The plan to escalate the number of U.S. soldiers and Marines, and to swell the ranks of the Afghan National Army, will not defeat or pacify the Taliban.

"What good are a quarter-million well-trained Afghan troops to a nation slipping into famine?" the officer asked. "What purpose does a strong military serve with a corrupt and inept government in place? What hope do we have for peace if the best jobs for the Afghans involve working for the military? What is the point of getting rid of the Taliban if it means killing civilians with airstrikes and supporting a government of misogynist warlords and criminals?

"We as Americans do not help the Afghans by sending in more troops, by increasing military spending, by adding chaos to disorder," he said. "What little help we do provide is only useful in the short term and is clearly unsustainable in the face of our own economic crisis. In the end, no one benefits from this war, not America, not Afghans. Only the CEOs and executive officers of war-profiteering corporations find satisfactory returns on their investments."

꩜

Congress has approved $345 billion for the war in Afghanistan, which includes more than $40 billion for training and equipping the army and police, according to the Special Inspector General for Afghanistan Reconstruction. The United States spends an estimated $500,000 to $1 million per soldier or marine per year in Afghanistan, depending on whether expenditures on housing and equipment are included along with pay, food, and fuel. These funds do not include medical costs and veterans' compensation. Foreign aid to Afghanistan, including food and development assistance, has totaled $17 billion since 2002, according to State Department and Congressional Research Service documents.

But it is not the financial cost of the war that makes the occupation of Iraq and Afghanistan so tragic, wasteful, and immoral. War as an instrument of change is brutal, savage, impersonal and counterproductive. It mocks the fantasy of individual heroism and the absurdity of utopian goals, such as the imposition of Western-style democracy or the liberation of women. In an instant, industrial warfare can kill dozens, even hundreds of people, who never see their attackers. The power of industrial weapons is indiscriminate and staggering. They can take down apartment blocks in seconds, burying and crushing everyone inside. They can demolish villages and send tanks, planes, and ships up in fiery blasts. The wounds, for those who survive, result in terrible burns, blindness, amputation, and lifelong pain and trauma. No one returns the same from such warfare. And once these weapons are employed, all talk of human rights is a farce. The explosive blasts of these weapons systems, for those of us who have witnessed them at work, inevitably kill and maim civilians, including children.

In Peter van Agtmael's *2nd Tour, Hope I Don't Die* and Lori Grinker's *Afterwar: Veterans from a World in Conflict*, two haunting books of war photographs, we see pictures of war which are almost always hidden from public view. They are shadows, for only those who go to and suffer from war can fully confront the visceral horror of it, but the books are at least an attempt to unmask war's savagery.

"Over ninety percent of this soldier's body was burned when a roadside bomb hit his vehicle, igniting the fuel tank and burning two other soldiers to death," reads a caption in van Agtmael's book. The photograph shows the bloodied body of a soldier in an operating room:

> His camouflage uniform dangled over the bed, ripped open by the medics who had treated him on the helicopter. Clumps of his skin had peeled away, and what was left of it was translucent. He was in and out of consciousness, his eyes stabbing open for a few seconds.

As he was lifted from the stretcher to the ER bed, he screamed "Daddy, Daddy, Daddy, Daddy," then "Put me to sleep, please put me to sleep." There was another photographer in the ER, and he leaned his camera over the heads of the medical staff to get an overhead shot. The soldier yelled, "Get that fucking camera out of my face."

"Those were his last words. I visited his grave one winter afternoon six months later," van Agtmael writes, "and the scene of his death is never far from my thoughts."[27]

"There were three of us inside, and the jeep caught fire," Israeli soldier Yossi Arditi says in Grinker's book. He is describing the moment a Molotov cocktail exploded in his vehicle. "The fuel tank was full and it was about to explode, my skin was hanging from my arms and face—but I didn't lose my head. I knew nobody could get inside to help me, that my only way out was through the fire to the doors. I wanted to take my gun, but I couldn't touch it because my hands were burning."

Arditi spent six months in the hospital. He had surgery every two or three months, about twenty operations, over the next three years.

"People who see me, see what war really does," he says.[28]

Filmic and most photographic images of war are shorn of the heart-pounding fear, awful stench, deafening noise, screams of pain, and exhaustion of the battlefield. Such images turn confusion and chaos, the chief elements of combat, into an artful war narrative. They turn war into porn. Soldiers and Marines, especially those who have never seen war, buy cases of beer and watch movies like *Platoon*, movies meant to denounce war, and as they do, they revel in the destructive power of weaponry. The reality of violence is different. Everything formed by violence is senseless and useless. It exists without a future. It leaves behind nothing but death, grief, and destruction.

Chronicles of war that eschew images and scenes of combat begin to capture war's reality. War's effects are what the state and the media, the handmaidens of the war-makers, work hard to keep hidden. If we really saw war, what war does to young minds and bodies, it would be impossible to embrace the myth of war. If we had to stand over the mangled corpses of schoolchildren killed in Afghanistan and listen to the wails of their parents, we would not be able to repeat clichés we use to justify war. This is why war is carefully sanitized. This is why we are given war's perverse and dark thrill but are spared from seeing war's consequences. The mythic visions of war keep it heroic and entertaining. And the media are as guilty as Hollywood. During the start of the Iraq war, television reports gave us the visceral thrill of force and hid from us the effects of bullets, tank rounds, iron fragmentation bombs, and artillery rounds. We tasted a bit of war's exhilaration, but were protected from seeing what war actually does to human bodies.

The wounded, the crippled, and the dead are, in this great charade, swiftly carted offstage. They are war's refuse. We do not see them. We do not hear them. They are doomed, like wandering spirits, to float around the edges of our consciousness, ignored, even reviled. The message they tell is too painful for us to hear. We prefer to celebrate ourselves and our nation by imbibing the myths of glory, honor, patriotism, and heroism, words that in combat become empty and meaningless. And those whom fate has decreed must face war's effects often turn and flee.

Saul Alfaro, who lost his legs in the war in El Salvador, speaks in Grinker's book about the first and final visit from his girlfriend as he lay in an army hospital bed.

"She had been my girlfriend in the military, and we had planned to be married," he says. "But when she saw me in the hospital—I don't know exactly what happened, but later they told me when she saw me she began to cry. Afterwards, she ran away and never came back."[29]

Public manifestations of gratitude are reserved for veterans who dutifully read from the script handed to them by the state. The veterans trotted out for viewing are those who are compliant and palatable, those we can stand to look at without horror, those willing to go along with the lie that war is the highest form of patriotism. "Thank you for your service," we are supposed to say. These soldiers are used to perpetuate the myth. We are used to honor it.

Gary Zuspann, who lives in a special enclosed environment in his parents' home in Waco, Texas, suffers from Gulf War syndrome. He speaks in Grinker's book of feeling like "a prisoner of war" even after the war had ended.

"Basically they put me on the curb and said, okay, fend for yourself," he says in the book. "I was living in a fantasy world where I thought our government cared about us and they take care of their own. I believed it was in my contract, that if you're maimed or wounded during your service in war, you should be taken care of. Now I'm angry."[30]

I went back to Sarajevo after covering the 1990s war for the *New York Times* and found hundreds of cripples trapped in rooms in apartment blocks with no elevators and no wheelchairs. Most were young men, many without limbs, being cared for by their elderly parents, the glorious war heroes left to rot.

Despair and suicide grip survivors. It is estimated that as many Vietnam veterans committed suicide after the war as were killed during it. The inhuman qualities drilled into soldiers and Marines in wartime defeat them in peacetime. This is what Homer taught us in *The Iliad*, the great book on war, and *The Odyssey*, the great book on the long journey to recovery by professional killers. Many never readjust. They cannot connect again with wives, children, parents, or friends, retreating into personal hells of self-destructive anguish and rage.

"They program you to have no emotion—like if somebody sitting next to you gets killed you just have to carry on doing your job and shut up," Steve Annabell, a British veteran of the Falklands War, says to Grinker. "When you leave the service, when you come back from a situation like that, there's no button they can press to switch your emotions back on. So you walk around like a zombie. They don't deprogram you. If you become a problem they just sweep you under the carpet."

"To get you to join up they do all these advertisements—they show people skiing down mountains and doing great things—but they don't show you getting shot at and people with their legs blown off or burning to death," he says. "They don't show you what really happens. It's just bullshit. And they never prepare you for it. They can give you all the training in the world, but it's never the same as the real thing."[31]

Those with whom veterans have most in common when the war is over are often those they fought.

"Nobody comes back from war the same," says Horacio Javier Benitez, who fought the British in the Falklands and is quoted in Grinker's book. "The person, Horacio, who was sent to war, doesn't exist anymore. It's hard to be enthusiastic about normal life; too much seems inconsequential. You contend with craziness and depression.

"Many who served in the Malvinas," he says, using the Argentine name of the islands, "committed suicide, many of my friends."[32]

"I miss my family," reads graffiti captured in one of van Agtmael's photographs. "Please God forgive the lives I took and let my family be happy if I don't go home again."

Next to the plea someone had drawn an arrow toward the words and written in thick, black marker: "Fag!!!"[33]

The disparity between what we are told or what we believe about war and war itself is so vast that those who come back are often rendered speechless. What do you say to those who advocate war as an instrument to liberate the women of Afghanistan or bring democracy to Iraq? How do you tell them what war is like? How do you explain that the very proposition of war as an instrument of virtue is absurd? How do you cope with memories of small, terrified children bleeding to death with bits of iron fragments peppered throughout their small bodies? How do you speak of war without tears?

Look beyond the nationalist cant used to justify war. Look beyond the seduction of the weapons and the pornography of violence. Look beyond Obama's ridiculous rhetoric about finishing the job or fighting terror. Focus on the evil of war. War begins by calling for the annihilation of the Other, but ends ultimately in self-annihilation. It corrupts souls and mutilates bodies. It destroys homes and villages and murders children on their way to school. It grinds into the dirt all that is tender and beautiful and sacred. It empowers human deformities—warlords, Shiite death squads, Sunni insurgents, the Taliban, al-Qaida and our own killers—who can speak only in the despicable language of force. War is a scourge. It is a plague. It is industrial murder. And before you support war, especially the wars in Iraq and Afghanistan, look into the hollow eyes of the men, women and children who know it.

III / Dismantling the Liberal Class

To those of us who still retain an irreconcilable animus against war, it has been a bitter experience to see the unanimity with which the American intellectuals have thrown their support to the use of war-technique in the crisis in which America found herself. Socialists, college professors, publicists, new-republicans, practitioners of literature, have vied with each other in confirming with their intellectual faith the collapse of neutrality and the riveting of the war-mind on a hundred million more of the world's people. And the intellectuals are not content with confirming our belligerent gesture. They are now complacently asserting that it was they who effectively willed it, against the hesitation and dim perceptions of the American democratic masses. A war made deliberately by the intellectuals! A calm moral verdict reluctantly passed after a penetrating study of inexorable facts! Sluggish masses, too remote from the world conflict to be stirred, too lacking in intellect to perceive their danger!

—RANDOLPH BOURNE,
"The War and the Intellectuals," 1917[1]

WOODROW WILSON, escorted by a troop of cavalry because of fears of anarchist bomb attacks, left the White House on a dreary, rainy April evening in 1917 for the Capitol to call on Congress to declare war on Germany. He made the twelve-minute journey without his family, who had gone on ahead, and entered the packed House of Representatives to enthusiastic applause.

He began his speech before the joint session of Congress in a quiet, conversational tone. He dryly listed the events that had transpired since the United States had severed diplomatic relations with Germany. He denounced German submarine warfare, which had resulted in the sinking of American cargo ships, as an attack against all humanity. He said that he had once thought armed neutrality would work, but had come to see that it was ineffectual.

"There is," Wilson said, "one choice we cannot make, we are incapable of making: we will not choose the path of submission and suffer the most sacred rights of our Nation and our people to be ignored or violated."

Chief Justice Edward Douglas White, a veteran of the Civil War who had fought on the Confederate side, was sitting with the other members of the Supreme Court in the front of the Speaker's stand, and he interrupted with applause that became contagious, spread through the assembly, and soon thundered throughout the chamber.

"With a profound sense of the solemn and even tragical character of the step I am taking," Wilson went on,

> and of the grave responsibilities which it involves, but in unhesitating obedience to what I deem my constitutional duty, I advise that the Congress declare the recent course of the Imperial German Government to be in fact nothing less than war against the government and the people of the United States; that it formally accept the status of belligerent which has thus been thrust upon it; and that it take immediate steps not only to put the country in a more thorough state of defense but also to exert all its power and employ all its resources to bring the Government of the German Empire to terms and end the war.

Justice White, a staunch segregationist who liked to regale listeners with tales of his personal war heroics that were too fantastic to be credible, at this point let out what to many who were in the chamber sounded like a Rebel yell. The crowd responded and rose to its feet in whoops and cheers. Wilson, who in 1916 had campaigned for reelection on the slogan "he kept us out of the war," had reversed himself. He had called on the Congress to commit United States troops to the brutal trench warfare and industrial slaughter that was tearing Europe apart and had already consumed the lives of millions of young men. He had done so although America was a fractious, divided nation that remained deeply skeptical about involving itself in Europe's self-slaughter. The country of one hundred million had 14.5 million people born outside the United States, including 2.5 million born in Germany, and hostility toward England, especially among nationalistic German and Irish immigrants, ran deep. Pacifism, a legacy of the costly fratricide of the Civil War, was championed by popular orators such as William Jennings Bryan and remained widespread. Many Americans who lived in remote, agricultural communities were deeply isolationist, distrustful of government, and ill informed about world affairs. This resistance would have to be overcome.

The decision to go to war, however, was quickly ratified. The Senate voted 82 to 6 for war. The House voted 373 to 50. War was declared on April 6, four days after Wilson's thirty-six minute address.

World War I ushered in the modern era. The war bequeathed industrial killing—wars fought with machines and sustained by industrial production—as well as vast wartime bureaucracies, which could for the first time administer and organize impersonal mass slaughter over months and years that left hundreds or thousands dead in an instant, many of whom never saw their attackers. Civil War battles rarely lasted more than two or three days. Battles in the new age of industrial warfare could rage for weeks and months with a steady flow of new munitions, mass-produced supplies, and mechanized transports that delivered troops by ship, rail, and motorized vehicles to the battlefield. A nation's entire industrial and organizational capacity, as well as its centralized systems of information and internal control, could be harnessed for war. World War I gave birth to the terrible leviathan of total war.

Just as ominously, the war unleashed radical new forms of mass propaganda and mass manipulation that made it possible to engineer public opinion through the technological innovations of radio, cinema, photography, cheap mass publications, and graphic art. Mass propaganda astutely exploited the new understanding of mass psychology, led by thinkers such as Gustave Le Bon (*The Crowd*), Wilfred Trotter (*Instincts of the Herd in Peace and War*), Graham Wallace (*Human*

Nature in Politics), and Gabriel Tarde (*On Opinion and Conversation*), as well as the work of pioneering psychologists such as Sigmund Freud.

The war destroyed values and self-perceptions that had once characterized American life and replaced them with fear, distrust, and the hedonism of the consumer society. The new mass propaganda, designed to appeal to emotions rather than disseminate facts, proved adept at driving competing ideas and values underground. It effectively vilified all who did not speak in the language imparted to the public by corporations and the state. For these reasons, it presaged a profound cultural and political shift. It snuffed out a brief and robust period of reform in American history, one that had seen mass movements, enraged at the abuses of an American oligarchy, sweep across the country and demand profound change. The rise of mass propaganda, made possible by industrial warfare, effectively killed populism.

The political upheavals in the years before the war had put numerous populists and reformers in positions of power, including the election of Socialist mayors in cities such as Milwaukee and Schenectady. While a few of these would linger until the 1950s, the war would chart a new course for the country. War propaganda not only bolstered support for the war—including among progressives and intellectuals—but also discredited dissidents and reformers as traitors.

The rise of mass propaganda signalled the primacy of Freud, who had discovered that the manipulation of powerful myths and images, playing to subconscious fears and desires, could lead men and women to embrace their own subjugation and even self-destruction. What Freud and the great investigators of mass psychology realized was that the emotions were not subordinate to reason. If anything, it was the reverse. Prior to World War I, much current American thinking, following post-Enlightenment European thought, relied on the assumption that reason could rule, that debate in the public sphere was driven most powerfully and effectively by strong, rational underpinnings. The dream was of a "pure dialectic," embodied in data, facts, postulates, deduction, or induction, stripped of emotion and conditioning. What Freud and the mass psychologists, and in turn, their godchildren, the mass propagandists, had rediscovered was a deep psychological truth grasped first and perhaps best by the philosophers and rhetoricians of Classical Greece. Greek philosophers did celebrate reason as *nous*, as a reflection of divine truth enacted in the human mind. But the Greek philosophers were trained in rhetoric before dialectics. Logical argumentation had to have a rhetorical, emotional resonance if it were to sway and shape public opinion. On the Pynx of Athens and later in the Forum of Rome, rhetors exercised powers of persuasion that appealed to emotions, alongside the appeal to reason and fact. Many Classical philosophers, beginning with Plato, warned that the appeal to emotion was only as good as the man making the appeal. But in twentieth-century mass propaganda, this warning was cast aside. The idea was to sway, and to use any means to do it. The moral aspect of public persuasion was pushed aside in pursuit of the targeted arousal of mass emotions. As the Greeks already knew, and Freud and his followers rediscovered, the illusion of "pure dialectic" was just that—an illusion.

The war, sold with simple slogans such as "the war to end all wars" or "the war to make the world safe for democracy," did not so much emasculate intellectuals, artists, and progressives as seduce them. The enthusiastic embrace of war by many intellectuals and dissidents stunned the few stalwarts, people like Randolph Bourne and Jane Addams, who watched in horror as the nation descended into a collective war madness. The great muckraking journalists, artists, and progressives who had used their talents to expose abuses of the working class joined the war effort.

Twelve thousand people, roused by German attacks on American cargo vessels and fiery denunciations in the press, rallied on March 22, 1917, in Madison Square Garden to call for war at a mass meeting organized by the American Rights Committee. William English Walling, Charles Edward Russell, Upton Sinclair, and nearly all other intellectual leaders in the Socialist Party, abandoning their opposition, issued a call for war the next day. The antiwar movement crumbled, with widespread defections including stalwarts such as Governor Arthur Capper of Kansas announcing on March 24 that the United States had to fight to defend itself against Germany's "murderous assaults on human life and human rights."[2] Preachers in the nation's most prominent pulpits blessed the call to arms, and the few voices that continued to resist the intoxication of battle were attacked. President John Grier Hibben of Princeton University, for example, refused to permit the pacifist David Starr Jordan, the former president of Stanford, to speak on the campus.

Jordan found refuge in the First Presbyterian Church in Princeton and tried to address the gathering but was booed by Princeton undergraduates. Huge rallies calling for war were held in Philadelphia, Denver, Boston, and Chicago, often addressed by progressive leaders and politicians. The beleaguered leaders of the Emergency Peace Federation, who tried to hold counter-rallies, were shouted down by crowds of war supporters, and were heckled and beaten by police.

"We have been doing the best we know to make known to the President and the Congressmen alternatives to war," Jordan reported:

> There would be no difficulty in the matter if the people concerned really wanted peace. Meanwhile, it is very evident that the Wall St. people are running this thing in their own interest, and that the thousands of conscientious men who think we . . . [should] do something for France or England are mere flies on the wheel by the side of the great prospects of having Uncle Sam endorse billions of European bonds and throw his money with Morgan & Company into the bottomless pit of war. . . . The Germans have behaved like sin, for such is the nature of war—but the intolerance and tyranny with which we are being pushed into war far eclipses [*sic*] the riotous methods which threw the Kaiser off his feet and brought on the crash in 1914.[3]

By the time war was declared by Congress, most of these last holdouts, including Jordan, let nationalism overcome principle and backed the war effort. There were still significant pockets of opposition within the population, but the antiwar movement had been decapitated.

"An intellectual class gently guiding a nation through sheer force of ideas into what the other nations entered only through predatory craft or popular hysteria or militarist madness!" Bourne wrote:

> A war free from any taint of self-seeking, a war that will secure the triumph of democracy and internationalize the world! This is the picture which the more self-conscious intellectuals have formed of themselves, and which they are slowly impressing upon a population which is being led no man knows whither by an indubitably intellectualized President. And they are right, in that the war certainly did not spring from either the ideals or the prejudices, from the national

ambitions or hysterias, of the American people, however acquiescent the masses prove to be, and however clearly the intellectuals prove their putative intuition.[4]

Wilson easily pushed through draconian laws to squelch dissent, but he hardly needed to have bothered. Congress passed the Espionage Act in 1917, which criminalized not only espionage but also speech deemed critical of the government. Wilson had hoped to include a provision for direct censorship of newspapers, but Congress denied his request. Next year Congress passed an amendment, known as the Sedition Act, that made it a crime to use "disloyal" or "profane" language that could encourage contempt for the Constitution or the flag. The Espionage Act and the Sedition Act became the coarse legal tools used by the Wilson administration to silence isolated progressives and the dwindling populist forces that questioned the war. Postmaster General Albert Burleson, empowered by the Espionage Act, cancelled the special mailing privileges of journals he condemned as unpatriotic, instantly hiking their postal rates and putting about a hundred out of business. A few thousand people, including the Socialist politician Eugene Debs, were arrested for their continued denunciation of the war and calls for draft resistance and strikes. Debs was imprisoned after making an antiwar speech in Canton, Ohio, in June 1918. The *Washington Post* wrote after his sentencing that "Debs is a public menace, and the country will be better off with him behind bars."[5] Debs spent more than two years in the Atlanta Federal Penitentiary until President Warren Harding commuted his sentence on Christmas Day 1921. Vigilante groups, roused by the enflamed war propaganda and nationalist call to arms, physically attacked and at times lynched war opponents.

Progressive politics had enjoyed an upsurge before the war, bringing on a golden era of American journalism and social reform, but that was now ended. Progressivism would flicker to life again in the 1930s with the Great Depression and then be crushed in the next war. Progressives in World War I shifted from the role of social critics to that of propagandists. They did this seamlessly. The crusades undertaken for the working poor in mill towns and urban slums were transformed into an abstract crusade to remake the world through violence, a war to end all wars. Addams acidly pointed out that "it is hard for some of us to understand upon what experience this pathetic belief in the regenerative results of war could be founded; but the world had become filled with fine phrases and this one, which afforded comfort to many a young soldier, was taken up and endlessly repeated with an entire absence of critical spirit."

The former socialists and activists were, perhaps, the most susceptible to Wilson's utopian dreams of a democratic League of Nations that would end warfare forever. Wilson, after all, came from the ranks of the liberal class. He was articulate and literate, knew many of them and was comfortable in the world of political theory and abstract thought. He wrote his own speeches. He reflected their high ideals. These intellectuals, once on the margins of society, became trusted allies in Wilson's crusade to recreate the world through violence. They were lauded and praised in public ways that were new and seductive. They no longer felt alienated from power but rather felt valued and appreciated by the elite. They lent their considerable skill to war propaganda and, in an intellectual and moral sense, committed suicide. Very few found the moral fortitude to resist. And their combined effort to sell the war fatally corrupted the liberal class.

"The intellectuals, in other words, have identified themselves with the least democratic forces in American life," Bourne lamented.

> They have assumed the leadership for war of those very classes whom the American democracy has been immemorially fighting. Only in a world where irony was dead could an intellectual class enter war at the head of such illiberal cohorts in the avowed cause of world liberalism and world democracy. No one is left to point out the undemocratic nature of this war liberalism. In a time of faith, skepticism is the most intolerable of all insults.

Arthur Bullard was a former history student of Wilson's at Princeton who went on to work as a reporter and foreign correspondent, including in Russia. He was typical of the intellectuals and activists who embraced the war and shifted their energy from social reform to state propaganda. Bullard, who often wrote under the pseudonym Albert Edwards for the pro-Bolshevik publication *The Masses* as well as *Harper's*, had sterling credentials as a muckraker and social activist. He had left Hamilton College after two years to serve as a probation officer for the New York Prison Association, spurred by the muckrackers' reports of the squalid conditions of the working class, and moved into University House on the Lower East Side. University House when he arrived was filled with radical writers as well as settlement house workers. It included the socialist writer William English Walling (a founder of the NAACP); Pulitzer Prize winner Ernest Poole; Howard Brubaker, who later became a columnist for the *New Yorker*; journalist Hamilton Hold, the editor of the weekly *Independent*, and author Walter Weyl, a founding editor of the *New Republic*. These writers produced articles and books on the housing and employment situation of workers on the Lower East Side, particularly the effects of inhuman working conditions and poverty on women and children. They were avowed socialists and fellow travelers with the revolutionaries seeking to topple the Russian Tsar Nicholas II. Poole, Walling, and Bullard, who was a press agent for the Friends of Russian Freedom in America, traveled to Russia in 1905 to cover the abortive revolution and its aftermath. They established contacts with radical Russian intellectuals, writers, artists, and revolutionaries. Bullard contributed a series of articles on Russia— he spoke some Russian—to *Harper's* and *Collier's*. In a report he wrote for *Collier's* in April 1906 under the pseudonym Albert Edwards, he told readers:

> My object in making this trip was to see how well the Russian troops could succeed in suppressing a revolutionary movement by sheer terrorism. I am convinced they cannot do it. They have failed to capture the leaders. They have failed to disarm the people. They have not succeeded in stamping out the revolutionary fire among the mass of the peasants. The indiscriminate executions, floggings, and burnings have only poured oil on the fire; it has turned the indignation into a personal determination for vengeance for murdered kindred; it has turned discontent into desperation, and hostility into hatred.

"General Orloff is a military man," he concluded, "and he was given orders to suppress the rebellion in these provinces. He did, and is doing it, as far as he can, but he has not enough soldiers, nor enough cartridges to do it thoroughly. The position of the Government has been perfectly logical—except for its premise, which is that this is the middle of the Dark Ages and that a state exists by the fear of its subjects."[6]

Bullard, who witnessed the power of revolutionary idealism and propaganda, believed that heavy censorship and secrecy laws that Wilson advocated would backfire, especially with many Americans viewing the war as one pushed down the throats of the nation by bankers and industrialists. The bankers and industrialists wanted to ensure that the massive loans to the European powers would be repaid, something that would not happen if Germany won the war. He grasped that a more potent weapon than overt repression could be found in mass propaganda. Propaganda could, he understood, feed the dark sentiments of nationalism and the lust for violence that made war possible. The public, he grasped, would, with the right kind of guidance, become enthusiastic war supporters. He sent a copy of his book *Mobilizing America* to Wilson in early 1917 in an effort to influence the president's management of the war. In it he argued that if the government controlled all the mechanisms of information, and used the creative arts to bolster its message, the country could be indoctrinated to support the war without resorting to overt forms of control.

"Truth and Falsehood are arbitrary terms," Bullard wrote. "There is nothing in experience to tell us that one is always preferable to the other. . . . There are lifeless truths and vital lies. . . . The force of an idea lies in its inspirational value. It matters very little whether it is true or false."

Bullard proposed to Wilson that the government form a large "publicity bureau, which would constantly keep before the public the importance of supporting the men at the front. It would requisition space on the front page of every newspaper; it would call for a 'draft' of trained writers to feed 'army stories' to the public; it would create a Corps of Press Agents. . . . In order to make democracy fight wholeheartedly," he said, "it is necessary to make them understand the situation."

Bullard, whose papers I sifted through one afternoon at the Seeley G. Mudd Manuscript Library at Princeton University, argued strenuously against Wilson's desire for overt censorship. Walter Lippmann, in a private letter to the president on March 11, reiterated Bullard's call for a government publicity bureau. He told Wilson the war had to be sold to a skeptical public by fostering "a healthy public opinion."[7] Lippmann, especially in his 1922 book *Public Opinion,* emerges as perhaps the darkest figure of the period. He assumes the intellectual role of the Grand Inquisitor, fearful of popular rule and brilliant enough to know how to manipulate public opinion. The war would prove him to be extremely prescient, and *Public Opinion* became a bible to the new power elite.

Wilson got the message. He agreed to set up the bureau Lippmann and Bullard proposed and turn it over to progressives and artists. "It is not an army we must shape and train for war, it is a nation," he stated.[8] A week after the war was declared, the president established the Committee for Public Information (CPI). The CPI, headed by a former muckraker named George Creel, which became popularly known as the Creel Commission, would become the first modern mass propaganda machine. Its goal was not, as Creel confessed, simply to impart pro-war messages but to discredit those who attempted to challenge the nation's involvement in the conflict. And Creel, who knew the world of journalism, set out to demolish decentralized and diverse systems of information. He recalled that during the period of neutrality before the war, the nation

> had been torn by a thousand divisive prejudices, with public opinion stunned and muddled by the pull and haul of Allied and German propaganda. The sentiment in the West was still isolationist; the Northwest buzzed with talk of a "rich man's war," waged to salvage Wall Street loans; men and women of Irish stock were "neutral," not caring who whipped England, and in every stage demagogues raved against "warmongers," although the Du Ponts and other so-called "merchants of death" did not have enough powder on hand to arm squirrel hunters.[9]

News, which had previously grown out of local discourses and public discussions, which reflected local public sentiment and concerns upward, would be dictated from above. It would have to deliver a consistent drumbeat of propaganda, a consistent pro-war narrative, and shut out or discredit dissenting views. It would have to leech off the news pages into every aspect of the nation's cultural life, from theater to film to novels to advertisements. The wide diversity of newspapers, and with them the diversity of opinions, concerns, and outlooks, had to be managed and controlled. All information about the war would come from one source, a practice that in later generations would be codified as "staying on message." There would be a total uniformity of ideas. Creel's efforts—his bureau would employ thousands by the war's end—had the twin effect of saturating the country with propaganda and dismantling the local, independent press. The committee would, by the time the war ended, see the president lionized by Secretary of State Robert Lansing as "the greatest propagandist the modern world has ever known."[10] No other president in American history did more to damage the independence and freedom of the press, or set back the cause of social reform, than Wilson.

The newspapers, with Creel feeding them propaganda packaged as news releases, began a relentless campaign of manipulation of public opinion thinly disguised as journalism. The papers not only published without protest the worst drivel handed to them by the CPI, including manufactured stories of German atrocities and war crimes, but in their news pages questioned the patriotism of dissenters.

"RADICALS AT WORK FOR GERMAN PEACE," read a June 24, 1917, headline in the *New York Times,* with a subhead adding, "Well-Financed Propaganda Has Ample Quarters and Staff and Is Flooding Country. TAKES IDEAS FROM RUSSIA[.] Proposes Council of Soldiers' and Workmen's Delegates Here to Run the War."

"A group of men and women, representing all shades of radical and pacifist opinion, have combined to carry on a campaign in this country to create sentiment in favor of peace along lines advocated by the most radical and visionary of Russia Revolutionists," the article began.

> In other words, the peace which they will agitate for in every part of the country will be just such a peace as persons best informed as to the views of the Kaiser and his absolutist followers say the German Government favors. It is not denied by some persons prominent in the new propaganda that if Germany should cease its submarine warfare they would advocate the United States deserting the Allies and concluding a separate peace with Berlin.
>
> In this new peace-at-any-price organization are a number of Germans and a great many radicals of other origin. The organization

is called the People's Council of America and is said to have the support of various organizations, such as the Collegiate Anti-Militarist League, two members of which were convicted last week of conspiracy to obstruct the military laws of the nation; the Emergency Peace Federation, which was so busy in the days immediately preceding the declaration of war against Germany, and the so-called American Union against Militarism.

The People's Council, as they call it, apparently has strong financial backing. It has a large suite of rooms in the Educational Building, at 70 Fifth Avenue, where a score of stenographers and secretaries are busy sending out letters and literature urging, among other things, the organization in the United States of a "Soldiers' and Workmen's Committee" such as now exists in Russia.

In one of the pamphlets now being mailed occurs this statement:

"It is hoped that our own People's Council will voice the peace will of America as unmistakably and effectively as the Council of Workmen's and Soldiers' Delegates in speaking for Russia."

Another document which is being mailed says that the organization is working for "an early, general and democratic peace, to be secured through negotiation and in harmony with the principles outlined by the new Russia," while in another place it denounces the President, by plain inference, when it is stated that "America has yielded the honor of leading in peace and is now a participant in the international carnage."

"Every day," another propaganda sheet issued in the name of the organization says, "the constitutional rights [of] free speech, free press and free assembly are being assaulted."

At the offices of the council it was frankly stated that the intention of those behind the agitation was to flood the country with propaganda, and that speakers and agitators would be sent to every part of the country. Joseph D. Cannon, a labor leader, has been delegated to agitate among the miners of the West; A. W. Ricker, a magazine editor, will try to gain a foothold for the organization among the farmers of the Northwest; James D. Maurer, the Pennsylvania labor agitator, will devote his efforts to the great labor centres in the State, while Professor L. M. Keasbey of the University of Texas and an Australian preacher named Gordon will try to bring the South into line against President Wilson and in favor of a peace which it is generally admitted is such a peace as the Germans would now accept.

Some of the people who are listed as "hard workers" in the organization are David Starr Jordan, who is the Treasurer; L. P. Lochner, the man who is generally credited with having persuaded Henry Ford to back the peace ship venture; the Rev. Dr. Judah L. Magnes, Algernon Lee, and Morris Hillquit, the Socialists who failed to get passports to Europe recently, where they wanted to attend the so-called Stockholm conference; Max Eastman, editor of a radical pamphlet; J. Schlossberg, a labor leader; Fola La Follette, a daughter of the Wisconsin Senator; Professor W. L. Dana of Columbia University, who, it was said at the offices of the organization, is also a prominent member of the Collegiate Anti-Militarist League; Mrs. Emily Greene Balch, and a score of other persons of similar views, and all of them violent opponents of the military policies of the Wilson Administration.

Here is a sample of the letters which the council is scattering over the country.

> Dear Friend: You will rejoice with us at the evidence of a powerful and rapidly growing sentiment for peace. The success of the First American Conference for Democracy and the Terms of Peace, and its remarkable climax at Madison Square Garden, have sent a ray of hope to hosts "that sat in darkness."
>
> You stood nobly by the Emergency Peace Federation, and I thank you again for your support. The federation is one of several organizations now being merged into the larger and more powerful movement represented by the People's Council. I am sure your loyal support will continue into the new organization.
>
> The Organizing Committee of the People's Council is undertaking a tremendous task. The People's Council meets on August 4. Before this time we must secure delegates to the People's Council from which the thousands of

organizations of workers, farmers, women, clergymen, anti-militarists, Socialists, single taxers, &c. We must send out organizers to explain the purpose of the council. We must arrange hundreds of public meetings, and flood the country with literature.

Fifty thousand dollars is needed before Aug. 1. We want 25,000 one dollar bills. A dollar contribution from 25,000 people means ten times more than the same amount from large contributors.

Will you not send us $1? Send more if you possibly can. Get your friends Interested—urge them to contribute— and do let us count on you.

Yours very sincerely,
REBECCA SHELLY
Financial Secretary.

That the activities of the organization will be closely watched by the Federal authorities can be stated on authority. Because of its evident strong financial backing and because it is out for the avowed purpose of attacking the policies of the Government and to stir up discontent over the conscription law, the proper authorities say the council "will bear watching," although its activities will in no wise be interfered with so long as it stays "within the law."

Members of the council admit that if they had their way France would not recover Alsace-Lorraine, Belgium would receive no indemnity for the destruction which the Germans have wrought, the Lusitania would be unavenged—in other words, the world would get a "German peace."[11]

⌒

The mass propaganda established during the war, which included journalists, entertainers, artists, and novelists, became the model for twentieth-century corporate and governmental advertising and publicity. The selling of the Iraq war by the administration of George W. Bush was lifted from the playbook of the CPI, as was the tactic used by ExxonMobil to use $16 million to fund a network of forty-three "grassroots" organizations opposed to the science of climate change, recruit scientists to publish non-peer-reviewed articles challenging the scientific evidence, and repeated placement of these "experts" on the national airwaves to manufacture public confusion. The use of these propaganda techniques has permitted corporations to saturate the airwaves with images and slogans that deify mass consumer culture. And it has meant the death, by corporate hands, of news.

"In 1909-1910, 58 percent of American cities had a press that was varied both in ownership and perspective," Stuart Ewen wrote in his classic *Captains of Consciousness.*

> By 1920, the same percentage represented those cities in which the press was controlled by an information monopoly. By 1930, 80 percent of American cities had given way to a press monopoly. The role and influence of advertising revenues multiplied thirteen-fold (from $200 million to $2.6 billion), and it was the periodicals, both the dailies and others, which acted as a major vehicle for this growth.[12]

Creel was, in many ways, the godfather of modern public relations. John Dos Passos called him "a little shrimp of a man with burning dark eyes set in an ugly face under a shock of curly hair."[13] He came from a poor Virginian family, fiercely loyal to the Confederate cause, which had migrated to Missouri after the Civil War. He had worked as a reporter for Kansas City newspapers and as a muckraking journalist for New York magazines. He was married to Blanche Bates, a well-known stage actress, and he was endowed with supreme self-confidence, boundless energy, and a penchant for a binary view of the world that painted reality in bold strokes of black and white. "To Creel," wrote journalist Mark Sullivan, "there are only two classes of men. There are skunks and the greatest man that ever lived. The greatest man that ever lived is plural and includes everyone who is on Creel's side in whatever public issue he happens at the moment to be concerned with." It had to be admitted, Creel wrote of himself, "that an open mind is not part of my inheritance. I took in prejudices with mother's milk and was weaned on partisanship."[14]

Creel's power—he had direct access to Wilson—was resented by many in Washington, and after his usefulness ebbed with the war's end, he would never regain his prominence, although he made many attempts. He was involved following the war in two shady business deals, the first as part of a sleazy Manhattan-based mail-order business, the Pelman Institute of America, which peddled a self-improvement scheme called "Pelmanism." It promised to teach people "how to think; how to use fully powers of which they are conscious; how to discover and to train the power of which they have been unconscious." It promised subscribers that "Pelmanism" produced salary increases "from 20 to 200 percent." He later was mixed up in the Teapot Dome oil scandal and admitted before a 1924 Senate investigation that he had accepted a check for $5,000 to convince Secretary of the Navy Josephus Daniels, whom he had worked with during the war, to lease two government-owned oil fields to private oil interests. He ran against Upton Sinclair in the 1934 Democratic primary for governor of California and lost. Franklin Roosevelt, who had had enough of Creel's arrogance during World War I, when Roosevelt had served as Assistant Secretary of the Navy, rejected Creel's requests to work in the Office of War Information during World War II. Creel ended his life as a fervent anticommunist and a champion of right-wing causes who worked with Senator Joseph McCarthy and Representative Richard Nixon during the Red Scare of the late 1940s. It was a fitting conclusion.

Creel knew that his task of selling the war would require emasculating powerful social movements that not only had opposed the war but also had exposed the brutality and ruthlessness of major industrialists such as John D. Rockefeller. Labor unions, progressive journalists, pacifists, isolationists, the large number of immigrants who disliked the British, and some one million Socialists, led by Debs—who announced at Cooper Union in New York City on March 7, 1917, that he would rather be shot as a traitor than "go to war for Wall Street"[15]—would prove to be obstacles to Wilson's war if left alone. The Industrial Workers of the World (IWW), or Wobblies, with some 100,000 members, and perhaps another 200,000 active supporters, denounced the war as capitalist exploitation, encouraged draft dodging, and called for strikes.

Wilson's initial worries about lukewarm public support proved well grounded. Enlistment rates were paltry with only seventy-three thousand young men volunteering for the army between April and the middle of May. The government was forced to institute conscription. It was then that Creel went to work.

Creel and his associates, which included artists, cartoonists, graphic designers, filmmakers, journalists, and public relations experts, saturated the cultural and intellectual life of the country with war propaganda. It did this by crossing the traditional boundaries of propaganda. It created the Division of Syndicated Features, one of nineteen divisions, which hired novelists, short-story writers, and essayists. These fiction writers masked the pro-war and pro-government message, in an example of social realism, in stories that reached an estimated twelve million people a month. Posters and ads in support of the war blanketed the country. Hollywood, which had a deserved reputation for sleaze, churned out war favourites such as *The Kaiser: The Beast of Berlin*, *Wolves of Kultur*, and *Pershing's Crusaders*. A movie titled *To Hell with the Kaiser* was so popular that Massachusetts riot police were summoned to deal with an angry mob denied admission. The film division nearly made enough money to pay for itself.

Creel's committee established direct relationships with eighteen thousand newspapers, eleven thousand national advertisers and advertising agencies, ten thousand chambers of commerce, thirty thousand manufacturers' associations, twenty-two thousand labor unions, ten thousand public libraries, thirty-two thousand banks, fifty-eight thousand general stores, 3,500 YMCA branches, ten thousand members of the Council of National Defense, one thousand advertising clubs, fifty-six thousand post offices, fifty-five thousand station agents, five thousand draft boards, one hundred thousand Red Cross chapters, and twelve thousand manufacturers' agents.[16] All were showered daily with war propaganda tailored specifically toward their interests and members. And the few institutions reluctant to spew out war propaganda were shut down.

In a 1920 memoir titled *How We Advertised America*, Creel wrote that the "war was not fought in France alone":

> It was the fight for the minds of men, for the "conquest of their convictions," and the battle-line ran through every home in every country.
>
> It was in this recognition of Public Opinion as a major force

that the Great War differed most essentially from all previous conflicts. The trial of strength was not only between massed bodies of
armed men, but between opposed ideals, and moral verdicts took
on all the value of military decisions. . . . In all things, from first to
last, without halt or change, it was a plain publicity proposition, a
vast enterprise in salesmanship, the world's greatest adventure in
advertising. . . .

There was no part of the great war machinery that we did not
touch, no medium of appeal that we did not employ. The printed
word, the spoken word, the motion picture, the telegraph, the cable,
the wireless, the poster, the sign-board—all these were used in our
campaign to make our own people and all other peoples understand
the causes that compelled America to take arms. . . . What we had to
have was no mere surface unity, but a passionate belief in the justice
of America's cause that should weld the people of the United States
into one white-hot mass instinct with fraternity, devotion, courage,
and deathless determination.

The committee manufactured daily news stories through its news
bureau that were run in the nation's newspapers. It provided a syndicated
news service to disseminate "facts" about the war. It had a foreign language division, with a large group of translators, to plant pro-American
stories in the foreign press. It established a speaker's bureau thanks to
which speakers, known as "four-minute men," would get up in
crowded movie houses, in churches, at civic functions, or even on the
street to deliver pro-war messages and raise money for Liberty Loan
drives. By the war's end Creel had some seventy-five thousand speakers
who gave four-minute talks on topics prepared for them by the committee. Creel called them "the stentorian guard." The CPI published
"Red, White and Blue Books," containing essays by prominent academics and historians, including John Dewey and Walter Lippmann, who
argued for the war. Newspapers were never directly censored but were
given guidelines and flooded with pro-war reports from the committee
that were reprinted as news.

"CPI posters were in every post office," Dos Passos wrote. "CPI information bulletins were on every bulletin board. Country weeklies and
trade journals were nourished on Creel's boilerplate. In an astonishing

short time George Creel had the entire nation—except of course the disreputable minority who insisted on forming their own opinions—repeating every slogan which emanated from the President's desk in the wordy war to 'make the world safe for democracy.' "[17]

The few figures who resisted, such as Bourne, Addams, Debs, Emma Goldman, or Bertrand Russell, became pariahs. The press accused them, with Creel's help, of being disloyal and pro-German. Addams, the socialist founder of Hull House in Chicago, which provided aid to poor and working-class families, was booed when she spoke against the war at Carnegie Hall and branded by the *New York Times* as unpatriotic. She noted the shift in the press as early as 1915, when the papers began to "make pacifist activity or propaganda so absurd that it would be absolutely without influence and its authors so discredited that nothing they might say or do would be regarded as worthy of attention." She went on to write, in *Peace and Bread in Time of War*, that "this concerted attempt at misrepresentation on the part of newspapers of all shades of opinion was quite new to my experience."[18] Voices of dissent were silenced under the onslaught. *Appeal to Reason*, a socialist journal founded in 1897 that provided an outlet for writers such as Jack London, Upton Sinclair, Mary "Mother" Jones, and Debs, had by 1902 the fourth highest circulation at 150,000 of any weekly in the nation. It opposed the war—not unusual for a publication at the start of the war—but its attempt to hold to its antiwar stance soon saw it come under tremendous pressure. The Espionage Act, making it an offence to publish material that undermined the war effort, effectively censored its content. *The Masses*, another left-wing journal, decided to cease publication for the duration of the war, but *Appeal to Reason* buckled and reluctantly agreed to back the war effort. The effect of Creel's work on American debate and culture was cataclysmic.

"German courses were dropped from schools and colleges," Dos Passos wrote.

> German dishes disappeared from the bills of fare. Sauerkraut became known as liberty cabbage, German measles was renamed. German clover appeared in the seed catalogues as crimson or liberty clover. All manifestations of foreign culture became suspect. German operas were dropped from the repertory. The drive against German music

culminated in the arrest of Dr. Carl Muck, the elderly and much admired conductor of the Boston Symphony Orchestra.[19]

The virus of nationalism infected every aspect of society. Dachshunds were renamed liberty dogs. The City University of New York reduced by one credit every course in German. Fourteen states banned the speaking of German in public schools. German-Americans, like Japanese-Americans in World War II, provided convenient scapegoats. An angry mob in Van Houten, New Mexico, accused an immigrant miner of supporting Germany. The mob forced him to kneel before them, kiss the flag, and shout, "To hell with the Kaiser." Robert Prager, a German-born coal miner, was accused in April 1918 by a crowd that swelled to 500 people of hoarding explosives outside of St. Louis. Prager, who had tried to enlist in the navy but had been rejected on medical grounds, was stripped, bound with an American flag, dragged barefoot and stumbling through the streets, and lynched as the mob cheered. At the trial of the leaders of the lynch mob, who appeared in court wearing red, white and blue ribbons, their defense counsel argued that the killing was justifiable "patriotic murder." It took the jury twenty-five minutes to return a not guilty verdict. One jury member shouted out, "Well, I guess nobody can say we aren't loyal now." The *Washington Post* wrote of the trial that "in spite of the excesses such as lynching, it is a healthful and wholesome awakening of the interior of the country." The explosives that Prager was alleged to be harboring were never found.

The severe weakening of populist forces during the war led to their obliteration when the war ended. The war propaganda, which used fear as its engine, instantly switched the target of its hatred from Germans to communists. During the Palmer Raids on November 7, 1919, carried out on the second anniversary of the Russian Revolution, more than ten thousand alleged communists and anarchists were arrested. Many were held for long periods without trial. When Russian-born émigrés such as Emma Goldman, Alexander Berkman, Mollie Steimer, and 245 others were released from prison, they were deported to Russia. By November 1922 *Appeal to Reason* was shut down.

"By a campaign of publicity and advertising on a scale history had never witnessed before, by chicanery and lying, by exaggeration and misrepresentation, by persistent and long-continued appeals to the basest as well as the noblest traits of man, by every imaginable and unprecedented manner and method, the great financial interests, eager for war and aided by the international Junkers, thrust humanity into the world war," wrote Berkman and Goldman in "Deportation: Its Meaning and Menace in 1919."

> Hatred, intolerance, persecution and suppression—the efficient "education" factors in the preparedness and war campaign—are now permeating the very heart of this country and propagating its virulent poison into every phase of our social life. But there is no more "Hun" to be hated and lynched. . . . But the Frankenstein and intolerance and suppression cultivated by the war campaign is there, alive and vital, and must find some vent for his accumulated bitterness and misery. Oh, there, the radical, the Bolshevik! What better prey to be cast to the Frankenstein monster?"

"Many people had long supposed liberalism to be the freedom to know and say, not what was popular or convenient or even what was patriotic, but what they held to be true," Addams wrote. "Now those very liberals came to realize that a distinct aftermath of the war was the dominance of the mass over the individual to such an extent that it constituted a veritable revolution in our social relationships."[20]

The CPI was closed on November 12, 1918, one day after the war ended. The activities of the committee's foreign division ended a few months later. The employees of the CPI, however, had no difficulty finding work. Political scientist Harold Lasswell, who wrote one of the best studies of the power of the new mass propaganda in his book *Propaganda Technique in the World War,* noted that most of the former CPI experts instantly gravitated to government and corporate offices in Washington and New York. The director of the CPI's Foreign Division, two years later, wrote that "the history of propaganda in the war would scarcely be worthy of consideration here, but for one fact—it did not stop with the armistice. No indeed! The methods invented and tried out in the war were too valuable for the uses of governments, factions, and special interests." Edward Bernays, Freud's nephew and the father of modern public relations, who had worked in Latin America for Creel, became a major figure on Madison Avenue and an advocate of mass propaganda as a tool for governmental and corporate control. "It was, of course, the astounding success of propaganda during the war that opened the eyes of the intelligent few in all departments of life to the possibilities of regimenting the public mind," wrote Bernays in his 1928 book *Propaganda*. "It was only natural, after the war ended, that intelligent persons should ask themselves whether it was not possible to apply a similar technique to the problems of peace."

There were critics of the new business of manufacturing public opinion. John Dewey challenged those who now routinely disguised propaganda as news. "There is uneasiness and solicitude about what men hear and learn," wrote Dewey, and the "paternalistic care for the source of men's beliefs, once generated by war, carries over to the troubles of peace." Dewey noted that the manipulation of information was visible in coverage of post-revolutionary Russia. The *Nation* agreed in 1919, arguing that "what has happened in regard to Russia is the most striking case in point as showing what may be accomplished by Government propaganda . . . Bartholomew nights that never take place, together with the wildest rumours of communism in women, and of murder and bloodshed, taken from obscure Scandinavian newspapers, are hastily relayed to the U.S., while everything favorable to the Soviets, every bit of constructive accomplishment, is suppressed."

The Hun, the object of hatred and scorn during the war, was supplanted by the Bolshevik. Social manipulation through fear, which had consolidated the power of the elite during the war, was employed again and again to ferret out those attacked as "internal enemies" and ward off external ones. But it was corporate advertising, rather than government witch hunts, which would prove the most deadly. News had to do battle with huge, sophisticated and well-funded propaganda campaigns. It would also be denied the tools of emotional persuasion perfected by mass propaganda. News would be restricted to fact, to balance and objectivity. The powerful techniques of appealing to emotion, of creating pseudo-events that a public could confuse with reality, of constantly taking the pulse of the public through surveys and opinion polls to appear to give people what they desired, would be left in the hands of the enemies of truth. The public would be trained, as Bourne wrote, to communicate in a language in which "simple syllogisms are substituted for analysis, things are known by their labels, [and] our heart's desire dictates what we shall see."

The war launched the destruction of American cultures—for we once had distinct regional cultures—through mass communication. It would turn consumption into an inner compulsion and eradicate difference. Old values of thrift, regional identity that had its own iconography, aesthetic expression and history, diverse immigrant traditions, self-sufficiency, and a press that was decentralized to provide citizens with a voice in their communities, were destroyed by corporate culture. New desires and habits were implanted by corporate advertisers to replace the old. Individual frustrations and discontents could be solved, corporate culture assured the populace, through the wonders of consumerism and cultural homogenization. American culture, or cultures, were replaced with junk culture and junk politics. And now, standing on the cultural ash heap, we survey the ruin. The slogans of advertising and mass culture have became the common idiom, robbing citizens of the language to make sense of the destruction. Manufactured commodity culture became American culture. As newspapers consolidated into chains, local and independent voices were silenced. The shift in the press from hatred toward the Hun to hatred toward the Red was seamless. Initial propaganda tied communists to the German war machine. On June 15, 1919, the *New York Times* summed up a Senate investigation into communism in which one anticommunist witness after another assured senators that Lenin and Trotsky were German agents and Germany had underwritten the Soviet revolution. "Experts" testified that the new Soviet regime enthusiastically supported "free-love" clinics and were "anti-Christ." One witness, Reverend George Simons, told the committee that "more than half of the agitators in the so-called Bolshevik revolution were Yiddish" and most of these "apostate Jews" had come from Manhattan's Lower East Side. Simons also assured the committee that the revolution had been financed by Germany, leading Senator Lee Overman of North Carolina to state that "it would be a very remarkable thing if the Bolshevik movement started in this country, financed by Germans, would it not?" Senator William King of Utah asked the same witness whether the Bolsheviks, "the males, rape and ravish and despoil women at will?" "They certainly do," was the answer. They are, Simons said, "the dirtiest dogs" he had ever seen in his life.[21]

The testimony was as fantastic and absurd as the host of manufactured atrocity stories of German soldiers entering convents to rape nuns, but it and disinformation like it galvanized the country into political passivity. The later anticommunist witch hunts differed little in their simplicity or crudity.

The *Times* summarized the committee's eight months of investigations with the headline "Senators Tell What Bolshevism in America Means." The newspaper reproduced from the report 29 "salient features which constitute the program of Bolshevism as it exists to-day in Russia and is presented to the rest of the world as a panacea for all ills." These included "the confiscation of all factories, mills, mines and industrial institutions and the delivery of the control and operation thereof to the employees therein"; "the absolute separation of churches and schools"; "the establishment, through marriage and divorce laws, of a method for the legalization of prostitution, when the same is engaged in by consent of the parties"; "the refusal to recognize the existence of God in its governmental and judicial proceedings"; and "the conferring of the rights of citizenship on aliens without regard to length of residence or intelligence."[22]

Civil and political discourse became poisoned by loyalty oaths, spy paranoia, and distrust of dissent. This manufactured fear used appeals to internal and external threats to persuade the country that it should devote a staggering half of all government spending to defense following World War II, and pour billions more into its intelligence service to prop up heinous dictators in Latin America, the Middle East, Asia, and Africa in the name of the battle worldwide against communism. The quaint literary serials, poems, local reports, town debates, and other forms of popular expression that had once been so prominent in the press, vanished from the pages of mass-produced newspapers. It was replaced by celebrity gossip; the new, angry rhetoric of the Cold War; and nationally syndicated columns. The papers became as commercialized and centralized as the rest of mass culture.

The business of mass propaganda brought vast sums of advertising revenue to all organs of mass communication. But corporate and government propaganda sharply narrowed the parameters of acceptable debate. It began the consolidation of the press by huge corporations that would end with nearly everything we see, hear, and read disseminated from roughly a half dozen corporations such as Viacom, Disney, General Electric, and Murdoch's News Corporation. And it turned news into the elite's echo chamber.

~

Liberal and radical movements at the turn of the twentieth century subscribed to the fiction that human diligence, moral probity, and reform, coupled with advances in science and technology, could combine to create a utopia on earth. It was, as the historian Sidney Pollard wrote, "the assumption that a pattern of change exists in this history of mankind . . . that it consists of irreversible changes in one direction only, and that this direction is towards improvement."[23] No longer would the poor have to wait for heaven. Justice and prosperity would arrive through human institutions.

The liberal class—buoyed by the rise of an independent press, militant labor unions, workers' houses, antipoverty campaigns, and the rising prosperity of the country bequeathed by the industrial revolution—embraced institutions, and especially the state, as tools for progress. This faith created a new form of liberalism that departed from "classical liberalism." While these two belief systems shared some of the same characteristics, including a respect for individual rights, the new liberal class was and remains distinctly utopian. It places its faith in practical state reforms to achieve a just society. Classical liberalism, while it embraced the goals of the Enlightenment, was colored by a healthy dose of skepticism about human perfectibility and acutely aware of the nature and potency of evil. Modern liberalism lost this awareness. Human institutions and government were seen as mechanisms that, under the right control, would inevitably better humankind.

Faith in human institutions was at the core of the Social Gospel, a Christian movement articulated at the turn of the century in books such as *Christianity and the Social Crisis*, published in 1907, and *Theology for the Social Gospel*, published a decade later, both of them written by the leading proponent of the movement, Walter Rauschenbusch. The Social Gospel replaced a preoccupation with damnation and sin with a belief in human progress. It spawned the Chautauqua movement, which had hundreds of chapters across the country. Chautauquan communities supported labor unions, collective bargaining, social services for the poor, hygiene programs, and universal education, although the movement was not free from many of the prejudices of its age and excluded Roman Catholics and African Americans. Organizations such as the Labor Temple in New York City, the University Settlement House in Chicago, and Washington Gladden's crusades to better the working conditions in Columbus, Ohio, were part of this intoxicating fusion of religion and reform, the Christian churches' version of the liberal class belief in the power of reform and human progress through good government. The Reverend Josiah Strong's declamation "that Christ came not only to save individual souls, but society" turned churches into temperance societies, labor halls, and soup kitchens. Salvation could be achieved through human agencies. The Social Gospel secularized traditional Christian eschatology and fused it with the utopian visions of material progress embraced by the wider liberal class.

The years before World War I had offered hope to liberal reformers. It was Ida Tarbell who in 1902 exposed the ruthless business practices of John D. Rockefeller and Standard Oil in *McClure's Magazine*. Her series, later published as a book, fueled a public outcry against Standard Oil. It was an important factor in the U.S. government's antitrust actions against the Standard Oil Trust, which eventually led to its breakup in 1911. Samuel Hopkins Adams, a contemporary of Tarbell, wrote a series of eleven articles for *Collier's* in 1905 called "The Great American Fraud." He exposed many of the false claims made by the manufacturers of patent medicines. Adams found that in some cases these medicines damaged people's health. The series led to the passage of the 1906 Pure Food and Drug Act. Upton Sinclair's exposé of inhumane conditions in the Chicago stockyards in 1906 in his muckraking novel *The Jungle* led to the passage of the 1906 Pure Food and Drug Act and the Meat Inspection Act. These exposés, which included Lincoln Steffens' exposure of municipal corruption, dovetailed neatly into the demands of those in the Social Gospel movement, labor unions, the progressive wing of the Democratic Party, or university sociology departments, which, when they were founded, focused on practical steps toward social reform.

The muckrakers and the Social Gospel reformers had been joined by militant labor organizations, including the anarcho-syndicalism of the IWW or Wobblies, which organized strikes by unskilled workers in New England textile mills, the Minnesota iron mines, and the steel industry in Pennsylvania. Before the war, the Wobblies led hundreds of thousands of industrial workers on walkouts. They conceived of themselves not simply as a union but a revolutionary movement. The Wobblies, unlike most other unions, included women, immigrants, and African Americans. They preached an uncompromising class struggle, as the movement's legendary leader, Bill Haywood, told delegates at the founding convention in 1905:

> Fellow workers, this is the Continental Congress of the working class. We are here to confederate the workers of this country into a working class movement that shall have for its purpose the emancipation of the working class from the slave bondage of capitalism. . . . The aims and objects of this organization should be to put the working class in possession of the economic power, the means of life, in control of production and distribution, without regard to capitalist masters.[24]

Socialism had wide appeal. Debs pulled a million votes in 1912. The Socialist Party printed twenty-nine English and twenty-two foreign-language weeklies, serving immigrant communities that diligently protected their languages and cultures. The party also published three English and six foreign language dailies. The United Mine Workers was primarily socialist. And Socialists were elected to Congress and became mayors in about a dozen major cities. The Socialists came close to defeating Samuel Gompers for the presidency of the American Federation of Labor.

And then, with war declared, it was over. Dwight Macdonald noted gloomily that "American radicalism was making great strides right up to 1914; the war was the rock on which it shattered."[25]

The cultural and social transformation, captured in E.P. Thompson's essay "Time, Work-Discipline, and Industrial Capitalism," following the war was much more than the embrace of an economic system or the triumph of undiluted nationalism. It was, as Thompson pointed out, part of a revolutionary reinterpretation of reality. It marked the ascendancy of mass propaganda and mass culture. Richard Sennet, in *The Fall of the Public Man*, targeted the rise of mass culture as one of the prime forces behind what he termed a new "collective personality . . . generated by a common fantasy." And the century's great propagandists would not only agree, but add to Sennet's argument that those who could manipulate and disseminate those fantasies could determine the directions taken and the opinions embraced by the "collective personality."

The suicidal impulses and industrial slaughter of World War I mocked the utopian vision of a heaven on earth and the inevitability of human progress embraced by the Social Gospel. The Swiss theologian Karl Barth, in *The Epistle to the Romans* (*Der Römerbrief*), published in 1918, tore apart the Social Gospel's naïve belief that human beings could link the will of God to human endeavors. Christians, Barth argued, could neither envision nor create the kingdom of heaven on earth. The liberal church never found an adequate response to Barth's critique. It retreated into a vague embrace of humanism and self-absorbed forms of spirituality.

After the war, as Stuart Ewen told me when we met in New York, all systems of public discourse, communication and expression were "systematically designed to avoid including any information or knowledge that might encourage people to evaluate the situation." Mass propaganda obliterated an informed public. "Except for those who seek out information internationally or through nontraditional sources," Ewen lamented, "the entire picture of the universe that is provided to people is one reduced to a comic strip."

"By the late 1920s, for example, you have the emergence of a fairly elaborate social psychological apparatus designed to take the temperature of public emotions, not for the purpose of reporting on what people feel but for the purpose for shaping what people feel," Ewen said:

> That institution, which starts out with the Psychological Corporation in the 1920s, grows into a major polling and survey research industry, which not only permeates the commercial world but begins to permeate academia. On that level, it has become more and more

pervasive. Almost every moment of human attention is being subjected to that kind of strategy. The resources that exist to give support to that are enormous. The amount of money that goes into the miseducation of the American people is far vaster and far more enthusiastically spent than that which goes into the education of the American people.

The liberal class, believing it had to fit its ideas into the new sloganeering of mass communications, began to communicate in the childlike vocabulary and simplistic sound bites demanded by commercial media. Intellectual debate, once a characteristic of the country's political discourse, withered. The liberal class became seduced by the need for popular appeal, forgetting, as Macdonald wrote, that "as in arts and letters, communicability to a large audience is in inverse ratio to the excellence of a political approach. This is not a good thing: as in art, it is a deforming and crippling factor. Nor is it an eternal rule: in the past, the ideas of a tiny minority, sometimes almost reduced to the vanishing point of one individual, have slowly come to take hold on more and more of their fellow men."[26]

The cultural embrace of simplification, as Macdonald warned, meant reducing a population to speaking in predigested clichés and slogans. It banished complexity and further pushed to the margins difficult, original, or unfamiliar ideas. The assault on radical and original thought, which by definition did not fit itself into the popular cultural lexicon, saw art forms such as theater suffer.

The radical current in theater of the 1920s and 1930s brought potent new ways of thinking to audiences who had neither the time nor the inclination to read social theory. The theater became one of the last effective ways in which artists could compete with corporate consumerist culture by appealing to emotion and fact. It opposed mass propaganda by using many of the same methods of commercial propaganda. Theater responded to the political upheavals preceding World War I, during the Depression and, in a final gasp, at the height of the Vietnam War with politically charged works that, like the organs of mass propaganda, were designed to make people feel. The Provincetown Playhouse in the 1920s performed the early plays of Eugene O'Neil and Susan Glaspell. The New Playwrights' Theatre, funded by the banker Otto Kahn, included the communist author Mike Gold, who wrote *Jews Without Money*, and left-wing artists such as Francis Edward Faragoh, Emjo Basshe, John Howard Lawson, and John Dos Passos. Lawson, who would become one of the Hollywood Ten, jailed for a year for refusing to answer before the House Un-American Activities Committee (HUAC), wrote a jazz play, *Processional*, about labor strife, prejudice, and violence in a Kentucky coal mining town.

Basshe wrote a manifesto for the New Playwrights, calling for "a theater which is as drunken, as barbaric, as clangorous as our age." A red flag was hoisted outside the Cherry Lane Theatre, on Commerce Street in Greenwich Village, which the New Playwrights rented for their second season. Dos Passos wrote the manifesto for their second season: "Towards a Revolutionary Theatre," in which he called for a theater that "draws its life and ideas from the conscious sections of the industrial and white collar working classes which are out to get control of the great flabby mass of capitalist society and mold it to their own purpose." These radicals sought to change content and theatrical form. The new social theater would be "somewhere between a high mass . . . and a Barnum and Bailey's circus."

During the New Deal, the Works Progress Administration (WPA) recruited Hallie Flanagan in 1935 to become the head of the Federal Theatre Project. This effort, which brought radicals and liberals together, became an effective tool for social change and perhaps was the last potent counterweight to the propaganda state. Production costs and scenic effects were limited. Money was used to pay salaries to the artists. Ticket prices were low. Theater suddenly became available to people across the country. The project split theater, as Flanagan noted, between commercial theater, whose aim was to make money, and those in the public theater who wanted to make a new social order. By the end of the first year the project had more than fifteen thousand men and women on its payroll, and by the time the project was shut down four years later, its productions had played to more than thirty million people in more than two hundred theaters and school auditoriums, on portable stages, and in public parks across the country.[27] Those working in the project were professional actors, directors, designers, writers, clowns, and musicians left unemployed by the financial collapse. They produced high-quality works that spoke to ordinary lives and the misery that had engulfed the country. Orson Welles and John Houseman directed the Negro Theatre Unit of the Federal Theatre Project in Harlem and set *Macbeth* in the Haitian court of King Henri Christophe. Voodoo witch doctors were recruited to play the weird sisters. The incidental music was composed by Virgil Thomson. The play, which premiered at the Lafayette Theatre on April 14, 1935, was sold out for each of its nightly performances. New plays, classical drama, modern drama, radio drama, puppet plays; Yiddish-, Spanish-, Italian-, and German-language theater; children's theater, dance drama, musicals, religious drama, vaudeville, and circuses—hundreds and hundreds of productions in every state of the union poured out of the project. It was the high point of American theater.

The productions—which took on factory owners, bankers, coal mine owners, government bureaucrats and industrialists—led to howls of protest from the power elite. *It Can't Happen Here,* a drama that illustrated how fascism could take hold in the United States, was based on the novel by Sinclair Lewis. It opened in twenty-one theaters in seventeen states on October 27, 1936. The *Hollywood Citizen-News* reported that "the project has been the target of criticism from sources holding the play will antagonize sympathizers of the Hitler and Mussolini regimes." Welles and Houseman were preparing to mount a production called *The Cradle Will Rock,* a musical written by Marc Blitzstein—who would be blacklisted in the 1950s—set in "Steeltown, U.S.A." The musical followed the efforts of a worker, Larry Foreman, to unionize steel workers. His nemesis is the heartless industrialist Mr. Mister, who controlled the press, the church, the arts, the local university, politics, the community's social organizations, and even the local doctor. *The Cradle Will Rock* spared no one, from Mr. Mister's philanthropic wife and spoiled children to Reverend Salvation, who used religion to bless war and capitalism, to the corrupt editor of the local paper, Editor Daily. Mr. Mister, a trustee of the local university, forced the college president to fire professors who did not laud the manly arts of war and capitalism to students. The artists Yasha and Dauber, considered themselves too "cultured" and dependent on the largesse of Mr. Mister's family to engage in politics. They sang with Mrs. Mister:

And we love Art for Art's sake,
It's smart, for Art's sake,
To Part, for Art's sake,
With your heart, for Art's sake,
And your mind, for Art's sake,
Be Blind, for Art's sake,
And Deaf for Art's sake,
And dumb, for Art's sake,
They kill, for Art's sake,
All the Art for Art's Sake[28]

Mr. Mister and Reverend Salvation, who preached peace and love before World War I was declared and blessed the war once it began, sang a duet:

War! War! Kill all the dirty Huns!
And those Austro-Hungarians
War! War! We're entering the war!
The Lusitania's an unpaid debt!
Remember Troy! Remember Lafayette!
Remember the Alamo! Remember our womanhood!
Remember those innocent unborn babies!
Don't let George do it, you do it,
Make the world safe for democracy!
Make the world safe for liberty!
Make the world safe for steel and the Mister family![29]

"Of course it's peace we're for," Reverend Salvation added. "This is the war to end all war."

"Amen," sang the chorus.

"I can see the market rising like a beautiful bird," Mister shouted.

"Collection!" Reverend Salvation announced to the congregation.

The show was scheduled to open June 17, 1937, at the Maxine Elliott Theatre on Broadway, with an elaborate set and a twenty-eight-piece orchestra. But at the last minute, Washington, bowing to complaints, announced that no new shows would be funded until after the beginning of the new fiscal year. The Maxine Elliott Theatre was surrounded by WPA security guards on June 14, since, the government argued, props and costumes inside were government property. Welles, Houseman, and Blitzstein rented the Venice Theatre and a piano. They met the audience outside the shuttered theater and marched the audience and the cast twenty blocks to the Venice. The procession invited onlookers to join them, and by 9 p.m., the Venice's 1,742 seats were filled. Actor's Equity had forbidden the cast to perform the piece "onstage." Blitzstein, who sat alone at the piano, was prepared to play and perform all the roles. Olive Stanton, a little-known relief actress who depended on her small WPA check to support her mother and herself, stood up from her seat when Blitzstein began and sang her opening number. It was an act of singular courage. The rest of the cast, scattered throughout the audience, stood and took over their parts. The poet Archibald MacLeish, who attended, thought it was one of the most moving theatrical experiences of his life. Houseman was promptly fired by the project and Welles quit. The two men would go on to found the Mercury Theater.

"This was obviously censorship under a different guise," Flanagan noted at the time.[30]

The Cradle Will Rock, like much of the popular work that came out of the Federal Theatre Project, addressed the concerns of the working class rather than those of the power elite. It excoriated greed, corruption, the folly of war, the complicity of liberal institutions in protecting the power elite, and the abuses of capitalism. Mr. Mister ran the town like a private plantation. "I believe newspapers are great mental shapers," he said. "My steel industry is dependent on them really."

"Just you call the News," Editor Daily responded. "And we'll print all the news. From coast to coast, and from border to border."

"O the press, the press, the freedom of the press," Editor Daily and Mr. Mister sang. "They'll never take away the freedom of the press. We must be free to say whatever's on our chest—with a hey-diddle-dee and ho-nanny-no for whichever side will pay the best."

"I should like a series on young Larry Foreman," Mr. Mister told Editor Daily, "who goes around stormin' and organizin' unions."

"Yes, we've heard of him," Editor Daily informed Mr. Mister. "In fact, good word of him. He seems quite popular with workingmen."

"Find out who he drinks with and talks with and sleeps with, And look up his past till at last you've got it on him."

"But the man is so full of fight, he's simply dynamite, Why it would take an army to tame him," Editor Daily said.

"Then it shouldn't be too hard to tame him," Mr. Mister answered.

"O the press, the press, the freedom of the press," the two sang. "You've only got to hint whatever's fit to print; If something's wrong with it, why then we'll print to fit. With a he-diddly-dee and a ho-nonny-no. For whichever side will pay the best."[31]

The kind of commercial censorship imposed on *The Cradle Will Rock* has been the favored tool, briefly disrupted by the Federal Theatre Project, used to dominate the theater and the arts since the era of World War I and the rise of the corporate state. Money, as in the rest of the liberal establishment, rewarded those who behaved and did not write or speak from the bottom up. For its four years, the Federal Theatre Project drew huge segments of the population, for whom the arts were often seen as elitist and inaccessible, into new and empowering forms of self-expression. But the power of art to shape and explain reality was something the power elite did not intend to extend to the working class.

"The most unique achievement of Federal Theatre, and the one that paradoxically was most responsible for its demise, was the creation of the *Living Newspaper*," said playwright and director Karen Malpede,

an indigenous form of documentary drama dramatizing hot-button subjects of national debate. *Triple-A Plowed Under, Power, One-Third of a Nation, Spirochete,* were researched by journalists, written by dramatists, acted by huge casts with full orchestras and explored the struggle of farmers, the debate over the Tennessee Valley Association's plan to bring subsidized electricity to the rural South; the reasons behind the housing crisis—"One-third of the nation is ill-housed, ill-fed," President Roosevelt had said—the race for the cure for syphilis. Labor intensive, provocative, using and inventing all sorts of non-realistic acting and staging techniques, the Living Newspapers, a new form of theater, were precursors of American 1960s experimentalism, documentary and collectively created political theater.[32]

The *Living Newspapers* were wildly popular. Sixty thousand people bought tickets to *Power* while the play was still being created. *The Nation* said it was a modern morality play: "Its theme is the search of Everyman for cheap electric power with which to make a better life." Harry Hopkins called it "a great show." It made him laugh and feel: "It's propaganda to educate the consumer who's paying for power. It's about time someone had some propaganda for him." The bolder and more popular the Federal Theatre Project became, the more it was accused of being a breeding ground for communism. In a popular children's play, *The Revolt of the Beavers*, actors dressed as beavers, rushing around on roller skates, overthrew an evil beaver king so all the beavers could eat ice cream, play, and be nine years old. Congressional critics attacked the beaver actors for disseminating communism.

The opponents of the New Deal, backed and funded by the business elite, announced that President Roosevelt had permitted communists to infiltrate the government and government-funded programs, such as the Federal Theatre Project. And that project was the first target of the Dies Committee, led by Texas democrat Martin Dies. The theater project was denounced in a series of hearings in August and November 1938. The Dies committee eventually became HUAC. Flanagan was asked about an article she had written titled "A Theatre Is Born," in which she described the enthusiasm of the federal theaters as having "a certain Marlowesque madness."

"You are quoting from this Marlowe," observed Alabama representative Joseph Starnes from the committee. "Is he a Communist?"

"The room rocked with laughter, but I did not laugh," Flanagan remembered. "Eight thousand people might lose their jobs because a Congressional Committee had so prejudged us that even the classics were 'communistic.' I said, 'I was quoting from Christopher Marlowe.'"

"Tell us who Marlowe is, so we can get the proper references, because that is all we want to do," Starnes said.

"Put in the record that he was the greatest dramatist in the period of Shakespeare, immediately preceding Shakespeare," Flanagan answered.

By 1939 the theater project was killed. The final performances of the Federal Theatre around the country were often poignant. The Ritz Theater in New York provided a new ending for *Pinocchio*. "Pinocchio, having conquered selfishness and greed, did not become a living boy,"

Flanagan wrote. "Instead he was turned back into a puppet." "So let the bells proclaim our grief," intoned the company at the finish, "that his small life was all too brief." The stagehands knocked down the sets in front of the audience, and the company laid Pinocchio in a pine box with the legend "Born December 23, 1938; Killed by Act of Congress, June 30, 1939."[33] At the Adelphi Theatre in New York, the play *Sing for Your Supper* reached its final climax with the "Ballad of Uncle Sam." The chorus sang:

> *Out of the cheating, out of the shouting . . .*
> *Out of the windbags, the patriotic spouting,*
> *Out of uncertainty and doubting . . .*
> *Out of the carpet-bag and the brass spittoon*
> *It will come again*
> *Our marching song will come again*[34]

The Federal Theater Project was the first of the WPA projects to go, "a reminder," Malpede said, "of the power of the theater." As Flanagan remembered:

If this first government theater in our country had been less alive it might have lived longer. But I do not believe anyone who worked on it regrets that it stood from first to last against reaction, against prejudice, against racial, religious, and political intolerance. It strove for a more dramatic statement and a better understanding of the great forces of our life today; it fought for a free theater as one of the many expressions of a civilized, informed, and vigorous life. Anyone who thinks those things do not need fighting for today is out of touch with reality.[35]

As for HUAC, it "terrorized and split the artistic community, and, worse, it led to the self-imposed censorship among American theater workers who, for the sake of their careers, largely fostered and accepted the notion that politics and art don't mix, that ipso facto, any play that was politically relevant had to be bad art," Malpede said. "The exceptions to the rule, of course, were Arthur Miller and Lillian Hellman, both defenders in their well-made plays of the earlier commitment to social justice as a necessary artistic theme. But the majority of American theater neutered itself, becoming prey to the basest commercial and escapist interests."

It was not until the civil-rights movement that theater regained its energy. African American artists and playwrights cut their ties with the commercial theater, along with many white artists, to speak out of their own experience. Barbara Ann Teer, a successful actress, moved uptown to Harlem and in 1968 began the National Black Theatre, mixing African ritual performance techniques with American Method acting. LeRoi Jones in 1964 wrote *Dutchman* and *The Slave* and changed his name to Amiri Baraka. He mounted a searing production called *Slave Ship*. Ntozake Shange in 1976 wrote *For Colored Girls Who Have Considered Suicide When the Rainbow Is Enuf*.

Judith Malina and Julian Beck's The Living Theatre, which had begun in 1947, produced Kenneth Brown's *The Brig*, set in a Marine prison during the Korean War. The Open Theater, founded by Joseph Chaikin, who had been an actor in the Living Theatre, created a series of plays like Jean-Claude van Itallie's *America Hurrah*, which denounced the sterility of American suburban life. The Living and the Open theaters harbored many pacifists. The founders of these theaters often spent time in jail for nonviolent civil disobedience against the Vietnam War. The turmoil of the 1960s, like the turmoil that roiled the country during the Depression, unleashed the energies of artists who took over café spaces of the Lower East Side. Sam Shepard and Maria Irene Fornés, as well as inventive producers such as Ellen Stewart of La MaMa, pushed back against the rigid constraints of commercial theater. The Bread and Puppet Theatre led antiwar marches. Peter Schumann's tragic Vietnamese puppet-women, their mourning faces painted on papier mâché masks, walked under the spreading wings of huge white birds—all the puppets being inhabited and animated by artist-activists. Crystal Field and George Bartenieff co-founded Theater for the New City, which became the producing home for many socially conscious artists. They hosted Angry Arts, a festival of opposition to the war by artists, and in 1991 they hosted a weekend of theater expressions against the Gulf War.

There was never much money behind these productions. But for most of this time it was still relatively inexpensive to live in New York.

Space could be rented without huge deposits. These new productions began to attract wider audiences, and eventually they attracted grant money from the Ford, Rockefeller, and Kaplan Foundations. Richard Nixon, who remained frightened enough of the counterculture to attempt to placate its demands, encouraged the National Endowment for the Arts, which had been founded in 1965 during the Lyndon Johnson administration. The NEA, at the start, funded the radical theater movements. Ticket prices were kept low, and, as in the 1930s, the productions attracted a wide and varied audience.

"What happened?" Malpede asked.

The Vietnam War finally ended, but the Peace Movement persisted in large numbers through the dirty wars in South America and the growing antinuclear movement. Yet, it became more and more difficult to produce socially conscious, poetic theater. The old dogma of the 1950s reasserted itself: art and politics don't mix. When Ronald Reagan was elected in 1980, he immediately ordered that NEA grants to small – read leftist – theaters be abolished. Reaganism eroded the public perception that a great democracy deserves great art.

"Without government support for funding innovation and the non-commercial, the theater began to institutionalize and to censor itself," Malpede went on.

The growing network of regional theaters became ever more reliant upon planning subscription seasons which would not offend any of their local donors, and the institutional theaters began to function more and more as social clubs for the wealthy and philanthropic. Sometimes, there was a breakthrough. *Angels in America* was one— the result, too, of an aggressive gay activist movement. But to a large degree, the theater no longer wanted to shake people up. The institutional theaters began to "develop" plays—a process geared to securing grants from the few foundations which still, in our age of austerity, fund the arts. Development means that most new plays receive a series of readings and workshops during which all sorts of dramaturges, literary managers, directors, and artistic directors give their "input," most often thoroughly confusing, especially to young playwrights, and frequently damaging whatever was authentic to begin with. Fewer and fewer of these plays ever reach production. As the economy worsens, fewer and fewer risks are taken. Some subjects are out of bounds altogether, including strong critiques of capitalism or American foreign policy, in other words, anything that might cause individual donors to stop donating.

Theater, once again unplugged from what gave it vitality, became increasingly mediocre and was produced as spectacle or celebrity-driven entertainment. Audiences dwindled and aged. Critical debate onstage was largely banished. Entertainment has become, as Macdonald wrote of his age, directed toward the mass, a set of statistics, what he called the "non-man." Mass art denies the existence of individual taste or experience, of an individual conscience, of anything that differentiates people from one another. Art is an individual experience. It forces us to examine ourselves. It broadens perspective. Entertainment masquerading as art, by contrast, herds viewers and audiences into the collective. It limits perspective to that experienced by the mass. "With the effective disempowering of artists, and with artists' collusion in their own disempowerment, the theater now serves no meaningful function," said Malpede. "It seldom startles, enlivens, enrages, or encourages its audience to become more fiercely aware of their own or of others' humanity."

Malpede's 2009 play *Prophecy*, which centers on the tragic effect of wars on individual lives from Vietnam, to the Israeli attacks in Lebanon and Gaza, to the war in Iraq, was not one a corporate sponsor would touch. It opened in London, where it won four stars in *Time Out London* and two Critics' Choice citations in 2008. But Malpede struggled to find a theater in New York. Her portrayal of Muslims as victims of indiscriminate Israeli and American violence, and its unrelenting condemnation of war, put it far outside the liberal spectrum.

"What is to be done?" Malpede asked of the commercial restraints on theater:

> Here I speak only from experience. My recent play *Prophecy* had six public readings, each packed with attentive and wildly enthusiastic audiences, yet was refused production by every theater that hosted

these readings and by others to whom the play was sent. One producer called the play "brilliant" but told me it was "too risky" and he
would "never produce" it at his theater. His was among the most
honest responses. Another producer told me she found the play
"very moving" when she read it, but is of the opinion that neither
critics nor audiences wish to "see anything about anything." Another
potential producer, who, after witnessing 150 people at the Kennedy
Center become totally engrossed in a reading and hearing their
amazingly positive feedback afterwards, wrote me, coolly, that he
"had received negative e-mails" and withdrew his offer to consider
the play. George Bartenieff, my partner, and I decided we had to produce the play ourselves. We had developed a devoted core audience,
and the play had no trouble attracting wonderfully talented actors. In
fact, I had written it for Najla Said and Kathleen Chalfant, and both
were eager to do it. Najla went to London, where *Prophecy* premiered
in a coproduction, which we partially funded, mainly from a small
pension fund of mine left over after I had been denied tenure at the
Tisch School of the Arts [at New York University] for "being an
artist," not a postmodern theorist. Bartenieff and I maintain a small
not-for-profit organization, Theater Three Collaborative, just for the
purpose of creating the sort of poetic, social theater we revere. We
had already produced [Malpede's] *The Beekeeper's Daughter*, about a
Bosnian refugee, and *I Will Bear Witness*, based on the Victor Klem-
perer diaries. After London, we set about raising the money mainly
from our core audience members, and finally completely depleting
my pension, to produce *Prophecy* in New York.

It is only when artists control their own work, as Malpede did with
her production of *Prophecy*, that great, socially relevant theater can be
sustained. The funding for this kind of work will never come out of the
world of corporate sponsorships which, like Mr. Mister, uses theater
and the arts as a diversion.

"The theater needs to be funded with public money, as it was in
Athens, where it began, and where all citizens were required to attend
the dramatic festival, because the theater is, when it functions, a corrective against the excesses of empire," Malpede said. "As such it remains
necessary to the functioning of a democratic state, and though it might

make the functionaries of such a state uncomfortable, it will and must be a beacon of truth. At its best, such a theater provides the experience of heightened feeling, heightened aliveness, heightened awareness of self and other. It makes us more human and humane, and, therefore, more able to take action in the world."

～

Malcolm Cowley chronicled the transformation of the artist as rebel to the artist as propagandist in *Exile's Return,* his intellectual history of the first half of the twentieth century. He noted that after World War I, the corporate class and the liberal class, including artists, sprang from the same communities and neighborhoods, went to the same schools, and merged into the same social class. The political opinions of the liberal class "were vague and by no means dangerous to Ford Motors or General Electric; the war had destroyed their belief in political actions. They were trying to get ahead, and the proletariat be damned. The economic standards were those of the small American businessman."[36]

Cowley questioned Max Weber's contention that the Puritan ethic—restraint, asceticism, guilt—was the primary value system demanded by capitalism. He argued that the "production ethic," which demanded "industry, foresight, thrift" was, in fact, the value system cherished by the now-lost machine age. The new corporate capitalism and mass production sustained themselves through the promotion of a new ethic that promoted leisure, self-indulgence, and wasteful consumption, activities that called for traits such as charm, a pleasant appearance, and likability. Consumption was more important than production. Cowley observed that after the war, artists, too, became devoted to self-expression, political cynicism, and hedonism, including the cult of the body. These values were embraced in the name of the counterculture, but they were also the core qualities corporate capitalism sought to inculcate in the public. This cult of the self was central, Cowley wrote, to the Bohemians and later the Beats.

Lawrence Lipton, who wrote a book on the Beats called *The Holy Barbarians,* argued that the Beats "expropriated" from the upper classes their arts, sins, and "privilege of defying convention." The Beats, like the Bohemians who populated Greenwich Village after World War I, also flaunted a self-indulgent hedonism that mirrored the ethic of the consumer culture. Lipton called this "the democratization of amorality." The Beats in the 1950s aided the dissipation of the intellectual class by abandoning urban centers, where a previous generation of public intellectuals, such as Jane Jacobs or Dwight Macdonald, lived and worked. They romanticized the automobile and movement. Russell Jacoby points out in *The Last Intellectuals* that the Beats had a peculiarly American "devotion to the automobile, the road, and travel, which kept them and then a small army of imitators crisscrossing the continent," as well as a populist "love of the American people."[37] The Beats not only bolstered the ethic of consumption and leisure as opposed to work, but also they "anticipated the deurbanization of America, the abandonment of the cities for smaller centers, suburbs, campus towns, and outlying areas."[38]

The new ethic of the liberal class, Cowley wrote, was one that embraced "the idea of salvation by the child," which proposed a new educational system "by which children are encouraged to develop their own personalities, to blossom freely like flowers, then the world will be saved by this new, free generation." It championed self-expression so that the individual can "realize his full individuality through creative work and beautiful living in beautiful surroundings." It fostered the cult of paganism, the idea that "the body is a temple in which there is nothing unclean, a shrine to be adorned for the ritual of love." It called for living for the moment, to "dwell in it intensely, even at the cost of future suffering." It defied all forms of Puritanism and demanded that "every law, convention or rule of art that prevents self-expression or the full enjoyment of the moment should be shattered and abolished." It supported female equality. It embraced the therapeutic culture, the belief that "if our individual repressions can be removed—by confessing them to a Freudian psychologist—then we can adjust ourselves to any situation, and be happy in it." The environment no longer needed to be altered, and "that explains why most radicals who became converted to psychoanalysis or glands or Gurdjieff [a popular mystic] gradually abandoned their political activism."[39]

Cowley noted that self-expression and paganism, however, only encouraged a demand for new products, from furniture to beach pajamas. The call to live for the moment, he argued, led people impulsively to purchase consumer goods, from automobiles to radios. Female equality was used to double the consumption of products such as cigarettes. The restlessness and fondness for self-imposed exile, embraced by Bohemians, intellectuals and artists, gave an allure to foreign objects and turned exotic locations into tourist destinations.[40]

Political rebels, Cowley noted, had all swiftly yielded to Woodrow Wilson's crusade to make the world safe for democracy and fight communism. And those few not seduced by the nobility of the war effort either fled to countries such as Mexico or were rounded up and sent to Leavenworth Penitentiary.

"Whatever course they followed, almost all the radicals of 1917 were defeated by events," Cowley wrote. "The Bohemian tendency triumphed in the Village, and talk about revolution gave way to psychoanalysis. The *Masses*, after being suppressed, and after temporarily reappearing as the *Liberator*, gave way to magazines like the *Playboy*, the *Pagan* (their names expressed them adequately), and the *Little Review*." [41]

Artistic expression soon became devoid of social purpose. It created, as Cowley wrote, "the religion of art" that "inevitably led into blind alleys." Abstract painting emerged as the artistic expression of this sterile form of rebellion, an outgrowth of the apolitical absurdist and Dada movements. There was no longer, as Cowley wrote, "any psychic basis common to all humanity. There was no emotion shared by all men, no law to which all were subject; there was not even a sure means of communication between one man and another."[42] Irving Howe noted that it was primarily Yiddish intellectuals who remained honest and connected to those they wrote and sang about because they were "too poor to venture on the programmatic poverty of Bohemia. . . . These intellectuals were thrown in with the masses of their people, sharing their poverty, their work, their tenements."[43] But the rest of the intellectual and artistic class were welcomed into the embrace of consumer culture, rushing out once large book advances were negotiated to buy the same consumer products that mesmerized the rest of society.

⌐

The liberal class was seduced by the ideology of progress—attained through technology and the amassing of national wealth, material goods, and comforts—and intimidated into supporting the capitalist destruction of reformist and radical movements. As long as the liberal class did not seriously challenge capitalism, it was permitted a place in the churches, the universities, the unions, the press, the arts, and the Democratic Party. Minimal reform, as well as an open disdain for Puritanism, was acceptable. A challenge to the sanctity of the capitalist system was not. Those who continued to attack these structures of capitalism, to engage in class warfare, were banished from the liberal cloisters.

The final purges of radicals included the blacklisting of writers, actors, directors, journalists, union leaders, politicians such as Henry Wallace, government employees, teachers, artists, and producers in the American film industry, in the late 1940s and early 1950s. The purge was done with the collaboration of the liberal class. Americans for Democratic Action (ADA), for example, backed the witch hunts. These purges proved useful to the most ambitious, and often most morally suspect, people within liberal institutions, especially those who wanted to dispose of rivals. "In the course of this battle liberals attacked liberals with more venom than they had ever directed at any economic royalist," observed an ADA supporter.[44] Henry Wallace, who ran for president as a third-party candidate in 1947 and 1948 and had been Franklin Roosevelt's vice president, was subjected to a vicious assault by the press and the liberal establishment. Wallace was discredited and finally exiled from political life as a communist sympathizer. The complicity of the liberal class was, in part, a product of insecurity, especially since many reformers and liberals had flirted with communism during the Depression, given the breakdown of capitalism in those years. But it was also the product of a craven careerism and desire for prestige and comfort.

The scurrilous newsletter *Counterattack,* published by a group of right-wing misfits, denounced what it called communist front groups including the Progressive Citizens of America, which it called the "biggest communist front," the Methodist Federation for Social Action, the Consumers Union, the National Lawyers Guild, and the Allied Labor News. The publication promised to expose "communist" labor unions. It published a book, called *Red Channels: The Report of Communist Influence in Radio and Television,* which listed the alleged communist affiliations of 151 actors, writers, musicians, and other radio and television entertainers. The newsletter and book were published by American Business Consultants, a group established in 1947 by three former FBI agents who were bankrolled by an upstate New York grocery chain magnate, Laurence Johnson, and later a former naval intelligence officer, Vincent Hartnett. It mounted a campaign against writers, including journalists such as Richard O. Boyer, who wrote profiles for the *New Yorker*, and the *New York Times* music critic Olin Downes. It attacked writers such as Dashiell Hammett and Ring Lardner Jr., as well as intellectuals including Albert Einstein. Radio and television personalities—many of them commentators and stars—were fired after being named in the pages of *Counterattack*. Those removed from the airwaves by nervous employers and sponsors included the Texas humorist and radio commentator John Henry Faulk; Ireene Wicker, the "Singing Lady," who had a popular children's television show; and Philip Loeb, who played the father on the popular sitcom *The Rise of the Goldbergs*. Loeb denied he was a communist, but the corporate sponsor of the show, General Foods, insisted he be removed.

The human cost of the blacklist was tragic. In his memoir *Inside Out: A Memoir of the Blacklist,* Walter Bernstein, a blacklisted screen writer, describes his friend Loeb as disconsolate. Loeb was the sole supporter of a mentally ill son whom he kept in a private treatment facility, and, as Bernstein wrote, "he was constantly afraid he would be unable to keep up the payments and his son would be moved to a state hospital for the insane." Loeb lost his apartment. He moved in for a time with the blacklisted comic and actor Zero Mostel, who, Bernstein wrote, "loved Loeb, a short, sweet, sad-eyed man."

Bernstein recounts how once or twice, Mostel and his wife Kate found Loeb

> shouting out the window at pedestrians below. Zero could never cheer him up, no matter how hard he tried. I never saw Loeb smile, even when Zero was at his hilarious best. He gave the impression he could not be touched. Finally, one day, he checked into a hotel and made sure he took enough pills to kill himself."[45]

A letter to the drama editor of the *New York Times* after Loeb's death said he "died of a sickness commonly called the blacklist."[46] The actress

Jean Muir, after being named, was removed from the cast of a television sitcom *The Aldrich Family*, in which she was supposed to appear as Mother Aldrich. The folk group the Weavers, which included Pete Seeger and the actress Lee Grant, all vanished from the public stage. Those who were blacklisted watched as friends, neighbors and acquaintances severed contact with them.

"My life revolved around those friendships," Bernstein wrote:

> They were almost entirely with other blacklisted people; we had circled the wagons and it was dangerous to step outside the perimeter. In the morning I tried to write—speculative scripts or articles or the occasional story—but they were desultory, lacking conviction. I seemed to need a validation I could not produce from myself alone. The days were aimless, as they had been when I was waiting to be drafted. I felt suspended; my real life was somewhere else, on hold, waiting to be resurrected when the country came to its senses. Finally, I had to admit I was depressed, a recognition that only added to the depression. A conspiracy was afoot to make me feel unworthy and I was giving it credence.[47]

Many, including Mostel, Faulk, Grant, and Seeger, and even Bernstein, would return to prominence in the 1960s, but the purges marked the last gasp of an era, one of progressive and radical artists who were allied with working-class movements and saw art as linked to the articulation and creation of a social and political consciousness. The broad, bold ideas and truths expressed by radical movements and artists before the witch hunts were effectively censored out of public discourse.

"The overall legacy of the liberals' failure to stand up against the anticommunist crusades was to let the nation's political culture veer to the right," writes Ellen Schrecker in *Many Are the Crimes: McCarthyism in America*:

> Movements and ideas that had once been acceptable were now beyond the pale. Though Communists and their allies were the direct victims, the mainstream liberals and former New Dealers within the Democratic Party were the indirect ones. Condoning the campaign against communism did not protect them from being denounced for

"losing" China or, like Supreme Court Justice Black, for supporting desegregation in the South. Moreover, because the left had been destroyed, when liberals came under attack they had to defend themselves from a more politically exposed position than they would otherwise have occupied. This may seem obvious, but it is a point that needs to be stressed. The disappearance of the communist movement weakened American liberalism. Because its adherents were now on the left of the political spectrum, instead of at the center, they had less room within which to maneuver.[48]

In the wake of the witch hunts, networks such as CBS forced employees to sign loyalty oaths. Walt Disney and Ronald Reagan, president of the Screen Actors Guild, cooperated in hounding out artists deemed disloyal. Those who refused to cooperate with the witch hunts or who openly defied HUAC instantly became nonpersons. One such resister was Paul Robeson, who went before the committee in June 1956. A celebrated singer and actor, Robeson, who was a communist sympathizer and vocal supporter of civil rights, was banned from commercial radio and television. He would end his life in obscurity. Although an African American, he encountered obstacles to performing afterward in black churches. Established liberal institutions, including the NAACP, the American Civil Liberties Union (where ACLU cocounsel Morris Ernst worked closely with FBI Director J. Edgar Hoover), Americans for Democratic Action, the American Association of University Professors, and the American Committee for Cultural Freedom either were silent or collaborated in the banishment of artists, teachers, writers, performers, scientists, and government officials.

The widespread dismissals of professors, elementary and high-school teachers, and public employees—especially social workers whose unions had advocated on behalf of their clients—were often carried out quietly. The names of suspected "reds" were routinely handed to administrators and school officials under the FBI's Responsibilities Program. It was up to the institutions, nearly all of which complied, to see that those singled out lost their jobs. There were rarely hearings. The victims did not see any purported evidence. They were usually abruptly terminated. Those on the blacklist were effectively locked out of their profession. Schrecker estimates that between ten thousand and twelve thousand people were blackballed through this process.

The fiercely anticommunist AFL-CIO, which subordinated itself to the Democratic Party, was permitted to flourish, while militant unions, including those in Hollywood, were ruthlessly purged or closed. The leadership of the CIO expelled several left-led unions in 1949 after disputes erupted over the party's initial support for Henry Wallace's presidential campaign. The CIO used the threat of further expulsions to stifle internal debate and discredit radicals, including anarchists, socialists, pro-Soviet communists, Trotskyists, and others who once played a vital role within the labor movement. Unions, formerly steeped in the doctrine of class struggle and filled with those who sought broad social and political rights for the working class, collaborated with the capitalist class and merged with the liberal establishment. The embrace of fanatical anticommunism was, in essence, an embrace of the suspension of civil liberties, including freedom of speech and the right to organize, values the liberal class claimed to support.

The Taft-Hartley Act, passed in 1948 and the single most destructive piece of legislation to the union movement, was a product of anticommunist hysteria. When it was passed, about half of all American workers belonged to labor unions. That figure has now dropped to twelve percent. The Taft-Hartley Act was devised as a revision of the National Labor Relations Act (NLRB) of 1935, known as the Wagner Act. It was one of the first new pieces of postwar legislation to roll back the gains made by workers under the New Deal. The Wagner Act, known as "the labor bill of rights," had created the NLRB, and it forbade employers from engaging in unfair labor practices. Although the gains by workers were made primarily in the North, since southern whites sought to block union organizing among blacks, the NLRB represented a major achievement for working men and women. To get it in place, Roosevelt had permitted the NLRB to exclude agricultural and domestic workers, a coded way to exclude blacks and keep southern politicians, who were mostly Democrats, behind him.

The Taft-Hartley Act, which is still law, prohibited jurisdictional strikes, wildcat strikes, solidarity or political strikes, and secondary boycotts—union strikes against employers who continue to do business with a firm that is undergoing a strike. The act forbade secondary or "common situs" picketing, closed shops, and monetary donations by unions to federal political campaigns. All union officers were forced to sign noncommunist affidavits or lose their positions. Heavy restrictions were placed on union shops, while individual states were allowed to pass "right-to-work laws" that outlawed union shops. The Federal Government was empowered to obtain legal strikebreaking injunctions if an impending or current strike "imperiled the national health or safety." The act effectively demobilized the labor movement. It severely curtailed the ability to organize and strike and purged the last vestiges of militant labor leaders from the ranks of unions. With the passage of Taft-Hartley the power of labor to fight back effectively against the corporate state died. Labor, once the beating heart of progressive radical movements, became as impotent as the arts, the media, the church, the universities, and the Democratic Party.

IV / Politics as Spectacle

What if the world is one kind of—of show! ... What if we are
all only talent assembled by the Great Talent Scout Up Above!
The Great Show of Life. Starring Everybody! Suppose enter-
tainment is the Purpose of Life!

—PHILIP ROTH, *"On the Air"*[1]

THE RADICAL upheavals of the 1960s were infused with the same hedonism and cult of the self that corrupted earlier twentieth-century counterculture movements. There was an open antagonism between most antiwar activists and the working class, whose sons were shipped to Vietnam while the sons of the middle class were often handed college deferments. Working-class high schools sent twenty to thirty percent of their graduates to Vietnam during the height of the war, while college graduates made up two percent of all troops sent to Vietnam in 1965 and 1966. Students who opposed the war were derided by the power elite, and many in the working class, as draft dodgers. Antiwar activists were portrayed as spoiled children of the rich and the middle class who advocated free love, drug use, communism, and social anarchy.

The unions remained virulently anticommunist, spoke in the language of militarism and the Cold War, and were largely unsympathetic to the civil-rights and antiwar movements. When student activists protested at the 1965 AFL-CIO Convention in San Francisco, chanting, "Get out of Vietnam!" the delegates taunted them by shouting, "Get a haircut." AFL-CIO president George Meany ordered the security to "clear the Kookies out of the gallery." Once the protesters were escorted out, Walter Reuther, president of the United Automobile

Workers and a leading force in the AFL-CIO, announced that "protestors should be demonstrating against Hanoi and Peking ... [who] are responsible for the war." The convention passed a resolution that read "The labor movement proclaim[s] to the world that the nation's working men and women do support the Johnson administration in Vietnam."[2]

Those that constituted the hard-core New Left, groups like Students for a Democratic Society (SDS), found their inspiration in the liberation struggles in Vietnam and the third world rather than the labor movement, which they considered bought off by capitalism. "With few exceptions, New Left radicals regarded the working class in the heart of the imperialist beast as a [big] part of the problem, and they looked elsewhere for allies," Sharon Smith writes.[3] Radicals turned to Mao Zedong, Joseph Stalin, and Leon Trotsky. And with that came an embrace of armed revolution. The Black Panthers, the Nation of Islam, and the Weather Underground Organization, severed from the daily concerns of the working class, became as infected with the lust for violence, quest for ideological purity, crippling paranoia, self-exaltation, and internal repression as the state system they defied. Only a few hundred radical Maoists, many of them living in communes in cities such as San Francisco, broke with the SDS and took jobs in factories as blue-collar workers in an attempt to organize the working class. But they were a tiny minority.

Protest in the 1960s found its ideological roots in the disengagement championed earlier by Beats such by Jack Kerouac, Allen Ginsberg, and William Burroughs. It was a movement that, while it incorporated a healthy dose of disrespect for authority, focused again on self-indulgent schemes for inner peace and fulfillment. The use of hallucinogenic drugs, advocated by Timothy Leary in books such as the *Politics of Ecstasy,* and the rise of occultism that popularized Transcendental Meditation, theosophy, the Hare Krishna branch of Hinduism, and renewed interest in Zen Buddhism and study of the *I Ching,* were trends that would have dismayed the Wobblies or the militants in the old Communist Party. The counterculture of the 1960s, like the commodity culture, lured adherents inward. It set up the self up as the primary center of concern. It, too, offered affirmative, therapeutic remedies to social problems that embraced vague, undefined, and utopian campaigns to remake society. There was no political vision.

Herman Hesse's *Siddhartha,* with its narrator's search for enlightenment, became emblematic of the moral hollowness of the New Left.

These movements, and the counterculture celebrities that led them, such as the Yippie leader Abbie Hoffman, sought and catered to the stage set for them by the television camera. Protest and court trials became street theater. Dissent became another media spectacle. Antiwar protesters in Berkeley switched from singing "Solidarity Forever" to "Yellow Submarine." The civil-rights movement, which was rooted in the moral and religious imperatives of justice and self-sacrifice, what Dwight Macdonald called nonhistorical values, was largely eclipsed by the self-centeredness of the New Left, especially after the assassinations of Malcolm X in 1967 and Martin Luther King Jr. a year later. And once the Vietnam War ended, once middle-class men no longer had to go to war, the movement disintegrated. The political and moral void within the counterculture meant it was an easy transition from college radical to a member of the liberal class. The 1960s counterculture, like the counterculture of the Bohemians or the Beats, was always in tune with the commercial culture. It shared commercial culture's hedonism, love of spectacle, and preoccupation with the self.

The moral vacuum of the counterculture disturbed religious radicals, such as Father Daniel Berrigan and his brother Philip, the *Catholic Worker* leader Dorothy Day, and the Reverend William Sloane Coffin, as well as stalwarts from the decimated Communist Party and old anarchists such as Dwight Macdonald and Murray Bookchin. The transition from street protester to grant applicant was, as Bookchin noted sourly, not hard, given the moral vacuum in the New Left.

"Radical politics in our time has come to mean the numbing quietude of the polling booth, the deadening platitudes of petition campaigns, carbumper sloganeering, the contradictory rhetoric of manipulative politicians, the spectator sports of public rallies and finally, the knee-bent, humble plea for small reforms," Bookchin wrote:

> in short, the mere shadows of the direct action, embattled commitment, insurgent conflicts, and social idealism that marked every revolutionary project in history. . . . What is most terrifying about present-day "radicalism" is that the piercing cry for "audacity"— "L'audace! L'audace! Encore l'audace!"—that Danton voiced in 1793

on the high tide of the French revolution would simply be *puzzling* to the self-styled radicals who demurely carry attaché cases of memoranda and grant requests into their conference rooms . . . and bull horns to their rallies.[4]

Macdonald argued that any movement that did not pay fealty to the nonhistorical values of truth, justice, and love inevitably collapsed. Once any class bowed to the practical dictates required by effective statecraft and legislation, or the call to protect the nation, it lost its voice. The naïve belief in human progress through science, technology, and mass production further eroded these nonhistorical values. The choice was between serving human beings and serving history, between thinking ethically and thinking strategically. Macdonald criticized Marxists for the same reason he criticized the liberal class: both subordinated ethics to another goal. By serving history and power, the liberal class, like the Marxists, surrendered their power and moral authority to the state. The capitulation of the liberal class, as Irving Howe noted, has bleached out all political tendencies: "It becomes a loose shelter, a poncho rather than a program; to call oneself a liberal one doesn't really have to believe in anything.[5]

In *Exile's Return*, Malcolm Cowley argues, like Macdonald and Howe, that the cultural and religious reformers of the early twentieth century unwittingly laid the foundations for their own dissolution. By extolling the power of the state as an agent of change, by accepting that increased comfort and consumption were the defining measures of human progress, they abetted the consumer society and the cult of the self, as well as the ascendancy of the corporate state. The trust in the beneficence of the state, which led most of these liberal reformers naïvely to back the war effort, ceded uncontested power to the state during the war, especially the power to shape and mold public perceptions. The state, once it held these powers, never gave them up.

The liberal class had placed its faith in the inevitability of human progress and abandoned the values, as Macdonald pointed out, that should have remained at the core of its activism. Mass culture, and the state—the repository of the hopes and dreams of the liberal class— should have been seen as the enemy. The breach between the liberal class and the radical social and political movements it once supported or sympathized with was total. This rupture has left the liberal class without a repository of new ideas.[6]

A recent exhibition at the Museum of Modern Art in New York illustrated the difference between an artistic movement that was, on one hand, integrated into social democracy and sought to eradicate the barriers between craftspeople and artists, and on the other, an artis- tic movement that served its elitist needs. The former was illustrated by Bauhaus at the MOMA, a huge retrospective of the German art movement. The latter was illustrated just a few floors below the Bauhaus exhibit, by MOMA's permanent collection of (mostly) American postwar art, a dreary example of flat, sterile, and self-referential junk. The iron control of the arts is vital to the power elite, as important as control of the political and economic process, the universities, the media, the labor movement, and the church. Art gives people a language by which they can understand themselves and their society. And the corporate power structure was determined to make sure artists spoke in a language that did not threaten their entitlement.

The liberal class, especially its most elitist and snobbish elements, was used to help distance art from the masses, portrayed as too unsophisticated and uneducated to appreciate or understand authentic artistic expression. Museums and their arrogant curators appointed themselves as the arbiters of high culture. These liberal institutions ruthlessly filtered out artistic expression that confronted or exposed the darker side of the power elite. The great philanthropic families, the Rockefellers, the Whitneys, the Paleys, the Blisses, the Warburgs, and the Lewisohns, many of whom also funded major universities, created the country's most important museum collections. They enriched and promoted their preferred artists. They championed abstract painters such as Jackson Pollock, who had abandoned his earlier radicalism.

Pollock, along with many other of the new abstract artists adopted by the elite, sought to turn the process of producing art into spectacle. These so-called action painters, as Neal Gabler writes, "used their canvases as a kind of movie screen for the creation of art and made themselves into romantic action heroes, bounding, thrashing, and raging their way across that canvas/screen and leaving art in their wake." Pollock spoke of literally being "in the painting as if," Gabler writes, "he were an actor in a film."[7] It would be left to Andy Warhol to point out that the most important art movement of the twentieth century wasn't cubism or surrealism or fauvism or minimalism or op or pop, to which [Warhol] himself nominally belonged. No, the most important art movement was celebrity. Eventually, no matter who the artist was and no matter what school he belonged to, the entertainment society made his fame his achievement and not his achievement his fame. The visual art, like so much else in American life, was a macguffin for the artist. It was just a means to celebrity, which was the real artwork.[8]

Wealthy art patrons backed organizations such as the Federation of Modern Painters and Sculptors, set up to counter the politically active Artists Congress. The Federation of Modern Painters and Sculptors was, as Max Kozloff wrote, "interested more in aesthetic values than in political action." Kozloff also pointed out the similarity between "American Cold War rhetoric" and the existentialist-individualist credos of Abstract Expressionist artists. Artistic expression became as domesticated and depoliticized as union activity, journalism, scholarship, and political discourse.

"The alleged separation of art from politics proclaimed throughout the 'free world' with the resurgence of abstraction after World War II was part of a general tendency in intellectual circles towards 'objectivity,' " wrote the art historian Eva Cockroft:

> So foreign to the newly developing apolitical milieu of the 1950s was the idea of political commitment—not only to artists but also to many other intellectuals—that one social historian, Daniel Bell, eventually was to proclaim the postwar period as "the end of ideology." Abstract Expressionism neatly fits the needs of this supposedly new historical epoch. By giving their painting an individualist emphasis and eliminating recognizable subject matter, the Abstract Expressionists succeeded in creating an important new art movement. They also contributed, whether they knew it or not, to a purely political phenomenon – the supposed divorce between art and politics which so perfectly served America's needs in the Cold War.[9]

Art schools have become as utilitarian as journalism schools. As the art historian Carol Becker notes, art schools train students not to be powerful in society but "to fit into the art world, but not into the world as it exists. You can see it in our public school system, where art is marginalized almost as some sort of leisure activity." Art, as Becker points out, "is relegated to a place of nostalgic longing, high culture, or entertainment. Most people if asked would say that art exists to infuse the world with beauty and vitality. It is not understood, except by the art world itself, as a legitimate arena for controversy and debate. In this society, art is not defined within the arena of real power—namely, politics."[10]

Art schools produce, along with departments devoted to the sciences and technologies, the specialist, the expert groomed to conform to the tastes of the power elite. These specialists must master narrow, arcane subjects and disciplines rather than reflect on and challenge systems of power. The specialists reign over tiny, often irrelevant kingdoms and ignore pressing moral and social questions that require a broader understanding of the human condition. The specialist cedes questions of power to the elite. The specialist justifies this moral abrogation by believing what he or she has been told. They are qualified only to speak about the minutiae of their area of study or discipline. And the specialist, once he or she corners an obscure topic, be it seventeenth-century porcelain or the role of gambling among nineteenth-century Russian aristocrats, locks out the nonspecialist through the use of unnecessarily obscure vocabulary and opaque data.

Liberal institutions and the power elite, from the media to museums to the universities, determine who is permitted to dominate these specialized fields. The wider society, conditioned to rely on the specialist—whether in finance, politics, or art—for its interpretation of reality, is fed approved assumptions. And this system is perfectly designed to reproduce itself. Universities, by demanding that professors attain doctorates, almost always written on narrow and obscure specializations approved by faculty committees, replenish their ranks with the timid and the mediocre.

The artist, like the specialist or the professor, is plugged into a system where he or she serves the interests and tastes of the power elite. The choice may be between high and low culture, but in each sphere members of the liberal class dare not risk losing their prestige and employment by defying the structures of power. Playwrights end up writing inane television scripts. Graphic artists draw and animate for corporations. Actors pay the rent doing commercials and voiceovers. Filmmakers, editors, and writers sell themselves to corporate advertising agencies. And those on the upper end of the cultural spectrum, the tenured professors and cultural critics, the lauded poets and art historians, speak and write only for one another like medieval theologians. Artistic expression, like scholarship, is sustained by a system of interlocking, exclusive guilds. And those who insist on remaining independent of these guilds, such as the documentary filmmaker Fred Wiseman, are locked out. Those who write, think, paint, film, or sculpt in ways that defy the specialists or the demands of commercialized mass culture must break from the institutions run by the liberal class.

Alan Magee, whose powerful images and sculptures of war and physical abuse explore the depravity of violence, entered the Illustration Department at the Philadelphia College of Art in 1967. He had no special interest in illustration. The department, however, was a place where art students were permitted to make representational paintings without apology. Fine-arts departments throughout the country, leaning toward the abstract and conceptual, saw representational art as by nature illustration. Those who gravitated to representational art were usually pegged as illustrators.

"As an art student I was searching for a language within the realist tradition that could carry contemporary ideas and issues," Magee told me.[11] "Surrealism provided one example of how representational art could communicate. I looked carefully at Magritte, and also at George Tooker, Philip Pearlstein, and the Canadian painter Alex Colville. Three paintings at the Philadelphia Museum of Art—Salvador Dalí's [*Soft Construction with Boiled Beans (Premonition of Civil War)*], Jan van Eyck's *Saint Francis Receiving the Stigmata*, and Andrew Wyeth's *Groundhog Day*—set me on my path as an aspiring illustrator.

"Outside our classrooms, inspiring work was beginning to appear in magazines, on posters, in European graphics," he said. "There was a lot to look at, to admire and measure oneself against. The magazine and book publishers were, by today's standards, inventive and politically courageous. The best art directors didn't get in the illustrator's way, or expect him to keep his eccentricities out of an assignment."

Magee began illustrating in New York in 1968. He said he was given nearly complete freedom in carrying out his work.

"I would be assigned, for example, a series of Graham Greene or Bernard Malamud books to read and to interpret in my own way," he said:

I looked for a symbolic or metaphorical equivalent to the writing whenever possible rather than making a literal depiction of the characters. My preliminary sketches were regularly accepted. The cynicism about the profits a book had to make hadn't really settled in, and the media conglomerates hadn't yet acquired the small publishing companies. That happened later, and the resulting erosion of the freedoms I had taken for granted was one of several reasons for my leaving that career and for concentrating on my own paintings.

"During the 1970s, in the fine-art world, the minimalist sculptor Donald Judd was installing polished aluminum boxes in galleries and art museums, Carl Andre was arranging rows of builder's bricks on museum floors, and many artists signed on to minimalism, conceptual art, and similar trends," Magee said. "These movements were no doubt partly aimed at asserting expanded possibilities for art. It was difficult to object to them. But the ascendancy of these opaque art practices did finally cordon off high art from the lives of ordinary people. Since then, 'significant' art has become ever more remote and inscrutable."

José Ortega y Gasset and Ernst Gombrich, Magee said, warned that modern art could evolve into a dehumanized enterprise. Ortega y Gasset suggested that intentionally obscure art would be used as an implicit insult to the lower classes when direct slurs were no longer regarded as acceptable. Gombrich predicted that membership in the modernist movement would be worn "like a badge" and that it would make analysis and criticism of particular artists and works of art from within the club impossible.

"Both of these predictions came to pass," Magee said:

I began to understand that art-world "discourses" could not be taken seriously, and I can remember a moment when it became clear to me that avant-garde art was not progressive or humanitarian—that it was, in a political sense, conservative, and was not looking for approval or comprehension from outside its privileged inner circle. I had naïvely believed that the modern art enterprise remained in some way linked to a gradual pull toward decency, a counterpart to various struggles for equality and fairness that were going on outside the world of art. The opposite was true. Tenderness and empathy had been banished from "important" art. They were not good for business. Today's sanctified works of art are essentially financial vehicles—stripped of burdensome humanity.

"But what is wrong with frivolity, art-world insider games, or with bewildering art objects being displayed in a museum?" Magee asked:

Nothing is wrong with these things, of course, unless they are piled up as in a blockade to make passage of any useful images or ideas very difficult. What disheartens me when I enter the contemporary wing of the Museum of Modern Art, although it could be any contemporary wing, anywhere, since there is now only one message, which is that a once-vital avenue of human connection is clogged with things that rebuke the notion of connection. I watch people wandering through these vast rooms looking somewhat glazed, half asleep—many of them, no doubt, suspecting that they are not clever enough or sufficiently educated to receive the blessing of high art. It saddens me that they came to experience art in good faith, believing that through it they might become uplifted, sensitized to life, as they would be if they had stayed home and read a good contemporary novel. Museum-goers are being deceived about the breadth of contemporary art and what it could offer them.

"Meaningful art is being created today, but as painter John Nava commented, the art that's been chosen to represent us all follows from Marcel Duchamp," Magee said. "His *Fountain*, a manufactured urinal signed 'R. Mutt,' which he submitted to the 1917 exhibition of the Society of Independent Artists in New York, was voted the most influential artwork of the twentieth century by five hundred selected British art-world professionals. Duchamp's point, intended to repudiate genteel aesthetics and to 'shock the squares,' was timely and well made, but it didn't need to be repeated for a century.

"My disappointment with the drift of official contemporary art is bound up with my admiration for certain movements and artists that were part of early European modernism—Dada, and German Expressionist art and film, for example—but all the arts seemed to soar in the 1920s and early '30s," he said. "And much of early modernism was moral, as John Gardiner used the term, even though, and because, it was brazenly coarse and defiant. Those modern artists, like early Christians, were outsiders. That sense of dissidence may be what attracts me to the graphics, poetry, film, music, and literature from that time and place.

"I have had to rewrite art history for my own purposes," Magee concluded:

> Maybe we all have to do that. I have to disregard the hierarchies of the art world to make space for artists in all fields who give me something authentic and who occasionally change my life. Some of these artists are well known. Others are like secrets completely invisible to those we call "art professionals." Among the artists in what I call "my working history of art" are the Czech animator and sculptor Jan Švankmajer, the Italian sculptor Giacomo Manzù, the Spanish painters Antonio López García and Cristóbal Toral, the French sculptors Louis Pons and Jacques Clavé, and the Swiss artist of "poetic machines," Paul Gugelmann. Then there are the Germans: Adolph Menzel, Otto Dix, Hannah Höch, and especially Käthe Kollwitz. I try to spread the word about these people rather than speaking negatively about the enormous mass of well-funded contemporary art that doesn't help.

"It seems to me that the biggest obstacle to the artist of conscience today is not, perhaps, the art world," said painter Rob Shetterly[12]:

> It's the mainstream media. When the corporate media chooses to ignore serious political art, it marginalizes it. Millions of people who might see, read, hear that art, don't. Their questions, ideas, feelings are not then validated by witnessing them portrayed accurately in art. Art tells many people it's OK to think and feel unpopular things. Without that assurance, people are often isolated with their own perception of reality and will retreat to official conformity and the comfort of patriotism, even when it betrays the ideals it is meant to support.

"I often think of the music of the 1960s—Phil Ochs, Dylan, Joan Baez, Odetta, Peter, Paul & Mary, etc," Shetterly said:

> That music about civil rights and the illegitimacy of the Vietnam War was everywhere. The corporate media had not yet learned that simply by not playing that music they could severely limit the spread of ideas. Millions of young people were radicalized to act for political causes, not by reading essays and taking courses, but by the spurring of art. Art told them their consciences were right. They could trust Bob Dylan and not LBJ or Nixon. Try to imagine the civil-rights or the antiwar movements without the music.

"This lesson was not lost on the corporate media after the '60s," Shetterly said:

> If their intent was to build a consensus good for profit, and that profit derived from war, exploitation, and imperialism, all they had to do was *not* report on or play art that carried a message of peace and resistance. It's not censorship. The artists are free to speak and produce. But not many people will know about it. And, because the corporate media, our sanctified free press, is now clearly part of the mechanism of propaganda for the military-industrial-congressional complex, artists have to attack the press as much as the war profiteers and elected liars, and thus have even less likelihood of being reported on. The media hates to have its biases exposed.

Shetterly's portrait series of radical Americans, from Sojourner Truth to Cindy Sheehan, called *Americans Who Tell the Truth*, have been held at arm's length by the media.

"I call lies lies, not differences of opinions," Shetterly said. "I call war crimes crimes, not mistakes. I call complicity of the media in lies and crimes just that. I point out that there has been, and is, frequently a profound antagonism between democracy and capitalism.

"Part of the bias against art of conscience in the art world comes from a serious belief that art has something to do with affirming our deepest humanity, our sense of beauty, our spiritual connections, our finest aspirations," Shetterly said:

Political art may call us to argue, be divisive, when we should be meditating. Shouldn't art be a refuge, a place for persistent reflection on the finer things? It is my belief that art should be, and can be, many things. If it is about beauty, it must also be about truth, even when that truth is ugly and anathema to the beautiful and powerful. A beautiful still life is never, in a certain sense, irrelevant. But if the survival of human life is in jeopardy, maybe it's important that some artists explore why with all of the urgency and truth that they can bring to bear.

"It's curious that we live at a time when 'art' is often described as literally anything the artist or the critic says it is," Shetterly said. "The media accepts this definition . . . except when the art's political."

"When we think about societies and civilizations of the past, what do we know about them?" Carol Becker asked.

We know them through their art, which is what endures and communicates the given psyche of the people at that time. When we look at art, we realize that the ideas we've taken from it define Western civilization, yet we devalue the place of the artist. We don't see what they do as legitimate, or even hard work. Take the art work of South African artist William Kentridge. He lived and created works during the apartheid years. He had this ability to shift and pivot the world at a time when no one wanted to confront or question power. So often artists are the ones who go into difficult situations. Doctors and others go into difficult situations in communities, too, but they don't make representations of those situations that transform how people see the world. All I'm saying is that I want artists to feel they could take leadership in the world, not that their work will simply be relegated to what we call "the art world."[13]

~~

"To train someone to operate a lathe or to read and write is pretty much education of skill," C. Wright Mills wrote in *The Power Elite*:

To evoke from people an understanding of what they really want out of their lives or to debate with them stoic, Christian, and humanist ways of living, is pretty much a clear-cut education of values. But to assist in the birth among a group of people of those cultural and political and technical sensibilities which would make them genuine members of a genuinely liberal public, this is at once a training in skills and an education of values. It includes a sort of therapy in the ancient sense of clarifying one's knowledge of one's self; it includes the imparting of all those skills of controversy with one's self, which we call thinking; and with others, which we call debate. And the end product of such liberal education of sensibilities is simply the self-educating, self-cultivating man or woman.

It is the ability, denied to the specialist, to turn personal troubles into social issues, as Mills wrote, to "see their relevance for his community and his community's relevance for them" that should be the culmination of artistic and intellectual vision. Many trapped in mass culture are "gripped by personal troubles, but they are not aware of their true meaning and source." And it is the task of the artist or the intellectual to "translate troubles into issues and issues into terms of their human meaning for the individual." The failure to make knowledge and artistic expression relevant to human reality—the goal of the Bauhaus movement in Weimar Germany—has left the public unable to "see the roots of his own biases and frustrations, nor think clearly about himself, nor for that matter about anything else."[14]

In his book *White Collar*, which includes a scathing chapter titled "Brains, Inc.," Mills argued that "men of brilliance, energy, and imagination" were no longer valued within universities. Colleges did not "facilitate, much less create, independence of mind." The professor had become part of "a petty hierarchy, almost completely closed in by its middle-class environment and its segregation of intellectual from social life . . . mediocrity makes its own rules and sets its own image of success." But the intellectuals outside the academy in the commercial sphere were no better. They had abandoned politics for administration and personal success. "The loss of will and even of ideas among intellectuals," he wrote, is due not simply to "political defeat and internal decay of radical parties." The liberal class who accepted its appointed slots in educational, state, institutional, and media bureaucracies had, Mills noted, sold their souls.[15]

The New Left of the 1960s turned out to be a mirage. The rupture within American politics was so severe that when the New Left arose, it had no roots. It existed in a historical vacuum. The counterculture of the 1960s, although it attracted a wide following at the height of the Vietnam War, never replicated the power of the Popular Front of 1930s, which had included the working class and mixed social, labor, and political movements. The New Left that rose in the 1960s, was, as the historian Ellen Schrecker writes, "a fractured, deracinated movement that could never reconstruct the ideological and cultural unity of its predecessors or overcome its own divisions. Even today, what passes for the left, the identity politics that all too often segregates rather than unifies its adherents, lacks the sense of interconnectedness that disappeared with the lost world of American Communism."[16] Protests, rather than disrupt manufacturing or the systems run by the power elite, usually became, as happened in the protests during the Chicago Democratic Convention in 1968, a media spectacle. The left and the right played their roles before the cameras. Politics had become theater.

The militancy of previous generations had been erased from collective consciousness. The counterculture, like the Beats before them, busied itself with disengagement rather than transformation. The appearance of decent and honorable political figures such as George McGovern and Eugene McCarthy may have offered a moment of hope, but the traditional Democratic establishment not only colluded with Richard Nixon to crush McGovern in the 1972 presidential election, but also swiftly rewrote party nominating rules so a McCarthy or a McGovern would never again be able to get the nomination. By now the domesticated liberal class, represented in the political arena by the Democratic Party, needed no prompting to defend the interests of the power elite. It was a full member of the club.

By the 1980s, the political sterility of the New Left found its academic expression in the embrace of French poststructuralist literary and cultural theory. The charade of protest was matched in the university by the charade of radical analysis. French theorists such as Jacques Derrida, Jacques Lacan, and Roland Barthes were adopted by American academics, who jettisoned the political projects that had influenced the work of the French academics, retreating instead into what they termed the science of language and meaning. They deciphered texts. They shifted Marxist analysis away from economic departments, most of which had been taken over by free-market ideologues anyway, to disciplines within the humanities, where Marxist critique would not threaten systems of power.

Marxists now became culture and literary critics. These theorists invested their energy in multiculturalism, with branches such as feminist studies, queer studies, and African American studies. The inclusion of voices often left out of the traditional academic canon certainly enriched the university. But multiculturalism, rather than leading to a critique of structures and systems that consciously excluded and impoverished the poor and the marginal, became an end in itself.

"Stripped of a radical idiom, robbed of a utopian hope, liberals and leftists retreat in the name of progress to celebrate diversity," Russell Jacoby writes. "With few ideas on how a future should be shaped, they embrace all ideas. Pluralism becomes a catchall, the alpha and omega of political thinking. Dressed up as multiculturalism, it has become the opium of disillusioned intellectuals, the ideology of an era without an ideology."

Political debate was replaced by multicultural discourse. Public values were subordinated to torturous textual analysis. There was nothing worth investigating, these poststructuralists insisted, outside of the text. This new group of "radical" theorists, including Gayatri Spivak, a postcolonial theorist; Paul Bové, the editor of the journal *boundary 2* and an English professor at The University of Pittsburgh; J. Hillis Miller, then of Yale; Gregory Ulmer of the University of Florida; and Marxist cultural historian Frederic Jameson, typified the trend. They wrap ideas in a language so obscure, so abstract, so preoccupied with arcane theory that the uninitiated cannot understand what they write. They make no attempt to reach a wider audience or enrich public life. Compared to the last generation of genuine, independent public intellectuals—Jane Jacobs, Paul and Percival Goodman, William H. Whyte, Lewis Mumford, C. Wright Mills, and Dwight Macdonald—they have produced nothing of substance or worth. Their work has no vision, other than perhaps calling for more diverse voices in the academy. It is technical, convoluted, self-referential, and filled with so much academic jargon that it is unreadable. This is a sample of what poststructuralists, in this case Jameson, believe passes for lucid thought:

In periodizing a phenomenon of this kind, we have to complicate the model with all kinds of supplementary epicycles. It is necessary to distinguish between the gradual setting in place of the various (often unrelated) preconditions for the new structure and the "moment" (not exactly chronological) when they all jell and combine into a functional system. This moment is itself less a matter of chronology than it is of a well-nigh Freudian *Nachträglichkeit*, or retroactivity: people become aware of the dynamics of some new system, in which they are themselves seized, only later on and gradually.[17]

While it seems on the surface to be a movement for social change, the campaign for cultural diversity, does little to perturb the power elite. It does not challenge economic or political structures that are rapidly disempowering the working class. Making sure people of diverse races or sexual orientations appear on television shows or in advertisements merely widens the circle of new consumers. Multiculturalism is an appeal that pleads with the corporate power structure for inclusion. The appeal was achieved politically with the election of Barack Obama. It has seen the establishment of multicultural departments in many universities. But it is a call, as Jacoby points out, for "patronage, not revolution"[18]:

> The radical multiculturalists, postcolonialists and other cutting-edge theorists gush about marginality with the implicit, and sometimes explicit, goal of joining the mainstream. They specialize in marginalization to up their market value. Again, this is understandable; the poor and the excluded want to be wealthy and included, but why is this multicultural or subversive?[19]

These radical theorists have internalized the rule that governs academia: write and teach what you want, but if you take a public stand that defies conventional mores and established structures, you risk your career. As long as academics write in the tortured vocabulary of specialization for seminars and conferences, where they are unable to influence public debate, they are free to espouse any bizarre or "radical" theory. The new Marxist academics, determined to adhere to a "scientific" analysis, have as much time for moral imperatives as the professors in the business schools with whom they share a faculty dining room. Universities hire by committee. It is not scholarship or ideas but collegiality and conformity committees prize most. And those who do receive tenure, after an average of seven years, long enough to integrate into the dominant culture, are rewarded for being conformists, not iconoclasts. "The trouble is that professors get their tenure by suppressing the expression of unpopular expression, not in order to express unpopular opinion," Jacoby writes. "The modern university, by its conservative inertia, has become the most hostile place for pursuing truth. And tenure, once deemed precious, has become the most wasted, irrelevant principle."[20]

Tenured academics are going the way of unionized steel workers. There are fewer and fewer tenure-track jobs—only about thirty-five percent of current academic positions offer tenure—and this percentage is declining. The scramble by desperate academics to placate the demands of college administrators and the university presses that will publish their work so they can get tenure, has only grown as the number of secure jobs diminishes. The majority of academics are itinerants who may teach in a series of schools over a career, or at two or three schools at a time, with no job security. Adjuncts are usually hired on contracts of a year or less. They are considered part-time employees and are ineligible for benefits. Many earn as little as $1,000 a course. The lack of job security further inhibits any propensity to write or speak about topics that have political or social relevance. It is better for one's career to stay away from politics and wallow in the arcane world of departmental intrigue and academic gibberish.

The media, like the university, are required to stay aloof from the issues of the day. The media, too, must assume the role of disinterested and impartial observers. This was, for those of us reporting on the wars in Central America, the Middle East, and the Balkans, an impossibility. It is difficult to witness human suffering and not feel. But to express these emotions in the newsroom, to express outrage at the atrocities committed by Salvadoran death squads, the killings by Bosnian Serbs, or especially the brutality of Israeli soldiers in Gaza, was to risk being reassigned or pushed aside by editors who demanded emotional disengagement. Those who feel in newsrooms are viewed as lacking impartiality and objectivity. They cannot be trusted. And the game I and others played was to mask our emotions and pretend that, no matter how horrible the crime, we were only clinical observers.

I spent seven years in the Middle East, five of them with the *New York Times* and four as the Middle East Bureau Chief for the paper. I spent months in Iraq during the dictatorship of Saddam Hussein, entered occupied Kuwait in the first Gulf War with the U.S. Marines, and then covered the long aftermath, when U.N. inspectors destroyed far more military equipment and stockpiles of weapons than were destroyed in the war itself. Those of us in Iraq after the first Gulf War understood that while Hussein was certainly a tyrant, he was not a threat to us or to Iraq's neighbors. The ruthless, secular Iraqi regime brutally disposed of Islamic militants and detested al-Qaida. It was a country so torn by ethnic antagonisms that any notion of creating a unified functioning democracy following an invasion and occupation was laughable. It was clear to all Arabists, including those in the State Department, the intelligence community, and the Pentagon, that we would not be greeted as liberators if we invaded, that the oil revenues would never pay for the reconstruction, and that democracy was not going to be implanted in Baghdad and radiate outward across the Middle East.

But to repeat these simple truths, which I did repeatedly in public forums before the war began, inflicted career wounds that saw me expelled from the *New York Times,* one of the liberal class's most revered institutions. My public stance against the war, repeated on national programs from *Charlie Rose* to NPR's *Fresh Air with Terry Gross*, angered the editors who argued that, as a news reporter, I had a duty to remain neutral.

The final confrontation with the *Times* was sparked by events in Rockford, Illinois, at Rockford College, where I had been invited to give the 2003 commencement address. I stood before about one thousand guests in May and spoke about the war. George W. Bush, decked out in a flight suit, had landed on the aircraft carrier USS *Lincoln* a couple of weeks before and spoken under a banner that read "Mission Accomplished."

The address, built around my book *War Is a Force That Gives Us Meaning*, was a harsh critique of empire and war. I walked to the podium at the end of the line of faculty. I wore a black academic gown and a borrowed hood with enough crimson in it to approximate my Harvard Divinity School colors. It was a windy day. I clutched the papers of my talk. The students, in the front, and the audience behind them sat in neat rows of folding chairs. There were black speakers mounted on poles to broadcast the talk.

"I want to speak to you today about war and empire," I began.

The killing, or at least the worst of it, is over in Iraq. Although blood will continue to spill—theirs and ours—be prepared for this. For we are embarking on an occupation that, if history is any guide, will be as damaging to our souls as it will be to our prestige, power, and security. But this will come later as our empire expands. And in all this we become pariahs, tyrants to others weaker than ourselves. Isolation always impairs judgment, and we are very isolated now.

We have forfeited the goodwill, the empathy the world felt for us after 9/11. We have folded in on ourselves, we have severely weakened the delicate international coalitions and alliances that are vital in maintaining and promoting peace. And we are part now of a dubious troika in the war against terror with Vladimir Putin and Ariel Sharon, two leaders who do not shrink in Palestine or Chechnya from carrying out acts of gratuitous and senseless acts of violence. We have become the company we keep.

The censure, and perhaps the rage, of much of the world—certainly one-fifth of the world's population which is Muslim, most of whom, I will remind you, are not Arab, is upon us. Look today at the fourteen people killed last night in several explosions in Casablanca. And this rage, in a world where almost fifty percent of the planet struggles on less than two dollars a day, will see us targeted. Terrorism will become a way of life.

At this point the crowd, restless and uneasy, began to mutter protests. There was a shout of "No!"

And when we are attacked, we will, like our allies Putin and Sharon, lash out with greater fury. The circle of violence is a death spiral; no one escapes. We are spinning at a speed that we may not be able to halt. As we revel in our military prowess—the sophistication of our military hardware and technology, for this is what most of the press coverage consisted of in Iraq—we lose sight of the fact that just because we have the capacity to wage war it does not give us the right to wage war. This capacity has doomed empires in the past.

"Modern western civilization may perish," the theologian Reinhold Niebuhr warned, "because it falsely worshipped technology as a final good."

The real injustices—the Israeli occupation of Palestinian land, the brutal and corrupt dictatorships we fund in the Middle East—will mean that we will not rid the extremists who hate us with bombs. Indeed, we will swell their ranks.

There was now a chorus of whistles and hoots.

"Once you master a people by force," I said, "you depend on force for control. In your isolation you begin to make mistakes."

"Where were you on September 11?" a man yelled.

"Fear engenders cruelty," I said. "Cruelty . . . fear, insanity, and then paralysis."

There were more hoots and jeers.

"Who wants to listen to this jerk?" someone cried out.

"In the center of Dante's circle," I said, "the damned remained motionless."

Horn blasts were unleashed.

"We have blundered into a nation we know little about and are caught between bitter rivalries and competing ethnic groups and leaders we do not understand," I continued:

We are trying to transplant a modern system of politics invented in Europe characterized, among other things, by the division of Earth into independent secular states based on national citizenship, in a land where the belief in a secular civil government is an alien creed. Iraq was a cesspool for the British when they occupied it in 1917. It will be a cesspool for us, as well.

"God bless America!" a woman cried.

I continued: "The curfews, the armed clashes with angry crowds that leave scores of Iraqi dead, the military governor, the Christian Evangelical groups who are being allowed to follow on the heels of our occupying troops to try and teach Muslims about Jesus, the occupation of the oilfields."

The microphone went dead. I stood looking out at the angry crowd, the wind whipping down the hillside. There were some people standing in the front. One woman was weeping. The crowd grew more agitated and several people rose to sing "God Bless America."

"Who wants to listen to this jerk?" a woman shouted.

I had to cut short my address and was removed by security before the awarding of the diplomas. The event dominated the broadcasts of the trash-talk right-wing commentators, from Rush Limbaugh to Fox News analysts. Clips of me being heckled and jeered, taken from home videos, were played repeatedly on the cable shows. The *Wall Street Journal* published an editorial denouncing me as an elitist and a pacifist and condemned my talk. The local paper, the *Rockford Register Star*, reported my address with the headline "SPEAKER DISRUPTS RC GRADUATION."

War, and especially war in the Middle East, were not abstractions to me. I spoke out of a reality few Americans understood. But my editors at the *New York Times* were furious. I had crossed the line once too often. I had dared to feel, to make a judgment, and to think independently. I was called into the *Times* offices at 229 West 43rd Street by an assistant managing editor, Bill Schmidt, and given a written reprimand for "public remarks that could undermine public trust in the paper's impartiality." The procedure meant that, under the rules established with the Newspaper Guild of New York, the next time I spoke out against the war I could be fired.

If I had repeated the mythic narrative of America—the narrative embraced by the power elite and the liberal institutions that serve them—the talk would not have attracted notice. If I had told the graduates that America was a great and noble country, that we were spreading democracy and virtue throughout the world, that globalism was empowering and enriching the world's poor, and that American soldiers were sacrificing their lives for our freedom and security, none of it would have been deemed controversial or political. The public statements of support for the invasion of Iraq by fellow reporter John Burns did not see him ousted from the paper. The approved mythic narrative is "neutral" and "apolitical" because it serves the empowered classes. Those who honor these myths remain valued members of the liberal class. Those who do not are banished.

The media are as plagued by the same mediocrity, corporatism, and careerism as the academy, the unions, the arts, the Democratic Party, and religious institutions. The media, like the academy, hold up the false ideals of impartiality and objectivity to mask their complicity with power. They posit the absurd idea that knowledge and understanding are attainable exclusively through vision, that we should all be mere spectators of life. This pernicious reduction of the public to the role of spectators denies the media, and the public they serve, a political role. As John Dewey has pointed out, public opinion is not formed when individuals possess correct representations of the government, even if such representations were possible. It is formed through discourse and discussion. But the reduction of the media and the public to the role of passive spectators cuts off the possibility of a conversation.[21]

Truth and news are not the same, as James W. Carey wrote. News is a signal that something is happening. It provides, in Carey's words, "degenerate photographs or a pseudo-reality of stereotypes. News can approximate truth only when reality is reducible to a statistical table: sports scores, stock exchange reports, births, deaths, marriages, accidents, court decisions, elections, economic transactions such as foreign trade and balance of payments."[22]

"The divorce of truth from discourse and action—the instrumentalization of communication—has not merely increased the incidence of propaganda," Carey wrote. It has also "disrupted the very notion of truth, and therefore the sense by which we take our bearings in the world is destroyed."[23]

Journalists, however, unlike academics, have to intersect with the public. They write and speak to be understood. And for this reason they are more powerful and more closely monitored and controlled than other writers and speakers. The commercial media, as C. Wright Mills pointed out, are essential tools for conformity. They impart to the public a sense of self. Media tell members of the public who they are. They tell them what their aspirations should be. They promise to help them achieve these aspirations. They offer a variety of techniques, advice, and schemes that promise eventual success.

The commercial media, as Wright notes, also help citizens feel as if they are successful and have met these aspirations, even if they have not. They tend to neglect reality (they don't run stories about how life is hard, fame and fortune elusive, hopes disappointed) and instead celebrate idealized identities—those that, in a commodity culture, revolve around the acquisition of status, money, fame, and power, or at least the illusion of these things. The media, in other words, assist the commercial culture in "need creation," prompting consumers to want things they don't need or have never really considered wanting. And catering to these needs, largely implanted by advertisers and the corporate culture, is a very profitable business. A major part of the commercial media revolves around selling consumers images and techniques to "actualize" themselves, or offering seductive forms of escape through entertainment and spectacle. News is filtered into the mix, but actual news is not the predominant concern of the commercial media.

Pick up any daily newspaper. At most, fifteen percent of the content in its pages is devoted to news. The rest is devoted to ways to feel or become a success. "This," Mills wrote, "is probably the basic psychological formula of the mass media today. But, as a formula, it is not attuned to the development of the human being. It is a formula of a pseudo-world which the media invent and sustain." [24]

Those who work inside commercial media outlets are acutely aware of the manipulation, even as the media publicly laud themselves for courage, honesty, and independence. This does not mean there is never any good journalism, just as the corruption within the academy does not preclude good scholarship. It means that myriad internal pressures, hidden from public view but faced every day by workers in the media world, make the production of good journalism and good scholarship very difficult. Reporters who persist in raising inconvenient questions, like academics who practice moral and independent scholarship, do not usually advance within liberal institutions.

"I'd written an article about Colgate-Palmolive having gone through a process to rebrand a type of toothpaste that they had bought in Asia that was named Darkie," remembered former *New York Times* reporter Doug McGill, who spent a decade at the paper:

Proctor & Gamble had bought this company, Hazel and Holly, which made the Darkie toothpaste. It was the best-selling toothpaste in Asia. The problem was that the brand mascot was a blackfaced minstrel. It was plastered over the toothpaste boxes. They obviously could not sell this in America, so they tried to find a name and an image that did not completely replace Darkie. It was too valuable as a brand, a name, and an image, but of course they wanted to erase the racist overtones. They eventually came up with Darlie. Instead of a minstrel in blackface, they used a silhouette of a Victorian dandy that looked a lot like the original Darkie. The story ran on the front page of the business section. The morning that the piece appeared in the paper, I got a telephone call. I was sitting at my desk in the business section. It was the head P.R. guy for Proctor & Gamble. I noticed the phone connection was scratchy. I asked him where he was calling from. He said, "I'm in a limousine. I'm going to the airport with Mr. Mark," meaning Ruben Mark, who was the CEO of the company. "I just want to let you know we really liked the article that you published. We like working with you as a journalist. As long as you keep writing stories like that, we would be very happy to work with you. Mr. Mark was wondering if you might be open for lunch some time." Then he proceeded to give me Ruben Mark's home telephone number. I said, "OK, well, thanks a lot, talk to you later," and I hung up the phone.[25]

"This was one of the first stories I had written for the business section," McGill remembered. "I had never heard anything quite so direct, the quid pro quo laid out so baldly: 'If you keep writing good stories, you will keep getting access to the CEO plus perks like lunches and home telephone numbers for future stories.' This is a signal example of what underpins a lot of big-time mainstream journalism.

"I wrote a story in 1983, while working as a reporter for the *New York Times,* about a proposed telephone rate hike in New York State," McGill went on:

The story had great interest in the New York area because it meant a rise in rates for New York customers. I was a metro reporter. I didn't know anything about rate hikes or telephone companies. I was smart enough to ask questions and write down answers. I had a street sense of accuracy and fairness, enough to get a story written. I got the information from the telephone company. I knew enough to call the people who were against the rate hike who were the consumer advocates. I got what they thought about the rate hike. Then I called the phone company to get their response to the critics of the rate hike. It was formulaic. It was the standard he-said-she-said formula. The *Times* published it on the front page of the paper. That night I was walking with the news editor to Grand Central Station. The editor asked jokingly: "Did you really understand the story you wrote today?" "Not a word of it," I said. And we both had a big laugh.

But inside, I didn't feel so good. It was a kind of arrogance. I was painting by numbers. I had written the story by calling up legislators who were sponsoring the proposal, and then calling up citizens' groups who were raising hell about it, and then getting back to the legislators for their reaction. I then stitched all the quotes together under a grand-sounding theme, and voilà! I'd been dutifully "objective" and gathered both sides of the story and made a "fair and balanced" front-page story for the *New York Times*. The point is, if anything unfair or truly nefarious was being done by the legislators, lobbyists, or citizens' groups in the process of getting this rate hike passed, I would have been blithely unaware of it. The principal actors in this story could have driven a bribe or a lie or a loophole or a simple unfairness right under my nose, and I wouldn't have suspected a thing. The he-said-she-said formula was all I needed to get on page one.

"During my last few years at the *Times*, I joked with my wife that my work there was all about making the world safe for millionaires," McGill told me. "There was no moral problem during the years when I was learning how to be a reporter, how to write a story, how to get published, etc. But when I finally saw what the *Times* as a corporate and political structure stands for, and the privileged constituencies that it serves, I had to ask whether I wanted my life and skills put in service of those particular people and values – and I did not.

"I was unconscious to the very powerful interests I was serving," he said:

I had never bellied up to the challenges to whether I wanted to serve power in this way. There were points during my ten years at the *Times* when I was writing about government. Power can be construed directly in those articles, but primarily I was a culture reporter for a long time, a metro reporter and then a business reporter. I was basically always a pawn in the big game. I had never thought through whether I was using the skills I had amassed for the best possible moral outcome. I knew people at the *Times* who literally got sick every time they walked through those revolving doors. I got that way. And I didn't know what was hitting me. I felt physically ill. It was my conscience. It was strong enough that I knew I needed to escape. When you work at the *New York Times*, it is like working at the White House. Nobody should have that power permanently. They should have it for a while and drop it. It is not the real world in there. I was getting too used to having mayors and governors and CEOs call me up, as if I were a friend, and pay for my dinners and give me their press releases and have me describe them in glowing terms. And this happened over and over. I wrote critical pieces. The former chairman of Christie's [auction house] lost his job because of me. The former head of the New York City Historical Society lost his job because of me and my reporting of how he squandered the endowment and let priceless treasures at the museum get rained on and destroyed. I did my bit. I did the investigative part. But overall, the *New York Times* is an entrenched source of power and does not serve those who are the neediest in society well or at all. When you have that amount of power, you need to spend a lot more time thinking about people who really need help.

And yet McGill, for all his problems with the paper, was quick to add that "the world without the *New York Times* would be a poorer place." He said that when the paper covered the U.S. government, New York City, or Washington, the moral problems he increasingly encountered as a reporter reached their apex: "That is when the conflicts of interest are the strongest." He said that the need for access to the powerful rammed news through "a weird distorting force field, to the point where it is difficult for readers to know where the story is coming from."

But despite these impediments, McGill fears, as do I, the loss of papers and liberal institutions as "a counterweight to government and corporate power." Newspapers, he said, were powerful enough to stand up to lawsuits and harassments and threats:

> No amount of blogging and Web sites, even when added up together, will equal that kind of counterweight. That is being lost. Journalism was born and reared in newspapers. Not in TV. Not in radio. There is so much institutional memory and practice and good that came up in newspapers that it will be a tragedy if it is lost, and it is being lost.

"The further you get from these distorting power sources, like New York City or Washington, and can write national or foreign stories, you can get indispensable reporting done by the same reporters who, in other realms, work in these distorting force fields," he said:

> There are two kinds of objectivities. There is one in quotes and one outside of quotes. The one in quotes is the corrupted objectivity of mainstream journalism. It is an ideology. It does not have an underlying rigor. It means a lot of things, with many of those things being contradictory. It can mean neutral, fair, balanced, and impartial. But you can have a story that is factual *and* unfair. You can have a story that is impartial but not factual. It is a bunch of practices adopted over time and lumped under this big word. When you look at the ideology, you see that unfortunately it is often serving laziness, rationalization, and, above all, the commercial purpose of the newspaper, and not the discovery and presentation of the truth. The objectivity outside of quotes is a method of inquiry that assures that the researcher gets as close as possible to the truth. It is patterned after scientific objectivity. It has its rules and its discipline. It requires verification through corroboration or through direct observation or any number of means. These are guidelines a reporter follows to get at the truth. And yet, it requires the utmost humility towards the idea of truth. The truth claim is the very last thing you arrive at, and only after intense methodological rigor and soul searching. Whatever you present is not going to be "objective," whatever that means. It will be

your best effort, but it will not be the truth, and it will be as slipshod and methodically easy as the he-said-she-said formula. There are two types of objectivity, and, like cholesterol, we want more of the good kind and less of the bad. Maybe there never was enough of the good objectivity to say that it is being lost with newspapers, but there are an awful lot of great reporters who are being lost. These great investigative journalists and reporters covering government, even if they were fighting with their newspapers, against the things we talked about, they worked to get the truth into the paper. And the best ones are being cut because the expensive forms of journalism are being cut. We are losing this culturally.

John Steinbeck, after visiting squatter camps filled with impoverished migrant workers in the San Joaquin Valley in California, filed a story for the *San Francisco News*. The poverty and filth in the camps appalled him. He found the people crushed, without hope, and on the brink of starvation. He wrote in his story about one family he had seen. The mother and father had built a hut by driving willow branches into the ground and wattling weeds. They had flattened tin cans and paper against them. The parents and three children, including a three-year-old with a distended belly caused by malnutrition, slept together on an old piece of carpet inside the crude hut. The youngest child had a gunnysack tied around his waist for clothing, had not had milk for two years, and was slow in his reactions. In the *News*, Steinbeck wrote:

> He will die in a very short time. The older children may survive. Four nights ago the mother had a baby in the tent, on the dirty carpet. It was born dead, which was just as well because she should not have fed it at the breast; her own diet will not produce milk.
>
> After it was born and she had seen that it was dead, the mother rolled over and lay still for two days. She is up today, tottering around. The last baby, born less than a year ago, lived a week. This woman's eyes have the glazed, faraway look of a sleepwalker's eyes.
>
> She does not wash clothes any more. The drive that makes for cleanliness has been drained out of her and she hasn't the energy. The husband was a share-cropper once, but he couldn't make it go. Now he has lost even the desire to talk.

He will not look directly at you, for that requires will, and will needs strength. He is a bad field worker for the same reason. It takes him a long time to make up his mind, so he is always late in moving and late in arriving in the fields. His top wage, when he can find work now, which isn't often, is a dollar a day.

The children do not even go to the willow clump any more. They squat where they are and kick a little dirt. The father is vaguely aware that there is a culture of hookworm in the mud along the river bank. He knows the children will get it on their bare feet.

But he hasn't the will nor the energy to resist. Too many things have happened to him.[26]

Steinbeck's *The Grapes of Wrath* was born at this moment out of profound human pain, injustice, and Steinbeck's capacity for empathy. It was an act of journalism, the best kind of journalism. His reporting flowed seamlessly into fiction, as it did with other great reporters, from Charles Dickens to George Orwell. In *Grapes of Wrath*, Steinbeck brought to life the Joad family's journey west from the Dust Bowl of the Great Plains. The Joads were not, in the sense of journalism, based on a single real family. They were a composite. But the ability to marry factual details with empathy and art effectively transmitted a reality, an experience, that has become part of our collective memory. Steinbeck's novel was the chronicle of the struggle of people to endure, made understandable by a mixture of allegory and fact. It took reality, as the Federal Theatre Project did, and transformed it into art. It challenged old myths and stereotypes—those who fled the Dust Bowl were scorned by many Americans—by appealing to human emotions.

⌒

Liberal institutions were created to make the world a better place. They were designed to give a voice to those who are shunted aside, abused, and ignored by the larger society. Throughout their history, they have promised to protect the common good, educate, and fight injustice. These institutions, when they function, keep alive qualities that defy the raw greed of unchecked capitalism. I am a product of these liberal institutions, in particular the church, the university—where I spent eight years, as an undergraduate and graduate student—and the media. I was, while a working journalist, a member of a labor union. The sermons preached from my father's pulpit, the study of literature, history, theology, the classics, and moral philosophy in college and graduate school, gave me a language to make sense of the world and define my place in it. It was journalism that permitted me to roam the world for two decades, every new foreign assignment the equivalent of another undergraduate degree. The languages I speak, the cultural literacy I possess, the grasp I have of political and economic systems, would not have been possible without these liberal institutions. I defied them in the end, but I am also deeply indebted to them. My anger is not directed against these institutions so much as those within them that failed when we needed their voices. These liberal principles were egregiously betrayed to protect careers, to preserve access to the powerful. Liberals conceded too much to the power elite. The tragedy of the liberal class and the institutions it controls is that it succumbed to opportunism and finally to fear. It abrogated its moral role. It did not defy corporate abuse when it had the chance. It exiled those within its ranks who did. And the defanging of the liberal class not only removed all barriers to neofeudalism and corporate abuse but also ensured that the liberal class will, in its turn, be swept aside.

The disease of the liberal class is the specious, supposedly "professional" insistence on objectivity. Before the rise of commercial newspapers, journals of opinion existed to influence public sentiment via arguments—not to stultify readers with lists of facts. Our oldest universities were formed to train ministers and inculcate into students the primacy of the common good. Labor unions had a vision of an egalitarian society that understood the inevitability of class struggle. Artists from Mark Twain to John Steinbeck sought not only to explain social, political, economic, and cultural reality, but also to use this understanding to fight for a social order based on justice. Movements that defied the power elite often started and sustained these liberal institutions, which were created as instruments of reform. One by one, these institutions succumbed to the temptation of money, the jargon of patriotism, belief in the need for permanent war, fear of internal and external enemies, and distrust of radicals, who had once kept the liberal class honest. And when it was over, the liberal class had nothing left to say.

In 1834 the *New York Sun* reported on a woman whose husband came home drunk and abusive once too often. It wrote of the event in a manner that would be impossible in today's cold, stripped-down reliance on fact: "As every sensible woman ought to do who is cursed with a drunken husband, she refused to have anything to do with him hereafter—and he was sent to the penitentiary." For comparison, here is the final sentence of a 1995 item from the *Ann Arbor News*, about a man who assaulted a prostitute after she refused to have sex with him: "Employees at the Ramada Inn Ann Arbor, 3750 Washtenaw Avenue, said the man and woman checked in around 2 a.m. Friday."[27]

The creed of "impartiality" and "objectivity" that has infected the liberal class teaches, ultimately, the importance of not offending the status quo. The "professionalism" demanded in the classroom, in newsprint, in the arts or in political discourse is code for moral disengagement. The righteous thunder of the abolitionist and civil-rights preachers, the investigative journalists who enraged Standard Oil and the owners of the Chicago stockyards, the theater productions such as *The Cradle Will Rock* that imploded the myths peddled by the ruling class and gave a voice to ordinary people, the unions that permitted African Americans, immigrants, and working men and women to find dignity and hope, the great public universities such as City College of New York that offered the children of immigrants a chance for a first-class education, the New Deal Democrats who understood that a democracy is not safe if it does not give its citizens an acceptable standard of living and protect the state from being hijacked by private power, are gone. The remnants of the liberal class, and the hollow institutions they inhabit, flee from those who speak in the strange and unfamiliar tongue of liberty and justice.

V / Liberal Defectors

But the secret of intellectual excellence is the spirit of criticism; it is intellectual independence. And this leads to difficulties which must prove insurmountable for any kind of authoritarianism. The authoritarian will in general select those who obey, who believe, who respond to his influence. But in doing so, he is bound to select mediocrities. For he excludes those who revolt, who doubt, who dare to resist his influence. Never can an authority admit that the intellectually courageous, i.e. those who dare to defy his authority, may be the most valuable type. Of course, the authorities will always remain convinced of their ability to detect initiative. But what they mean by this is only a quick grasp of their intentions, and they will remain for ever incapable of seeing the difference.

—KARL POPPER, *The Open Society and Its Enemies*[1]

THE LIBERAL class's disposal of its most independent and courageous members has long been part of its pathology. The liberal class could afford this rate of attrition as long as the power elite remained accountable to the citizenry, managed power with a degree of responsibility and justice, governed so that it could still respond to the common good, and accepted some of the piecemeal reforms proposed by the liberal class. But as the state was slowly hijacked by corporations, a process that began after World War I, accelerated after World War II and was completed with ruthless efficiency over the past thirty years, the liberal class purged itself of the only members who had the fortitude and vision to save it from irrelevance.

The final phase of total corporate control, which began with Ronald Reagan, saw the steady assimilation of corporate ideology into liberal thought. It meant that the liberal class was forced to discard the principle tenets of liberalism. The liberal class, its institutions controlled by corporations, was soon mouthing the corporate mantra that economics and the marketplace, rather than human beings, should guide political and economic behavior. Free-market capitalism, a distinctly illiberal belief system, soon defined liberal thought.

By the time the touted benefits of globalization—the belief that workers around the world would become wealthier, that the market would lift the developing world out of poverty, that tearing down trade barriers would benefit citizens from both the developed and developing worlds, that peace and prosperity would inevitably result from interconnected global economies—were exposed as a sham, it was too late. The liberal class had driven critics of this utopian fiction from their midst. The liberal class was complicit in the rise of a new global oligarchy and the crushing poverty visited in globalization's wake on the poor and the working class. It abetted the decline of the middle class—the very basis of democracy. It has permitted, in the name of progress, the dismantling of the manufacturing sector, leaving huge pockets of postindustrial despair and poverty behind.

But it would be a mistake to assume that the liberal class was simply seduced by the utopian promises of globalism. It was also seduced by careerism. Those who mouthed the right words, who did not challenge the structures being cemented into place by the corporate state, who assured the working class that the suffering was temporary and would be rectified in the new world order, were rewarded. They were given public platforms on television and in the political arena. They were held up to the wider society as experts, sages, and specialists. They became the class of wise men and women who were permitted to explain in public forums what was happening to us at home and abroad. The *New York Times* columnist Thomas Friedman, a cheerleader for the Iraq war and globalization, became the poster child for the new class of corporate mandarins. And although Friedman was disastrously wrong about the outcome of the occupation, as he was about the effects of globalization, he continues, with a handful of other apologists, to dominate the airwaves.

"My initial support for the war [in Iraq] was symptomatic of unfortunate tendencies within the foreign policy community, namely the disposition and incentives to support wars to retain political and professional credibility," wrote Leslie Gelb in *Foreign Policy* in a mea culpa for the whole liberal establishment after the invasion of Iraq. "We 'experts' have a lot to fix about ourselves, even as we 'perfect' the media. We must redouble our commitment to independent thought, and embrace, rather than cast aside, opinions and facts that blow the common—often wrong—wisdom apart. Our democracy requires nothing less."

Independent thought, as Gelb and many of those who backed the war understood, is an instant career killer. Doors shut. No longer are you invited on the television talk shows, given grants, feted in the university, interviewed on CNN, invited to the Council on Foreign Relations, given tenure, or asked to write op-ed pieces in the *New York Times*. There is no cost to being wrong if the policies of the power elite are lauded. There is, however, a tremendous cost to being defiant, even if that defiance is prescient and correct. The liberal class, seeking personal and financial advancement as well as continued entrée into the inner circles of power, is not concerned with the moral but the practical.

"Nothing in my view is more reprehensible than those habits of mind in the intellectual that induce avoidance, that characteristic turning away from a difficult and principled position which you know to be the right one, but which you decide not to take," wrote Edward Said. "You do not want to appear too political; you are afraid of seeming controversial; you want to keep a reputation for being balanced, objective, moderate; your hope is to be asked back, to consult, to be on a board or prestigious committee, and so to remain within the responsible mainstream; someday you hope to get an honorary degree, a big prize, perhaps even an ambassadorship."

"For an intellectual these habits of mind are corrupting *par excellence*," Said went on. "If anything can denature, neutralize, and finally kill a passionate intellectual life it is the internalization of such habits. Personally I have encountered them in one of the toughest of all contemporary issues, Palestine, where fear of speaking out about one of the greatest injustices in modern history has hobbled, blinkered, muzzled many who know the truth and are in a position to serve it. For despite the abuse and vilification that any outspoken supporter of Palestinian rights and self-determination earns for him or herself, the truth deserves to be spoken, represented by an unafraid and compassionate intellectual."[2]

In *The Treason of Intellectuals*, Julien Benda argued that it is only when intellectuals are *not* in pursuit of practical aims or material advantages that they can serve as a conscience and a corrective. "For more than two thousand years until modern times, I see an uninterrupted series of philosophers, men of religion, men of literature, artists, men of learning (one might say almost all during this period), whose influence, whose life, were in direct opposition to the realism of the multitudes," Benda wrote.

Once intellectuals transfer their allegiance to the practical aims of power and material advantage, they emasculate themselves as intellectuals. They disregard unpleasant truths and morality to influence or incorporate themselves into systems of power. Stanley Hoffman denounced the liberal class for the bond between the scholarly world and the world of power in his 1977 essay "An American Social Science: International Relations" in *Daedalus* magazine. Academics and researchers, he notes, were "not merely in the corridors but also the kitchens of power." What had once been an intellectual exchange had become a professional one. Liberal foundations, Hoffman writes, had became "a golden halfway house between Washington and academia." Scholars saw themselves as efficient Machiavellians who were there to advise "the Prince on how best to manage his power and on how best to promote the national interest." Scholarship became directed toward a tiny elite in the hope of shaping policy. And the closer scholars came to the centers of power, the greater the temptation was to "slight the research and to slant the advocacy for reasons either of personal career or of political or bureaucratic opportunity." This meant that the scholar "may still be highly useful as an intelligent and skilled decision-maker—but not as a scholar." Hoffman argued that "the greatest hope for the science would lie in blowing up the bridge that leads across the moat into the citadel of power."[3]

Benda wrote that intellectuals in the past had been indifferent to popular passions. They gazed "as moralists upon the conflict of human egotisms." They "preached, in the name of humanity or justice, the adoption of an abstract principle superior to and directly opposed to these passions." These intellectuals were not, Benda concedes, very often able to prevent the powerful from "filling all history with the noise of their hatred and their slaughters." But they did "prevent the laymen from setting up their actions as a religion, they did prevent them from thinking themselves great men as they carried out these activities." In short, Benda asserted, "humanity did evil for two thousand years, but honored good." But once the intellectuals began to "play the game of political passions," those who had "acted as a check on the realism of the people began to act as its stimulators."[4]

Those within the liberal class who challenge the orthodoxy of belief, who question reigning political passions, are usually removed from liberal institutions. The list of apostates, those once feted and then ruthlessly banished by the liberal class, is long. It includes all those who refused, in the end, to "be practical" and serve power.

Sydney Schanberg arrived at the *New York Times* in 1959 after attending Harvard University on scholarship. He was soon promoted to a job on the city desk, sent as a reporter to the Albany bureau, and then became a foreign correspondent. He covered Vietnam and the India-Pakistan War and opened a bureau for the paper in Singapore in April 1973. He went to Indonesia, Japan, the Philippines, and repeatedly to Cambodia, where in, 1975, he was nearly killed after staying behind to cover the conquest of Phnom Penh by the Khmer Rouge, reporting for which he won a Pulitzer Prize. He tells this story in his book *The Death and Life of Dith Pran*, made into the film *The Killing Fields*. The slaughter he witnessed in Cambodia and the disappearance of his assistant and friend Dith Pran into the Khmer Rouge gulags left him angry and troubled at the vast disparity between the official announcements and indifference in Washington and the human misery he witnessed. When he returned to the newspaper, he became an institutional problem.

"In his work, he seemed like a sickened man; sick of the official lying, sick of safe little men sitting in Washington offices and playing God with the lives of foreign strangers, sick of too much pain, too much bullshit, too much death," wrote Pete Hamill in a profile of Schanberg in the *Village Voice*. "He was also laced with guilt; the normal guilt that the living feel after surviving catastrophe, specific guilt because his assistant Dith Pran had been left behind."[5]

Schanberg was appointed the assistant metropolitan editor and later the metropolitan editor. He pushed his reporters to cover the homeless, the poor, and the victims of developers. The social movements built around the opposition to the Vietnam War, however, had disbanded, and with them had gone many alternative publications. The commercial press, no longer shamed into good journalism by renegade publications such as *Ramparts*, had less and less incentive to challenge the power elite. Many in the establishment viewed Schanberg's concerns as relics of a dead era. He was removed from his position as metropolitan editor and given a column about New York. He used the column, again, to decry the abuse of the powerful, especially developers, against the poor. The editor of the paper, Abe Rosenthal, began to refer acidly to Schanberg as the resident "Commie" and address him curtly as "St. Francis." Rosenthal, who met William F. Buckley almost weekly for lunch, and the publisher, Arthur "Punch" Sulzberger, grew increasingly annoyed with Schanberg's attacks on their powerful and wealthy friends. Schanberg soon became a pariah. He was not invited to the paper's table at two consecutive Inner Circle dinners held for New York reporters. The senior editors and the publisher did not attend the previews for the film *The Killing Fields*. His days at the newspaper were numbered.

The city Schanberg continued to profile in his column did not look like the glossy ads in the *Times* fashion section or the Sunday magazine. Schanberg's city was one in which thousands of homeless people were sleeping on the streets. It was one where there were long lines at soup kitchens. It was a city where the mentally ill were tossed onto sidewalks or locked up in jails. He wrote of people who were unable to afford housing and New Yorkers who were being displaced by the greed of overzealous developers. He profiled landlords who charged exorbitant rent that drove out the working and middle class. He soon was denied even his column. He left the paper to work for *New York Newsday* and later the *Village Voice*. Schanberg knew the rules. But he refused to serve his own career interests or the "practical" concerns of his editors.

"I heard all kinds of reports over the years that the wealthy patrons of the Metropolitan Museum of Art would often get to use the customs clearance provided to the museum to import personal items, including jewelry, which was not going to the museum," Schanberg said when we met in his apartment on Manhattan's Upper West Side. "I can't prove this, but I believe it to be true. Would the *Times* investigate this? Not in a million years. The publisher at the time was the chairman of the board of the museum. These were his friends."[6]

"And yet they do more than anyone else, although they leave out a lot of things," Schanberg said of the paper:

> There are stories on their blackout list. But it is important the paper is there because they spend money on what they choose to cover. Most of the problem of mainstream journalism is what they leave out. But what they do, aside from the daily boilerplate, press releases and so forth, is very, very important to the democratic process.

"Papers function as a guide to newcomers, to immigrants, as to what the ethos is, what the rules are, how we are supposed to behave," Schanberg added:

> That is not always good, obviously, because this is the consensus of the establishment. But papers, probably more in the earlier years than now, print texts of things people will never see elsewhere. It tells them what you have to do to cast a vote. It covers things like the swearing in of immigrants. They are a positive force. I don't think the *New York Times* was ever a fully committed accountability paper. I am not sure there is one. I don't know who coined the phrase Afghanistanism, but it fits for newspapers. Afghanistanism means you can cover all the corruption you find in Afghanistan, but don't try to do it in your own backyard. The *Washington Post* does not cover Washington. It covers official Washington. The *Times* ignores lots of omissions and worse by members of the establishment.

"Newspapers do not erase bad things," Schanberg went on:

> Newspapers keep the swamp from getting any deeper, from rising higher. We do it in spurts. We discover the civil-rights movement. We discover the women's rights movement. We go at it hell-bent because now it is kosher to write about those who have been neglected and

treated like half-citizens. And then when things calm down it becomes easy not to do that anymore.

South African justice Richard Goldstone was another high-profile apostate from the liberal class. On the international stage, he engendered a clash with the liberal elite much like that which Michael Moore kindled in Hollywood and Schanberg did at the *New York Times*.

The United Nations Human Rights Council created a fact-finding mission in 2009 to investigate violations of humanitarian and human-rights law in the war in Gaza. Goldstone, who is Jewish, headed the mission, and his name was associated with the report for the United Nations that resulted. The Israeli government refused to cooperate with Goldstone's mission. Its findings were not what Israeli liberal orthodoxy found acceptable. The report detailed human-rights violations carried out by the Palestinians, but it blamed most of the heavy loss of life on the government of Israel. The Goldstone report investigated Israel's twenty-two-day air and ground assault on Gaza that took place from December 27, 2008, to January 18, 2009. The report found that Israel used disproportionate military force against Hamas militants in the Gaza Strip while failing to take adequate precautions to protect the civilian population against the military assault. The Israeli attack killed 1,434 people, including 960 civilians, according to the Palestinian Center for Human Rights. More than six thousand homes were destroyed or damaged, leaving behind some $3 billion in destruction in one of the poorest areas on Earth. Hamas rockets fired into Israel during the assault killed no Israelis.

But the report did not limit itself to the twenty-two-day attack: it went on to indict the occupation itself. It examined the beginning of the occupation and condemned Israel for the border closures, the blockade, and for the wall, or security barrier, in the West Bank. It had two references to the right of return—the right of displaced Palestinians and their descendants to return and settle in Israel—and investigated Israeli torture. It criticized the willful destruction of the Palestinian economy. Goldstone, like Moore, immediately felt the wrath of the liberal class. His name was vilified and because of threats and an effort by a Zionist group to bar him, he decided in April 2010 not to risk attending his grandson's bar mitzvah in South Africa. An arrangement was finally struck that allowed him to attend, after great controversy, both in South Africa and Israel.

Goldstone is the quintessential Jewish liberal, a champion of human rights and international law. He has long and close ties to Israel. His mother was an activist in the Zionist movement. His daughter moved to Israel. He is a member of the board of governors of Hebrew University, where he also has an honorary degree. But Goldstone, like Moore and Schanberg, dared to place his conscience above his career. And the rage of the liberal class directed toward Goldstone was the rage of those who, because of him, had their complicity with power and acts of injustice exposed.

"*Liberal* has a distinct connotation," Norman Finkelstein said when we spoke:

> It means to believe in the rule of law. It means to believe in international institutions. It means to believe in human rights. Amnesty International and Human Rights Watch are liberal organizations. What the Goldstone phenomenon registers and catalyzes is the fact that it is impossible to reconcile liberal convictions with Israel's conduct. Too much is now known about the history of the conflict and the human-rights record and the so-called peace process. It is impossible to be both liberal and defend Israeli policy. That was the conflict that confronted Goldstone. I very much doubt he wanted to condemn Israel.[7]

"Israeli liberalism always had a function in Israeli society," said Finkelstein, whose book *This Time We Went Too Far* examines the 2008 Israeli attack on Gaza:

> When I talk about liberals, I mean people like A. B. Yehoshua, David Grossman, and Amos Oz. Their function was to issue these anguished criticisms of Israel, which not only extenuated Israeli crimes but exalted Israeli crimes. "Isn't it beautiful, the Israeli soul, how it is anguished over what it has done." It is the classic case of having your cake and eating it. And now something strange happened. Along comes a Jewish liberal and he says, "Spare me your tears. I am only interested in the law."

"Goldstone did not perform the role of the Jewish liberal," Finkelstein said, "which is to be anguished, but no consequences. And all of a sudden Israeli liberal Jews are discovering, hey, there are consequences for committing war crimes. You don't just get to walk into the sunset and look beautiful. They can't believe it. They are genuinely shocked. 'Aren't our tears consequences enough? Aren't our long eyes and broken hearts consequences enough?' 'No,' he said, 'you have to go to the criminal court.'"

The campaign against Goldstone took the form of venomous denunciations of all activists and jurists. It includes a bill before the Israeli parliament, the Knesset, making it possible to imprison the leaders of Israeli human-rights groups if they failed to comply with crippling new registration conditions. Human-rights activists from outside Israel who work in the Palestinian territories were rounded up and deported. The government refused to issue work visas to employees of 150 nongovernmental organizations (NGOs) operating in the West Bank and East Jerusalem, including Oxfam, Save the Children, and Médecins Sans Frontières (Doctors Without Borders). The new tourist visas effectively barred these employees from Palestinian territory under Israeli occupation. Professor Naomi Chazan, the Israeli head of the New Israel Fund (NIF), which has donors in the United States, was vilified by ultranationalist groups such as Im Tirtzu. Chazan had spoken out on human-rights issues in Israel, and Im Tirtzu claimed the NIF was connected with groups that had funneled anti-Israel information to the Goldstone mission. Israeli officials pressured foreign donors to the NIF, as well as other human-rights groups, to halt contributions. Chazan had written a column for the *Jerusalem Post*. The paper terminated the column. Billboards sprouted up around Tel Aviv and Jerusalem with a grotesque caricature of Chazan. Groups such as Im Tirtzu had branded her as an agent for Hamas and Iran, with a horn growing from her forehead. "Naomi-Goldstone-Chazan," the caption on the billboard read. Im Tirtzu included among its financial backers the ministries of right-wing Christian pastor John Hagee and the New York Central Fund, which also supports extremist settler organizations.

"This is the first time the human-rights dimension of the Israel-Palestine conflict has moved center stage," Finkelstein noted:

It has temporarily displaced the fatuous peace process. It is the first time that human-rights reports have counted. There are literally, because I have read them, tens if not hundreds of thousands of pages of accumulation of human rights reports condemning Israel going back roughly to the first *intifada* [a Palestinian uprising against Israeli rule, 1987–1993] to the present. The human-rights organizations since the 1990s have been quite sharp in their criticism of Israel human-rights policy, but nobody ever reads the reports. They are never reported on, with maybe a couple of exceptions, in the mainstream media. The Goldstone report was the first time the findings of these human-rights organizations moved center stage. People stopped talking about the peace process and started talking about Israel's human-rights record.

Finkelstein was cut off by the liberal class from the start of his career as an academic. He studied a 1984 book by Joan Peters, *From Time Immemorial.* The book was widely praised by Jewish intellectuals such as Barbara Tuchman, Saul Bellow, and Martin Peretz. But Finkelstein's research showed that it was a hoax. *From Time Immemorial* made the mendacious claim that the land of Palestine was largely unpopulated when Jewish settlers arrived. Finkelstein's research discredited a legal document, central to Peters's book, which denied Palestinians rights to the land in Palestine. He soon found himself at war with the powerful Israeli lobby. But he refused to back down, continuing his scholarship, which demolished myths surrounding Israel and exposed Israel's political and financial exploitation of the Nazi Holocaust. This work swiftly turned him into a pariah. He was pushed out of numerous universities, including New York University, Hunter College, and DePaul University in Chicago, although his review committee at DePaul had recommended him for tenure.

He has spent most of his academic career as an adjunct professor earning $15,000 to $18,000 annually. Yet his work, including *Image and Reality of the Israel-Palestine Conflict,* published in 1995, is one of the finest and most important by any scholar on Israeli relations with the Palestinians. His writing is driven by a relentless search for truth and his compassion for the Palestinians and their suffering. This compassion, he often says, comes from his experience as the son of Holocaust survivors. In the suffering of the Palestinians, he saw the suffering his mother and father endured in the Warsaw ghetto and later the Nazi death camps. Unlike many of his critics, Finkelstein understands the lessons of the Holocaust, and of war. He has applied them to the fight against the abuse and suffering of others, even if this abuse is being carried out by Israel.

Liberals are expected by the power elite to police their own. The Harvard law professor Alan Dershowitz plays this role. He has used his position to mount campaigns against liberal dissidents such as Finkelstein and Middle East studies departments in universities such as Columbia. The use of prominent liberals to do the dirty work of the power elite is an old and effective tactic. In the late 1940s into the 1950s, the philosopher Sidney Hook, a former Trotskyist, enthusiastically supported the purging of communists from their posts in universities to avoid "playing into the hands of native reaction which would like to wipe out all liberal dissent." Hook, who argued that leftists, communists, radicals, and those he termed "ritualist liberals" endanger freedom, understood that the power elite would only accept criticism that did not defy corporate structures and ideologies. It would never permit radical critics to achieve positions of prominence within liberal institutions. He feared that unless the liberal class acted as enforcers of proper doctrine it would collide with the power elite. Hook defended this purging as "the enforcement of the proper professional standards." He called this "a matter of ethical hygiene and not of political heresy or persecution." Hook encouraged his fellow academics to "name names" in the 1950s hunt for communists within the universities, drawing an analogy between communists and drug dealers. He founded several groups, such as the Congress for Cultural Freedom, which took CIA money to counter and discourage American intellectuals from favoring cooperation with the Soviet Union. And the power elite rewarded him for his service. The anti-liberal National Association of Scholars offers a $2,500 Sidney Hook Award every year to "uncommon service in the defense of intellectual freedom and academic integrity."

Schanberg, Goldstone, and Finkelstein violated the unwritten code, one established in the anticommunist hysteria of the twentieth century, between the power elite and the liberal class. The liberal class is expected to mask the brutality of imperial war and corporate malfeasance by deploring the most egregious excesses while studiously refusing to question the legitimacy of the power elite's actions and structures. When dissidents step outside these boundaries, they become pariahs. Specific actions can be criticized, but motives, intentions, and the moral probity of the power elite cannot be questioned.

The liberal class has ossified. It has become part of the system it once tried to reform. It continues to speak in the language of technical jargon and tepid political reform, even though the corporate state has long since gutted the mechanisms for actual reform. The failure by the liberal class to adjust to the harsh, new reality of corporate power and the permanent war economy, to acknowledge its own powerlessness, has left the liberal class isolated and despised. The liberal class has died because it refused to act as if anything had changed. It ignored the looming environmental and economic collapse. It ignored the structural critique that might pull us back from the horrific effects of climate change and a global depression. Our power elite and their liberal apologists lack the ideas and the vocabulary to make sense of our new and terrifying reality.

We have entered a historical vacuum. The systems built around the old beliefs have failed, but new alternatives have yet to be articulated. The longer the power elite and the liberal class speak in words that no longer correspond to reality, the more an embittered and betrayed populace loses faith in traditional systems of government and power. The inability of liberals and the power elite to address our reality leaves the disenfranchised open to manipulation by the demagogues. The moral nihilism Dostoyevsky feared with the collapse of the liberal class inevitably leads to social chaos.

Alan Greenspan, the former head of the Federal Reserve Board, once treated with reverential deference by the power elite and the liberal class, announced in 2008, "I made a mistake in presuming that the self-interest of organizations, specifically banks and others, were such that they were best capable of protecting their own shareholders and their equity in their firms."[8]

Greenspan exposed the folly of the liberal experts and economists, who had promoted a baseless belief in the power of free markets to self-regulate and solve the world's problems. In holding up what amounts to a strenuously defended utopianism, these leaders ignored three thousand years of economic and human history to serve a corporate ideology. All the promises of the free market have turned out to be lies.

The mechanisms of control, which usually work to maintain a high level of fear among the populace, have produced, despite these admissions of failure, the "patriotic" citizen, plagued by job losses, bankrupted by medical bills, foreclosed on his or her house, and worried about possible terrorist attacks. In this historical vacuum, the "patriotic" citizen clings to the privilege of being a patriot—or, perhaps, the double privilege of being white and a patriot. The retreat into a tribal identity is a desperate attempt to maintain self-worth and self-importance at a time of deep personal and ideological confusion. The "patriotic" citizen, although abused by the actual policies of the state, unfailingly supports widespread surveillance and permanent war. The "patriotic" citizen does not question the $1 trillion in defense-related spending. The "patriotic" citizen accepts that the eighteen military and civilian intelligence agencies, most of whose work is now outsourced to private corporations, are held above government. The "patriotic" citizen accepts the state's assertion that it needs more police, prisons, inmates, spies, mercenaries, weapons, and troops than any other industrialized nation. The "patriotic" citizen objects when anyone suggests that military budgets can be cut, that troops need to come home, that domestic policies need more attention than the pursuit of permanent war. The military-industrial lobbies have ensured that military budgets are untouchable. The "patriotic" citizen admires the military and somehow pretends that the military is not part of the government. In the name of patriotism, the most powerful instruments of state power and control are effectively removed from public discussion. We endure more state control than at any time in U.S. history. And the liberal class, whose task was once to monitor and protest the excesses of the power elite, has assisted in the rout.

The failure by the liberal class to articulate an alternative in a time of financial and environmental collapse clears the way for military values of hypermasculinity, blind obedience, and violence. A confused culture disdains the empathy and compassion espoused by traditional liberalism. This cruelty runs like an electric current through reality television and trash-talk programs, where contestants endure pain and humiliation while they betray and manipulate those around them in a ruthless world of competition. These are the values championed by an increasingly militarized society and the manipulation and dishonesty on Wall Street. Friendship, trust, solidarity, honesty, and compassion are banished for the unadulterated world of competition.

This hypermasculinity, the core of pornography, fuses violence and eroticism, as well as the physical and emotional degradation of women. It is the language employed by the corporate state. Human beings are reduced to commodities. Corporations, which are despotic, authoritarian enclaves devoted to maximizing profit and ensuring that all employees speak from the same prompt cards, have infected the wider society with their values. Hypermasculinity crushes the capacity for moral autonomy, difference, and diversity. It isolates us from one another. It has its logical fruition in Abu Ghraib prison, the wars in Iraq and Afghanistan, along with our lack of compassion for our homeless, our poor, our mentally ill, our unemployed, our sick, and our gay, lesbian, transgender, and bisexual citizens. It is the antithesis of liberalism.

In his two-volume 1987 study entitled *Male Fantasies*, which draws on the bitter alienation of demobilized veterans in Germany following the end of World War I, Klaus Theweleit argues that a militarized culture attacks all that is culturally defined as the feminine, including love, gentleness, compassion, and acceptance of difference. It sees any sexual ambiguity as a threat to male "hardness" and the clearly defined roles required by the militarized state. The elevation of military values as the highest good sustains the perverted ethic, rigid social roles, and emotional numbness that Theweleit explored. It is a moral cancer that the liberal class once struggled against. The collapse of liberalism permits the hypermasculinity of a militarized society to redefine the nation. Sexual metaphors of abuse and rape are used to justify imperial and military power. And once the remnants of the liberal class adopt the heartless language of sexual violence, they assent, consciously or not, to the rule of corporate greed and violence.

Tom Friedman, interviewed in 2003 by Charlie Rose, used this hypermasculine, sexualized language of violence to justify the invasion and occupation of Iraq. It was a window into the moral and intellectual collapse of the liberal class. The old liberal columnists at the *New York*

Times, writers such as Anthony Lewis, would have never descended to Friedman's crudity. These older liberals were domesticated by corporate capitalism, but they retained some moral and intellectual independence. Friedman and the new liberal class has none.

What Islamic extremists needed to see, Friedman told Rose, "was American boys and girls going house to house, from Basra to Baghdad, and basically saying, 'Which part of this sentence don't you understand? You don't think, you know we care about our open society, you think this bubble fantasy, we're just gonna let it grow? Well, *suck on this*.' That, Charlie, is what this war is about. We could have hit Saudi Arabia, it was part of that bubble. Could have hit Pakistan. We hit Iraq because we could."[9]

Capitalism, as Marx understood, when it emasculates government and escapes its regulatory bonds, is a revolutionary force. And this revolutionary force is plunging us into a state of neofeudalism, endless war, and more draconian forms of internal repression. The liberal class lacks the fortitude and the ideas to protect the decaying system. It speaks in a twilight rhetoric that no longer corresponds to our reality. But the fiction of democracy remains useful, not only for corporations, but also for the bankrupt liberal class. If the fiction is exposed as a lie, liberals will be forced to consider actual resistance, which will be neither pleasant nor easy. As long as a democratic façade exists, liberals can engage in a useless moral posturing that requires no sacrifice or commitment. They can be the self-appointed scolds of the Democratic Party, acting as if they are part of the debate, vindicated by their pathetic cries of protest.

~

The best opportunities for radical social change exist among the poor, the homeless, the working class, and the destitute. As the numbers of disenfranchised dramatically increase, our only hope is to connect ourselves with the daily injustices visited upon the weak and the outcast. Out of this contact we can resurrect, from the ground up, a social ethic, a new movement. We must hand out bowls of soup. Coax the homeless into a shower. Make sure those who are mentally ill, cruelly abandoned on city sidewalks, take their medication. We must go back into America's segregated schools and prisons. We must protest, learn to live simply and begin, in an age of material and imperial decline, to speak with a new humility. It is in the tangible, mundane, and difficult work of forming groups and communities to care for others that we will kindle the outrage and the moral vision to fight back, that we will articulate an alternative.

Dorothy Day, who died in 1980, founded the Catholic Worker movement with Peter Maurin in the midst of the Great Depression. The two Catholic anarchists published the first issue of the *Catholic Worker* newspaper in 1933. They handed out twenty-five hundred copies in Union Square for a penny a copy. The price remains unchanged. Two Catholic Worker houses of hospitality in the Lower East Side soon followed. Day and Maurin preached a radical ethic that included an unwavering pacifism. They condemned private and state capitalism for its unfair distribution of wealth. They branded the profit motive as immoral. They were fervent supporters of the labor movement, the civil-rights movement, and all antiwar movements. They called on followers to take up lives of voluntary poverty. And when the old Communist Party came under fierce attack in the 1950s during the anticommunist purges, Day, although not a communist, was one of the only activists to denounce the repression and attend communist demonstrations.

The Catholic Worker refused to identify itself as a not-for-profit organization. It never accepted grants. It did not pay taxes. It operated its soup kitchen in New York without a city permit. The food it still provides to the homeless is donated by people in the neighborhood. There are some 150 Catholic Worker houses around the country and abroad, although there is no central authority. Some houses are run by Buddhists, others by Presbyterians. Religious and denominational lines are irrelevant. Day cautioned that none of these radical stances, which she said came out of the Gospels, ensured temporal success. They were not practical. She wrote that sacrifice and suffering were expected parts of the religious life. Success, as the world judges it, should never be the final criterion for the religious and moral life, or for the life of resistance. Spirituality, she said, was rooted in the constant struggle to fight for justice and be compassionate, especially to those in need. And that commitment was hard enough without worrying about its ultimate effect. One was saved in the end by faith, faith that acts of compassion and justice had an intrinsic worth, even if these acts had no disernable practical effect.

Those within the Worker worry that economic dislocation will empower right-wing, nationalist movements and the apocalyptic fringe of the Christian Right. This time around, they say, the country does not have the networks of labor unions, independent media, community groups, and church and social organizations that supported them when Day and Maurin began the movement. They note that there are fewer and fewer young volunteers at the Worker. The two houses on the Lower East Side depend as much on men and women in their fifties and sixties as they do on recent college graduates.

"Our society is more brutal than it was," Martha Hennessy, Day's granddaughter, told me over tea at the Catholic worker house in New York. "The heartlessness was introduced by Reagan. Clinton put it into place. The ruthlessness is backed up by technology. Americans have retreated into collective narcissism. They are disconnected from themselves and others. If we face economic collapse, there are many factors that could see the wrong response. There are more elements of fascism in place than there were in the 1930s. We not only lack community, we lack information."[10]

As our society begins to feel the disastrous ripple effects from the looting of our financial system, the unraveling of our empire, the effects of climate change and the accelerated impoverishment of the working and middle classes, hope will come only through direct contact with the destitute, and this hope will be neither impartial nor objective. The ethic born out of this contact will be grounded in the real and the possible. This ethic, because it forces us to witness suffering and pain, will be uncompromising in its commitment to the sanctity of life.

"There are several families with us, destitute families, destitute to an unbelievable extent, and there, too, is nothing to do but to love," Day wrote of those she had taken into the Catholic Worker house:

> What I mean is that there is no chance of rehabilitation, no chance, so far as we see, of changing them; certainly no chance of adjusting them to this abominable world about them—and who wants them adjusted, anyway?

What we would like to do is change the world—make it a little simpler for people to feed, clothe, and shelter themselves as God intended them to do. And to a certain extent, by fighting for better conditions, by crying out unceasingly for the rights of the workers, of the poor, of the destitute—the rights of the worthy and the unworthy poor, in other words—we can to a certain extent change the world; we can work for the oasis, the little cell of joy and peace in a harried world.[11]

Father Daniel Berrigan broke into a draft board in Catonsville, Maryland, on May 17, 1968, with eight other activists, including his brother, Father Philip Berrigan. The group removed several hundred draft files of young men who were to be sent to Vietnam. They carted the files outside and burned them in two garbage cans with homemade napalm to protest the war. Father Berrigan was tried, found guilty, spent four months as a fugitive from the FBI, was apprehended, and sent to prison for eighteen months. There would be many more "actions" and jail time after his release from prison, including a sentence for his illegal entry into a General Electric nuclear missile plant in King of Prussia, Pennsylvania, on September 9, 1980, with seven other activists, where they poured blood and hammered on Mark 12A warheads.

Berrigan, unbowed at eighty-seven when I met him, sat primly in a straight-backed wooden chair in his upper Manhattan apartment. The afternoon light slanted in from the windows, illuminating the collection of watercolors and religious icons on the walls.[12] Time and age had not blunted this Jesuit priest's fierce critique of the American empire or his radical interpretation of the Gospels. "This is the worst time of my long life," he said with a sigh. "I have never had such meager expectations of the system. I see those expectations verified in their paucity and their shallowness every day I live.

"We are talking, even in the length of years I've had, we are talking short term," he said:

It is very important to keep that kind of perspective. We haven't lost everything because we have lost today. The biblical evidence for the survival of any empire is not very large; in fact, the whole weight of biblical history goes in the other direction. They all come down.

According to the Book of Revelation, Babylon self-destructs. There is not even a hint of an enemy at the gates. "Fallen! Fallen! is Babylon the Great." I think we are somewhere in that orbit where the fall of the towers was symbolic as well as horribly actual. The thing is bringing itself down by a willful blindness that is astonishing. I happen to go very strongly with the Buddhist understanding that the good is to be done because it is good, not because it goes somewhere. I put a secret footnote in my mind. I believe if it is done in that spirit it will go somewhere, but I don't know where. I don't think the Bible grants us to know where goodness goes, what direction, what force. There is a biblical ignorance about all this that is very revealing. . . . I have come to the conclusion that the stronger a series of events in a lifetime hearken to the Bible, the less one will know about outcome. That was true from Abraham to Jesus. I have never been seriously interested in the outcome. I was interested in trying to do it humanly and carefully and nonviolently and let it go. My impression being that the tactic is of secondary importance. If we are talking real, we are talking about a community with a common spirit, the ability to open the Bible with a common understanding. In this world death seems often redundantly powerful. And yet we have the resurrection to cope with.[13]

The trial of the Catonsville Nine altered resistance to the Vietnam War, moving activists from street protests to repeated acts of civil disobedience, including the burning of draft cards. It also signaled a seismic shift within the Catholic Church, propelling radical priests and nuns led by the Berrigans, Thomas Merton, and Dorothy Day to the center of a religiously inspired social movement that challenged not only church and state authority but also the myths and ideologies Americans used to define, enrich, and empower themselves.

"Dorothy Day taught me more than all the theologians," Berrigan said. "She awakened me to connections I had not thought of or been instructed in, the equation of human misery and poverty and warmaking. She had a basic hope that God created the world with enough for everyone, but there was not enough for everyone *and* war-making."

Berrigan's relationship with Day led to a close friendship with the writer and Trappist monk Thomas Merton. Merton's "great contribution to the religious left," Berrigan said, "was to gather us for days of prayer and discussion of the sacramental life. He told us, 'Stay with these, stay with these, these are your tools and discipline, and these are your strengths.'

"He could be very tough," Berrigan noted of Merton. "He said, 'You are not going to survive America unless you are faithful to your discipline and tradition.' " Merton's death at fifty-three—a few weeks after Berrigan's trial—left Berrigan "deaf and dumb."

"I could not talk or write about him for ten years," he said. "He was with me when I was shipped out of the country, and he was with me in jail. He was with his friend."

The distractions of the world are for Berrigan just that: distractions. The presidential election campaign between Barack Obama and John McCain, under way when we spoke, did not preoccupy him, and when I asked him about it, he quoted his brother, Philip, who said that "if voting made any difference it would be illegal." He was critical of the Catholic Church, saying that Pope John Paul II, who marginalized and silenced radical nuns and priests like the Berrigans, "introduced Soviet methods into the Catholic Church," including "anonymous delations, removals, scrutiny, and secrecy, and the placing of company men into positions of great power." He estimated that "it is going to take at least a generation to undo appointments of John Paul II."

Berrigan despaired of universities, especially Boston College's decision to give an honorary degree to Secretary of State Condoleezza Rice, and to invite then-attorney general Michael Mukasey to address the law school. "It is a portrayal of shabby lives as exemplary and to be honored," he said. And he has little time for secular radicals or the liberal class who stood with him forty years ago but who have now "disappeared into the matrix of money and regular jobs or gave up on their initial discipline."

"The short fuse of the American left is typical of the highs and lows of American emotional life," he said. "It is very rare to sustain a movement in recognizable form without a spiritual basis of some kind."

While all empires rise and fall, Berrigan said, it is the religious and moral values, and the nonhistorical values, of compassion, simplicity, love, and justice that endure and alone demand fealty. The current decline of American power is part of the cycle of human civilizations, although, he said ruefully, "the tragedy across the globe is that we are pulling down so many others. We are not falling gracefully. Many, many people are paying with their lives for this."

Berrigan argued that those who seek a just society, who seek to defy war and violence, who decry the assault of globalization and degradation of the environment, who care about the plight of the poor, should stop worrying about the practical, short-term effects of their resistance.

Berrigan is sustained, he said, by the Eucharist, his faith, and his religious community. No resistance movement can survive without a vigorous, disciplined spiritual core:

> The reason we are celebrating forty years of Catonsville and we are still at it, those of us who are still living—the reason people went through all this and came out on their feet—was due to a spiritual discipline that went on for months before these actions took place. We went into situations in court and in prison and in the underground that could easily have destroyed us and that did destroy others who did not have our preparation.

The decline of the Catholic Church, traditional Protestant denominations, and liberal Jewish synagogues, institutions that once had a place for radicals from Martin Luther King Jr. to Abraham Heschel to Dorothy Day to the Berrigans, was a body blow to the liberal class. These religious institutions, which purged radicals as ruthlessly as their secular counterparts, became as useless as the other pillars of the liberal establishment.

"The Unitarians represented the far fringe of the Social Gospel movement, and make it easy to see its fundamental flaw," the Rev. Davidson Loehr, a Unitarian-Universalist minister in Austin, Texas, told me:

> In the late 1970s, Unitarians started saying that the trouble was that their children didn't know what to tell their friends they believed. When I heard it in grad school at The University of Chicago, I thought no, the trouble is that neither the adults nor the ministers knew what mattered. The U.U.'s then took a fatal turn. They essentially conducted a poll, to find what members and attendees of the

churches happened to believe—in other words, what beliefs had they brought in with them? From this weird process the Seven Principles were born, as "What U.U.'s Believe." Yet looking through them, they're simply the generic beliefs shared by all cultural liberals, whether they were religious or not. They had projected their beliefs onto a platform, then worshiped them. So they collapsed into a narcissism that has grown weaker and more desperate since they adopted those Seven Dwarfs in 1985. It became and is even worse.

The Unitarians, like all white moderate-to-liberal Christians and Jews, have seen their role as speaking up for the downtrodden. It's fair to say that the early civil-rights movement would not have succeeded without the white liberal support. But this changed in the 1960s and 1970s, when Martin Luther King Jr. and Malcolm X didn't want white folks speaking for them, and had far more charismatic speakers themselves. Same with the women's movement. Betty Friedan, Gloria Steinem, Germaine Greer were miles ahead, and wanted to speak for themselves. After Stonewall, the gays also spoke for themselves. This left white liberals with no useful role in society. They were welcome to follow the black, women, gay leaders, but not to speak for them. When they could no longer speak for anybody, they—and by *they* I mean the faculties of good humanities divisions and women's studies—started the political correctness movement. The inane brilliance of this was that, by inventing disadvantaged groups, nobody could say they didn't have the right to speak for them.[14]

"By bringing 'heaven' down to earth with the Social Gospel, religious and political liberals lost any framework that could critique the things they happened to believe," Loehr said. "Individual rights have to be balanced by our responsibility to the larger wholes. But why? In the name of what? Few seem to know or care. Cowardice has become one of the identifying traits of moderate-to-liberal religions.

"Even in the Middle Ages, theologians knew the difference between wisdom and knowledge," Loehr said:

They wrote often of the categorical distinction between *sapientia* and *scientia*. *Sapientia* is the Latin word for wisdom, as in our self-flattering species name, *homo sapiens*. Seven centuries ago, theologians taught that the only knowledge that really mattered was the kind of knowledge that leads to wisdom, that tells us who we most deeply are and how we should live, the demands of love, and the nature of allegiance and responsibility. Even the ancient Greek word *filosofia*, the love of wisdom, was about the wisdom that leads to a fulfilling life— not factoids and syllogisms.

People have always ascribed human qualities to God. We say things like "God says" and "God tells us," as though God were a humanoid who spoke only through the mouths of priests, prophets and shamans. But now, in our newspapers and on television every day, we hear people saying, "Science says" and "Science tells us." Let's be clear: there is no such thing as science spelled with a capital *S*. There are many sciences, and many scientists. Scientists say things and don't always agree. But when we construct a sentence that begins with the words *Science says*, we have created a humanoid fiction, named it Science, and begun to trust it in the way we once trusted God. Once capitalized, both words are linguistic idols.

Preachers and lay people may say, "In a church, through rituals and traditions, black-robed priests proclaim the revelations of God, helping us learn the beliefs and wisdom that can lead to our salvation." Scientists and many lay people say, "In a laboratory, under controlled conditions, following the rituals of the scientific method, white-robed scientists proclaim the new theories and discoveries of Science, helping us to gain the understanding and the knowledge that can lead us both toward a good life, and Progress."

During the twentieth century, the churches lost even more of their fundamental contributions. Psychologists took over the role of hearing confessions and forgiving sins—for both the laity and the ministers. Books, movies, radio, and television took over the role of providing the most persuasive fictions. Virtually all our best movies are about good and evil, because we created them, and we wonder about good and evil. A long list of literary fictions and film plotlines have allowed people to enter easily into their fantasies, to try on different roles for themselves: *Star Trek*, *Star Wars*—"The Force be with you"—*Rocky*, *Rambo*, Clint Eastwood's tough characters, *Lord of the Rings*, *Harry Potter*, *Superman*, *Batman*, *Iron Man*, etc. With the giant leap forward of the movie *Avatar*, our best professional storytellers can blur the line between fantasy and reality, making it even easier for people to enter the stories.

An important part of this, I think, is that people know all these stories are fictions. If they were told that all these things were factually true, they'd reject them. This also makes it easier to recognize that biblical stories are also fictions—but not as attractive as the best movies. In graduate school, the Catholic theologian David Tracy made some little waves when he wrote that our religious/theological stories are "useful fictions," or even "necessary fictions." If so, they have a long way to go to be as attractive as all the other fictions we have today.

Christianity certainly has—through Jesus and the best of the Hebrew prophets—some profound wisdom, without any doubt. But once you claim to exalt the Wisdom Tradition—as the Jesus Seminar also did—then there's no reason to stop with Christianity. All wisdom (and alleged wisdom) is on the table. Then it's easy to see and say things that are almost impossible to say from within Christianity. "Jesus was so young. It's a pity he didn't live to 70-80, as Socrates, Plato, Aristotle, the Buddha, Lao Tzu and Confucius had, and grow into a less idealistic and more realistic vision." Questions like this, I think, take the discussion outside of Christianity (or any single religion) and into a field that might be called the best sort of humanism (à la Shakespeare and Montaigne). But it's hard for professors and preachers paid to be Christians to make that move, for lots of reasons.

Ministers know that if they're going to preach on a story from the Bible, they have to tell the people the story first, since most of them have never read it. I remember Borges writing that we die twice, once when the body gives out, and then the second and final death, "when there is no one left to tell our story." I think this is the state of most Christian churches today.

I. F. Stone, perhaps more than any journalist in the twentieth century, lived a life dedicated to the values Day and Macdonald held out as the only hope for real transformation. Stone, born and raised by Russian immigrants in Philadelphia, was one of the most famous reporters in the nation by the end of World War II. He was a regular on television news programs and had easy access to those in power. He traveled with underground Jewish survivors of the Nazi Holocaust on leaky transports to British-occupied Palestine and wrote a series of reports that dramatically boosted the circulation of the New York newspaper *PM*. He covered the war for Israeli independence. And he was a confidant of many in the administration of Franklin Roosevelt.

And then, challenging President Harry Truman's loyalty program and the establishment of NATO, Stone disappeared from public view and was swallowed up in the hysteria over communism. He became a nonperson. He began an address to a rally against the hydrogen bomb in February 1950 with the words "FBI agents and fellow subversives"[15] He was soon under daily FBI surveillance. His passport was not renewed. And he was blacklisted as a reporter. Even the *Nation*, the centerpiece of the liberal intelligentsia, would not give him a job. He was forty-four and wrote that such actions made him "feel for the moment like a ghost."[16]

Stone gathered up a few stalwarts from his old magazine and newspaper audience—although not enough to cover expenses—and launched a newsletter in 1953 called *I. F. Stone's Weekly*. Stone did what the muckrakers did before the war, but rather than write for huge mass weeklies, he self-published his work in his basement. Stone's work exposed the damage done to journalism by mass culture. The stories that Stone broke were ignored by most organizations. It was Stone who punctured the Johnson administration's assertion that U.S. ships had been attacked in the Gulf of Tonkin. He pointed out that "one bullet embedded in one destroyer hull is the only proof we have been able to muster that the . . . attacks took place."[17] In an appendix of a State Department white paper meant to justify an expansion of the war, he found that in the months between June 1962 and January 1964 only 179 of approximately 7,500 weapons captured from the Vietcong had come from the Soviet bloc. The remainder, ninety-five percent, came from U.S. arms provided to the South Vietnamese.

He did this reporting while shut out of the big news conferences and confidential background briefings given to well-placed Washington reporters. The establishment reporters, he conceded, knew things he did not, but "a lot of what they know isn't true."[18] What those journalists called objectivity "usually is seeing things the way everybody else sees them,"[19] Stone said. By the time he closed the weekly nearly two decades later, it had seventy thousand subscribers, and he had become a journalistic icon.

Stone was that curious hybrid of intellectual and journalist. He was as conversant in theater, art, literature, poetry, and the classics—he knew Latin and mastered Greek at the end of his life to write a book on the trial of Socrates—as he was in the intricacies of the New Deal, the permanent war economy, and the labor movement. His fierce independence and razor-sharp intellect, like George Orwell's, often made him a scourge to the liberal class as well as the right. He detested orthodoxy. He consistently stood on the side of those who would have remained unheard without him. He may have been a supporter of Israel, but he had the courage to write in 1949 that Deir Yassin, an Arab village attacked in 1948 by Zionist paramilitary, who killed more than one hundred residents, was a village "whose Arabs were massacred by Irgunists with biblical ferocity, a shameful page in the history of the Jewish war of liberation."[20] American Jewish organizations offered to promote his book on the war for Israeli independence if he deleted one sentence calling for a binational Arab-Jewish state made up of Palestine and Trans-Jordan. He refused. The book languished in obscurity.

Stone would not sell out. He never forgot, as he famously quipped, that "every government is run by liars."[21] He was expelled from the National Press Club after he and a black former federal judge were refused luncheon service. He promptly joined the black newspapermen's club. He declared Malcolm X "savagely uncompromising" after his assassination, seeing perhaps a bit of himself in the brilliant leader who read *Paradise Lost* and Herodotus in prison. Malcolm X, Stone stated, "drove home the real truth about the Negro's position in America. It may not be pleasant, but it must be faced . . . No man has better expressed his people's trapped anguish."[22] Yet as the New Left became anarchic and its fringes began to embrace violence in the 1960s, he was as withering in his critique of the 1960s radicals as he was of the government it defied. "Lifelong dissent has more than acclimated me cheerfully to defeat," Stone wrote:

> It has made me suspicious of victory. I feel uneasy at the very idea of a Movement. I see every insight degenerating into dogma, and fresh

thoughts freezing into lifeless party lines. Those who set out nobly to be their brother's keeper sometimes end up by becoming his jailer. Every emancipation has in it the seeds of a new slavery, and every truth easily becomes a lie."[23]

It is only when radicals such as Stone exist that the commercial media wake from their slumber. Figures like Stone, in essence, shame the press into good journalism. The news media reached their peak in the 1960s and 1970s with the publication of the Pentagon Papers, the coverage of Watergate, and the reporting of the Vietnam War. This reporting took place against a backdrop of social unrest, including the civil-rights movement and the antiwar movement, and a discrediting of established centers of power. The commercial media reported on the realities of the Vietnam War and the excesses committed by the CIA and the FBI only when public sentiment began turning against the war. Mass movements acquired, if not formal political power, at least enough power to demand a voice. The acceptable debate between the two wings of the power elite broke down. The alternative press, including magazines such as *Ramparts*, exposed egregious assaults on civil liberties directed at those outside the circles of established power and ignored by the liberal class. The pressure was an example of how important radical movements are for the vitality of the liberal class.

Government harassment of the underground press, especially after Richard Nixon took office in 1969, was ignored by commercial media. The FBI pressured record companies to cancel advertisements in alternative publications. Papers such as the *Rat* in New York City and the *NOLA Express* in New Orleans were under constant FBI surveillance. During 1969 and 1970 the editor of Miami's *Daily Planet* was arrested twenty-nine times and acquitted twenty-eight times, posting a total of $93,000 in bond money. FBI harassment included phony letter-writing campaigns and three phony underground newspapers, along with three phony news services. Army intelligence burglarized the *Free Press* in Washington.[24]

But once Richard Nixon began to use illegal tactics against the liberal establishment, the commercial press fought back. The Watergate scandal, mythologized as an example of a vigorous free press, in fact illustrates the deference the liberal class pays to privilege and power, as

Edward Herman and Noam Chomsky point out in their book *Manufacturing Consent*. Nixon had long engaged in similar illegalities against antiwar groups and dissidents such as Daniel Ellsberg, as well as against alternative publications, such as *Ramparts*, with little or no reaction from the liberal class. Nixon's fatal mistake was to use these illegal tactics on the liberal class itself. Once the Democratic Party and the liberal class became the targets of Nixon's illegalities, the media were empowered to expose abuses they had previously ignored.

"History has been kind enough to contrive for us a 'controlled experiment' to determine just what was at stake during the Watergate period, when the confrontational stance of the media reached its peak," Herman and Chomsky wrote:

> The answer is clear and precise: powerful groups are capable of defending themselves, not surprisingly; and by media standards, it is a scandal when their position and rights are threatened. By contrast, as long as illegalities and violations of democratic substance are confined to marginal groups or dissident victims of U.S. military attack, or result in a diffused cost imposed on the general population, media opposition is muted and absent altogether. This is why Nixon could go so far, lulled into a false sense of security precisely because the watchdog only barked when he began to threaten the privileged.[25]

Howard Zinn in the *People's History of the United States* examined history through the eyes of Native Americans, immigrants, slaves, women, union leaders, persecuted socialists, anarchists and communists, abolitionists, antiwar activists, civil rights leaders, and the poor. Zinn's work has been castigated by many academic historians, largely because he broke with the mold of writing about the great and the powerful. Zinn related history as it was experienced by people and he imploded numerous national foundation myths from the hijacking of the American Revolution by the wealthy, slave owning elite to the treachery exhibited by European settlers towards Native Americans. Zinn also exposed the clay feet of the founding fathers, including George Washington, who was the richest man in the nation after the revolution, and national idols such as Abraham Lincoln, whose opposition to slavery was never emphatic or even principled. Zinn's honesty perhaps explains why the FBI, which released its 423-page file on Zinn in July 2010, saw him as a threat.

Zinn, who died in January 2010 at the age of eighty-seven, did not advocate violence or support the overthrow of the government, something he told FBI interrogators on several occasions. He was rather an example of how independent intellectual thought deeply disturbs the myths perpetuated by the power elite. Zinn's work was based on a fierce moral autonomy and personal courage and was, for this reason, branded as "political." Zinn was a threat not because he was a violent revolutionary or a communist but because he was fearless and told the truth.

The cold, dead pages of the FBI file stretch from 1948 to 1974. At one point, five agents are assigned to follow Zinn. Agents make repeated phone calls to employers, colleagues and landlords seeking information. The FBI, although Zinn is never suspected of carrying out a crime, eventually labels Zinn a high security risk. J. Edgar Hoover, who took a personal interest in Zinn's activities, on January 10, 1964, drew up a memo to include Zinn "in Reserve Index, Section A," a classification that permitted agents to immediately arrest and detain Zinn if there was a national emergency. Muslim activists, from Dr. Sami Al-Arian to Fahad Hasmi, can tell you that nothing has changed.

The Zinn file exposes the absurdity, waste and pettiness of our national security state. And it seems to indicate that our security agencies prefer to hire those with mediocre or stunted intelligence, dubious morality, and little common sense. Take for example this gem of a letter, complete with misspellings, mailed by an informant to then FBI Director Hoover about something Zinn wrote.

"While I was visiting my dentist in Michigan City, Indiana," the informant wrote, "this pamphlet was left in my car, and I am mailing it to you, I know is a DOVE call, and not a HOCK call. We have had a number of ethnic groups move into our area in the last few years. We are in a war! And it doesn't look like this pamphlet will help our Government objectives."

Or how about the meeting between an agent and someone identified as Doris Zinn. Doris Zinn, who the agent says is Zinn's sister, is interviewed "under a suitable pretext." She admits that her brother is "employed at the American Labor Party Headquarters in Brooklyn." That is all the useful information that is reported. The fact that Zinn did not have a sister gives a window into the quality of the investigations and the caliber of the agents who carried them out.

FBI agents in November 1953 wrote up an account of a clumsy attempt to recruit Zinn as an informant, an attempt in which they admitted that Zinn "would not volunteer information" and that "additional interviews with Zinn would not turn him from his current attitude." A year later, after another interrogation, an agent wrote that Zinn "concluded the interview by stating he would not under any circumstances testify or furnish information concerning the political opinions of others."

The FBI spent years following Zinn, and carefully cutting out newspaper articles about their suspect, to amass the inane and the banal. One of Zinn's neighbors, Mrs. Matthew Grell, on February 22, 1952, told agents that she considered Zinn and another neighbor, Mrs. Julius Scheiman, "to be either communists or communist sympathizers" because, the agents wrote, Grell "had observed copies of the Daily Workers in Mrs. Scheiman's apartment and noted that Mrs. Scheiman was a good friend of Howard Zinn."

The FBI, which describes Zinn as a former member of the Communist Party, something Zinn repeatedly denied, appears to have picked up its surveillance when Zinn, who was teaching at Spelman, a historically black women's college, became involved in the civil rights movement. Zinn served on the Student Nonviolent Coordinating Committee. He took his students out of the classroom to march for civil rights. Spelman's president was not pleased.

"I was fired for insubordination," Zinn recalled. "Which happened to be true."

Zinn, in 1962, decried, "The clear violations by local police of Constitutional rights" of blacks and noted that "the FBI has not made a single arrest on behalf of Negro citizens." The agent who reported Zinn's words added that Zinn's position was "slanted and biased." Zinn in 1970 was a featured speaker at a rally for the release of the Black Panther leader Bobby Seal held in front of the Boston police headquarters. "It is about time we had a demonstration at the police station," Zinn is reported as telling the crowd by an informant who apparently worked with him at Boston University. "Police in every nation are a blight and the United States is no exception."

"America has been a police state for a long time," Zinn went on. "I believe that policemen should not have guns. I believe they should be disarmed. Policemen with guns are a danger to the community and themselves."

Agents muse in the file about how to help their unnamed university source mount a campaign to have Zinn fired from his job as a professor of history at Boston University.

"[Redacted] indicated [Redacted] intends to call a meeting of the BU Board of Directors in an effort to have Zinn removed from BU. Boston proposes under captioned program with Bureau permission to furnish [Redacted] with public source data regarding Zinn's numerous antiwar activities, including his trip to Hanoi, 1/31/68, in an effort to back [Redacted's] efforts for his removal."

Zinn and the Catholic priest Daniel Berrigan had traveled together to North Vietnam in January 1968 to bring home three prisoners of war. The trip was closely monitored by the FBI. Hoover sent a coded teletype to the president, the secretary of state, the director of the CIA, the director of the Defense Intelligence Agency, the Department of the Army, the Department of the Air Force and the White House situation room about the trip. And later, after Berrigan was imprisoned for destroying draft records, Zinn repeatedly championed the priest's defense in public rallies, some of which the FBI noted were sparsely attended. The FBI monitored Zinn as he traveled to the Danbury Federal Prison in Connecticut to visit Berrigan and his brother Philip.

"Mass murders occur, which is what war is," Zinn, who was a bombardier in World War II, said in 1972, according to the file, "because people are split and don't think . . . when the government does not serve the people, then it doesn't deserve to be obeyed. . . . To be patriotic, you may have to be against your government."

Zinn testified at the trial of Daniel Ellsberg, who gave a copy of the Pentagon Papers to Zinn and Noam Chomsky. The two academics edited the secret documents on the Vietnam War, sections of which had appeared in the *New York Times*, into the four volumes that were published in 1971.

"During the Pentagon Papers jury trial, Zinn stated that the 'war in Vietnam was a war which involved special interests, and not the defense of the United States,'" his FBI file reads.

By the end of the file one walks away with a profound respect for Zinn and a deep distaste for the buffoonish goons in the FBI who followed and monitored him. There is no reason, with the massive expansion of our internal security apparatus, to think that things have improved. There are today 1,271 government organizations and 1,931 private companies working on programs related to counterterrorism, homeland security and intelligence in about ten thousand locations across the United States, the *Washington Post* reported in an investigation by Dana Priest and William M. Arkin. These agencies employ an estimated 854,000 people, all of whom hold top-secret security clearances, the Post found. And in Washington, DC, and the surrounding area, thirty-three building complexes for top-secret intelligence work are under construction or have been built since September 2001. Together, the paper reported, they occupy the equivalent of almost three Pentagons or twenty-two U.S. Capitol buildings—about 17 million square feet.

We are amassing unprecedented volumes of secret files, and carrying out extensive surveillance and harassment, as stupid and useless as those that were directed against Zinn. And a few decades from now maybe we will be able to examine the work of the latest generation of dimwitted investigators who have been unleashed upon us in secret by the tens of thousands. Did any of the agents who followed Zinn ever realize how they wasted their time? Do those following us around comprehend how manipulated they are? Do they understand that their primary purpose, as it was with Zinn, is not to prevent terrorism but discredit and destroy social movements as well as protect the elite from those who would expose them?

Zinn knew that if we do not listen to the stories of those without power, those who suffer discrimination and abuse, those who struggle for justice, we are left parroting the manufactured myths that serve the interests of the privileged. Zinn set out to write history, not myth. He found that challenging these myths, even as a historian, turned one into a pariah.

The descent of Ralph Nader, from being one of the most respected and powerful public figures in the country to being an outcast, illustrates perhaps better than any other narrative the totality of our corporate coup and the complicity of the liberal class in our disempowerment.

Nader's marginalization was not accidental. The corporations, which grew tired of Nader's activism, mounted a campaign to destroy him. It was orchestrated to thwart the legislation that Nader and his allies, who had once belonged to the Democratic Party and the liberal class, enacted to prevent corporate abuse, fraud, and domination. And by the time he was shut out of the media and the political process with the election of Ronald Reagan, the government was firmly in the hands of corporations.

"The press discovered citizen investigators around the mid-1960s," Nader told me when we spoke one afternoon in Princeton:[26]

> I was one of them. I would go down with the press releases, the findings, the story suggestions, and the internal documents and give it to a variety of reporters. I would go to Congress and generate hearings. Oftentimes, I would be the lead witness. What was interesting was the novelty. The press gravitates to novelty. They achieved great things. There was collaboration. We provided the newsworthy material. They covered it. The legislation passed. Regulations were issued. Lives were saved. Other civic movements began to flower.

"Ralph Nader came along and did serious journalism. That is what his early stuff was, such as *Unsafe at Any Speed*," the investigative journalist David Cay Johnston told me:

> The big books they put out were serious, first-rate journalism. Corporate America was terrified by this. They went to school on Nader. They said, "We see how you do this. You gather material, you get people who are articulate, you hone how you present this." And the corporations copycatted him with one big difference: they had no regard for the truth. Nader may have had a consumer ideology, but he was not trying to sell you a product. He is trying to tell the truth as best as he can determine it. It does not mean it is the truth. It means it is the truth as best as he and his people can determine the truth. And he told you where he was coming from.[27]

Between 1966 and 1973, Congress passed twenty-five pieces of consumer legislation, nearly all of which Nader had a hand in authoring.

The auto and highway safety laws, the meat and poultry inspection laws, the oil pipeline safety laws, the product safety laws, the updated flammable fabric laws, the revised Clean Air Act, the revisions to the Federal Water Pollution Control Act, the Environmental Protection Agency, Occupational Safety and Health Act (OSHA), and the Environmental Council in the White House transformed the political landscape. By 1973, Nader was named the fourth most influential person in the country after Richard Nixon, Supreme Court Justice Earl Warren, and AFL-CIO president George Meany.

"Then something very interesting happened," Nader told me:

> The pressure of these meetings by the corporations like General Motors, the oil companies, and the drug companies with the editorial people, and probably with the publishers, coincided with the emergence of the most destructive force to the citizen movement mise-en-scène: Abe Rosenthal, the editor of the *New York Times*. Rosenthal was a right-winger from Canada who hated communism, came here, and hated progressivism. The *Times* was not doing that well at the time. Rosenthal was commissioned to expand his suburban sections, which required a lot of advertising. He was very receptive to the entreaties of corporations, and he did not like me. I would give material to Jack Morris in the Washington bureau, and it would not get in the paper.

Rosenthal, who banned social critics such as Chomsky from being quoted in the paper, decreed that no story built around Nader's research could be published unless there was a corporate response. Corporations, informed of Rosenthal's dictate, refused to comment on Nader's research. This effectively killed the stories. The *Times* set the agenda for national news coverage. Once Nader disappeared from the *Times*, other major papers and networks did not feel compelled to report on his investigations. He found it harder and harder to be heard.

Much as Mr. Mister of *The Cradle Will Rock* hires a detective to spy on his enemies, General Motors hired detectives to dig up dirt on Nader's personal life. They found none. The company had Nader followed in an attempt to blackmail him. They sent an attractive woman to his neighborhood Safeway in a failed bid to seduce him while he was shopping. GM's campaign was exposed and led to a public apology by the company. Nader was awarded $425,000 in damages, which he used to fund citizen action groups.

But far from ending the effort to destroy Nader, the defeat in court only spurred corporations to unleash a more sophisticated and well-funded attack. Lewis Powell, who was the general counsel to the U.S. Chamber of Commerce and would later be appointed to the Supreme Court, wrote a memo in August 1971 that expressed corporate concern over Nader's work: "Perhaps the single most effective antagonist of American business is Ralph Nader, who—thanks largely to the media—has become a legend in his own time and an idol of millions of Americans." Powell goes on to recommend: "There should be no hesitation to attack the Naders, the Marcuses, and others who openly seek destruction of the system. There should not be the slightest hesitation to press vigorously in all political arenas for support of the enterprise system. Nor should there be reluctance to penalize politically those who oppose it.

"Moreover," Powell went on:

> much of the media—for varying motives and in varying degrees— either voluntarily accords unique publicity to these "attackers," or at least allows them to exploit the media for their purposes. This is especially true of television, which now plays such a predominant role in shaping the thinking, attitudes and emotions of our people. One of the bewildering paradoxes of our time is the extent to which the enterprise system tolerates, if not participates in, its own destruction.[28]

The eight-page memo, entitled "Attack on American Free Enterprise System," became the blueprint for corporate dominance. Powell's memo led to the establishment of the Business Roundtable, which amassed enough money and power to direct government policy and mold public opinion. It inspired the activities of the Heritage Foundation, the Manhattan Institute, the Cato Institute, Citizens for a Sound Economy, and Accuracy in Academe. The memo detailed ways corporations could shut out those who, in "the college campus, the pulpit, the media, the intellectual and literary journals," were hostile to corporate interests. Powell called for the establishment of lavishly funded think tanks and conservative institutes to churn out ideological tracts that attacked government regulation and environmental protection. His memo led to the successful effort to place corporate-friendly academics and economists in universities and on the airwaves, as well as drive out those in the public sphere who questioned the rise of unchecked corporate power and deregulation. It saw the establishment of monitoring organizations that pressured the media to report favorably on corporate interests. And it led to the building of legal organizations to promote corporate interests in the courts and press for the appointment of sympathetic judges to the bench.

Corporations poured hundreds of millions into the assault. They invented bogus disciplines, including cost-benefit and risk-management analysis, all geared to change the debate from health, labor, and safety issues to the rising cost of big government. They ran sophisticated ad campaigns to beguile voters. These corporations wrenched apart, through lavish campaign donations and intensive and shady lobbying, the ties between Nader's public interest groups and his supporters in the Democratic Party. Washington, by the time they were done, was besieged with twenty-five thousand corporate lobbyists and nine thousand corporate action committees.

When Reagan, the corporate pitchman, swept into office, he set out to dismantle some thirty governmental regulations, most put into place by Nader and his allies. All of them curbed the activities of corporations. The Reagan White House gutted twenty years of Nader legislation. And Nader, once a fixture on Capitol Hill, was thrust into the wilderness.

Nader, however, did not give up. He turned to local community organizing, assisting grassroots campaigns around the country, such as the one to remove benzene, known to cause cancer, from paint in GM car plants. But by the time Bill Clinton and Al Gore took office, the corporate state was unassailable. Nader and his citizen committees were frozen out by Democrats as well as Republicans. Clinton and Gore never met with Nader while in office, despite Gore's reputed concern for the environment.

"We tried every way to get the Democrats to pick up on issues that really commanded the felt concerns and daily life of millions of Americans," Nader says in the documentary *An Unreasonable Man*, "but these were issues that corporations didn't want attention paid to, and so when people say, "Why did you [run for president] in 2000, I say, 'I'm a twenty-year veteran of pursuing the folly of the least worse between the two parties.'"[29]

Establishment liberals express a fascinating rage—and *rage* is the right word—against Nader in *An Unreasonable Man*. Todd Gitlin and Eric Alterman, along with a host of former Nader's Raiders, attack Nader, a man they profess to have once admired. The most common charge is that Nader is an egomaniac. Their anger is the anger of the betrayed. But they were not betrayed by Nader. They betrayed themselves. They bought into the facile argument of "the least worse" and ignored the deeper, subterranean corporate assault on our democracy that Nader has always addressed. The anger they express is the anger of an exposed liberal class.

It was an incompetent, corporatized Democratic Party, along with the orchestrated fraud by the Republican Party, which threw the 2000 election to Bush. It was not Nader's fault. Nader received only 2.7 percent of the vote in 2000 and got less than one-half of one percent in 2004. All of the third-party candidates who ran in 2000 in Florida—there were about half a dozen—got more votes than the 537 that separated Bush and Gore. Why not go after the other third-party candidates? And what about the ten million Democrats across the country who voted in 2000 for Bush? What about Gore, whose campaign was so timid and empty—he *never* mentioned global warming—that he could not even carry his home state of Tennessee? And what about the 2004 Democratic presidential candidate, Senator John Kerry, who got up like a Boy Scout and told us he was reporting for duty and would bring us "victory" in Iraq?

Nader argues that there are few—he never said *no*—differences between the Democrats and the Republicans. And during the Bush administration the Democrats proved him right. They authorized the war in Iraq. They stood by as Bush stacked the judiciary with "Christian" ideologues. They let Bush, in violation of the Constitution, pump hundreds of millions of taxpayer dollars into faith-based organizations that discriminate based on religious creed and sexual orientation. They permitted American children to get fleeced by No Child Left Behind. They did not protest when federal agencies began to propagate "Christian" pseudoscience about creationism, reproductive rights, and homo-sexuality. And the Democrats let Bush further dismantle regulatory agencies, strip American citizens of constitutional rights under the Patriot Act and other draconian legislation, and thrust impoverished Americans aside through passage of a corporate-sponsored bankruptcy bill. And then the Democrats helped transfer hundreds of billions of taxpayer dollars to Wall Street. It is a stunning record. If the Democratic Party and the liberal class had challenged corporate welfare, corporate crime, the Wall Street bailouts, and issues such as labor law reform, if it stood up to these corporate behemoths on behalf of the working and middle classes, rather than mutter thought-terminating clichés about American greatness, they could rally a disgusted public behind them.

There are a few former associates who argue that Nader is tarnish-ing his legacy, and by extension their own. But Nader's legacy is undi-minished. He fights his wars against corporate greed with a remarkable consistency. He knows our democratic state is being hijacked by the same corporate interests that sold us unsafe automobiles and danger-ous and shoddy products.

"I don't care about my personal legacy," Nader says in *An Unrea-sonable Man*. "I care about how much justice is advanced in America and in our world day after day. I'm willing to sacrifice whatever 'repu-tation' in the cause of that effort. What is my legacy? Are they going to turn around and rip seat belts out of cars, air bags out of cars?

"It was off to the races," Nader said to me:

> You could hardly keep count of the number of right-wing corporate-funded think tanks. These think tanks specialized, especially against the tort system. We struggled through the Nixon and early Ford years, when inflation was a big issue. Nixon did things that horrified conservatives. He signed into law the Occupational Safety and Health Administration, the Environmental Protection Agency, and air and water pollution acts because he was afraid of popular opinion, fol-lowing the rumble that came out of the 1960s. He was the last Repub-lican president to be afraid of liberals.

"There was, before we were silenced, a brief, golden age of journal-ism," Nader lamented. "We worked with the press to expose corporate abuse on behalf of the public. We saved lives. This is what journalism should be about. It should be about making the world a better and safer place for our families and our children, but then it ended, and we were shut out.

"We were thrown on the defensive, and once we were on the defensive, it was difficult to recover," Nader said:

> The break came in 1979, when they deregulated natural gas. Our last national stand was for the Consumer Protection Agency. We put everything we had on that. We would pass it during the 1970s in the House on one year, then the Senate during the next session, then the House later on. It ping-ponged. Each time we would lose ground. We lost it because Carter, although he campaigned on it, did not lift a finger compared to what he did to deregulate natural gas. We lost it by twenty votes in the House, although we had a two-thirds majority in the Senate waiting for it. That was the real beginning of the decline. Then Reagan was elected. We tried to be the watchdog. We put out investigative reports. They would not be covered.

"The press in the 1980s would say, 'Why should we cover you?'" Nader continued:

> "Who is your base in Congress?" I used to be known as someone who could trigger a Congressional hearing pretty fast in the House and Senate. They started looking towards the neoliberals and neocons and the deregulation mania. We put out two reports on the benefits of regulation, and they, too, disappeared. They did not get covered at all. This was about the same time that Tony Coelho taught the Democrats, starting in 1979 when he was head of the House Campaign Finance Committee, to start raising big-time money from corporate interests. And they did. It had a magical influence. It is the best example I have of the impact of money. The more money they raised, the less interested they were in any of these popular issues. They made more money when they screwed up the tax system. There were a few little gains here and there. We got the Freedom of Information [Act] through in 1974. And even in the 1980s we would get

some things done, [the General Services Administration] buying air-bag-equipped cars, the drive for standardized air bags. We would defeat some things here and there, block a tax loophole and defeat a deregulatory move. We were successful in staunching some of the deregulatory efforts.

Nader, locked out of the legislative process, decided to send a message to the Democrats, who were now beholden to corporate donors. He went to New Hampshire and Massachusetts during the 1992 primaries and ran as "None of the above." In 1996 he allowed the Green Party to put his name on the ballot before running hard in 2000 in an effort that spooked the Democratic Party. The Democrats, fearful of his grassroots campaign, blamed him for the election of George W. Bush, an attack that found fertile ground among those who had abandoned rational inquiry for the sound bites of television news.

Nader's status as a pariah corresponded with an unchecked assault on the working class by corporations and their tacit allies in the liberal class. Long-term unemployment, millions of foreclosures, crippling personal debts and bankruptcies, the evaporation of savings and retirement accounts, and the crumbling of the country's infrastructure are taking place as billions in taxpayer subsidies, obscene profits, bonuses, and compensation are doled out to corporate overlords. The drug and health-insurance companies, subsidized with billions in taxpayer funds, will soon legally force us to buy their defective products while remaining free to raise co-payments and premiums, especially if we get seriously ill. The oil, gas, coal, and nuclear power companies have made a mockery of Barack Obama's promises to promote clean, renewable energy. We are rapidly becoming a third-world country, cannibalized by corporations, with two-thirds of the population facing severe financial difficulty and poverty.

"You have a tug of war with one side pulling," Nader said:

The corporate interests pull on the Democratic Party the way they pull on the Republican Party. If you are a "least-worst" voter, you don't want to disturb John Kerry on the war, so you call off the anti-war demonstrations in 2004. You don't want to disturb Obama because McCain is worse. And every four years both parties get worse. There is no pull. That is the dilemma of the *Nation* and the *Progressive* and other similar publications. There is no breaking point. What is the breaking point? The criminal war of aggression in Iraq? The escalation of the war in Afghanistan? Forty-five thousand people dying a year because they can't afford health insurance? The hollowing out of communities and the movement of jobs to fascist and communist regimes overseas that know how to put the workers in their place? There is no breaking point. And when there is no breaking point, you do not have a moral compass.

The system is broken. And the consumer advocate who represented the best of our democracy, and the best of the liberal class, was broken with it. As Nader pointed out after he published *Unsafe at Any Speed* in 1965, it took only nine months for the Federal Government to regulate the auto industry for safety and fuel efficiency. Three years after the collapse of Bear Sterns, however, there is still no adequate financial reform. The large hedge funds and banks, from Citibank to Goldman Sachs, are using billions in taxpayer subsidies to engage once again in the speculative games that triggered the first financial crisis and will almost certainly trigger a second. The corporate media, which abet our vast historical amnesia, do nothing to remind us how we got here. They speak in the empty slogans handed to them by public relations firms, corporate paymasters, and the sound-bite society.

"If you organize one percent of the people in this country along progressive lines, you can turn the country around, as long as you give them infrastructure," Nader said:

> They represent a large percentage of the population. Take all the conservatives who work in Wal-Mart. How many would be against a living wage? Take all the conservatives who have preexisting conditions. How many would be for single-payer, not-for-profit health insurance? When you get down to the concrete, when you have an active movement that is visible and media-savvy, when you have a community, a lot of people will join. And lots more will support it. The problem is that most liberals are estranged from the working class. They largely have the good jobs. They are not hurting.

"The real tragedy is that citizens' movements should not have to rely on the commercial media, and public television and radio are disgraceful. If anything, they are worse," Nader said:

> In thirty-some years, [Bill] Moyers has had me on twice. We can't rely on the public media. We do what we can with Amy [Goodman] on *Democracy Now!* and Pacifica stations. When I go to local areas, I get very good press, TV, and newspapers, but that doesn't have the impact, even locally. The national press has enormous impact on the issues. It is not pleasant having to say this. You don't want to telegraph that you have been blacked out, but on the other hand you can't keep it quiet. The right wing has won through intimidation.

This intimidation works especially well in a culture of permanent war. In the months leading up to the war in Iraq, there were many credible critics, including former U.N. inspectors such as Hans Blix, who questioned the lies used to justify the invasion and occupation, but the media refused to include independent voices. The case for war, any war, is almost always presented without significant comment or criticism from the liberal class. Liberals are reduced to arguing over tactics.

The *Philadelphia Inquirer*, for example, published a front-page analysis the day after Hans Blix undermined President Bush and Secretary of State Colin Powell's plans to demand a U.N. Security Council war resolution. Blix had reported that the U.N. inspection teams were making progress. The *Inquirer* responded by writing: "President Bush now faces an unpleasant choice. He must decide whether to launch a final round of diplomacy aimed at repairing the breach with many U.S. allies and thus winning broader backing for war, or to abandon the United Nations, ignore global opinion, and launch an invasion with whatever allies will follow."[30] The third choice, not going to war at all, was never raised.

Martin Luther King Day has become a yearly ritual that seeks to turn a black radical into a red-white-and-blue icon. It has become a day that allows us to pat ourselves on the back for "overcoming" racism and "fulfilling" King's dream. It is a day filled with old sound bites about little black children and little white children that, given the state of America, would enrage King. Most of our great social reformers are sanitized for mainstream public consumption after their deaths, and turned into harmless props of American glory. King was not only a socialist but also fiercely opposed to American militarism. He was aware, especially at the end of his life, that racial justice without economic justice was a farce.

"King's words have been appropriated by the people who rejected him in the 1960s," said James Cone, who teaches at Union Theological Seminary in New York and is the author of *Martin & Malcolm & America*:

> So by making his birthday a national holiday, everybody claims him even though they opposed him while he was alive. They have frozen King in 1963 with his "I Have a Dream" speech. That is the one that can best be manipulated and misinterpreted. King also said, shortly after the Selma march and the riots in Watts, "They have turned my dream into a nightmare."

"Mainstream culture appeals to King's accent on love, as if it can be separated from justice," Cone said:

> For King, justice defines love. It can't be separated. They are intricately locked together. This is why he talked about *agape* love and not some sentimental love. For King, love was militant. He saw direct action and civil disobedience in the face of injustice as a political expression of love because it was healing the society. It exposed its wounds and its hurt. This accent on justice for the poor is what mainstream society wants to separate from King's understanding of love. But for King, justice and love belong together.[31]

Malcolm X, who could never be an establishment icon because of his refusal to appeal to the white ruling class and the liberal elite, converged with King's teachings in the last months of his life. But it would be wrong to look at this convergence as a domestication of Malcolm X. Malcolm influenced King as deeply as King influenced Malcolm. At the end of their lives, each saw the many faces of racism and realized that the issue was not simply sitting at a lunch counter with whites—blacks in the North could in theory do this—but rather being able to afford the lunch. King and Malcolm were both deeply informed by their faith. They adhered to belief systems, one Christian and the other Muslim, that demanded strict moral imperatives and justice.

King, when he began his calls for integration, argued that hard work and perseverance could make the American dream available for rich and poor, white and black. This is the staple message and mythology embraced by the liberal class. King grew up in the black middle class. He was well educated and comfortable in the cultural and social circles of the liberal class. He admitted that until his early twenties, life had been wrapped up for him like "a Christmas present." He naïvely thought that integration was the answer. He trusted, ultimately, in the liberal, white power structure to recognize the need for justice for all of its citizens. Like most college-educated blacks, he shared the same value system and preoccupation with success as the liberal whites with whom he sought to integrate.

But this was not Malcolm's America. Malcolm grew up in urban poverty in Detroit, dropped out of school in eighth grade, was shuttled between foster homes, was abused, hustled on city streets, and eventually ended up in prison. There was no evidence in his hard life of a political order that acknowledged his humanity or dignity. The white people he knew did not exhibit a conscience or compassion. And in the ghetto, where survival was a daily battle, nonviolence was not a credible option.

"No, I'm not an American," Malcolm said:

> I'm one of 22 million black people who are the victims of Americanism. One of the . . . victims of democracy, nothing but disguised hypocrisy. So I'm not standing here speaking to you as an American, or a patriot, or a flag-saluter, or a flag-waver—no, not I! I'm speaking as a victim of this American system. And I see America through the eyes of the victim. I don't see any American dream; I see an American nightmare![32]

King came to appreciate Malcolm's insights, especially after he confronted the insidious racism in Chicago. A visit to the Watts section of Los Angeles in 1965, two days after riots there, shook King, as did a dialogue with residents, in which they informed him that from their viewpoint, the vote was nice, but jobs would be better. As King said on the second anniversary of the Montgomery bus boycott, "any religion that professes to be concerned with the souls of men and is not concerned with the slums that damn them, the economic conditions that cripple them, is a spiritually moribund religion in need of new blood."[33]

"King began to see that Malcolm was right in what he was saying about white people," Cone explains. "Malcolm saw that white people did not have a conscience that could be appealed to to bring justice for African Americans. King realized that near the end of his life. He began to call most whites 'unconscious racists.' "

The crude racist rhetoric of the past has now been replaced by a refined, polite variety. We pretend there is equality and equal opportunity while ignoring the institutional and economic racism that infects our inner cities and fills our prisons, where a staggering one in nine black men between the ages of 20 and 34 is incarcerated. There are more African American men behind bars than in college. "The cell block," the poet Yusef Komunyakaa, told me, "has replaced the auction block."

The fact that prisons and urban ghettos are populated primarily with people of color is not an accident. It is a calculated decision by those who wield economic and political control. For the bottom third of African Americans, many of whom live in segregated enclaves in cities such as Detroit or Baltimore, little has changed over the past few decades. Life, in fact, has often gotten worse. But this is not a narrative acceptable to the liberal class, which speaks of a postracial America. The liberal class continues to insist that hard work is the route to a better life.

In the last months of his life, King began to adopt Malcolm's language, reminding listeners that the ghetto was a "system of internal colonialism."

"The purpose of the slum," King said in a speech at the Chicago Freedom Festival, "is to confine those who have no power and perpetuate their powerlessness. . . . The slum is little more than a domestic colony which leaves its inhabitants dominated politically, exploited economically, segregated and humiliated at every turn." Coming close to a teaching Malcolm had long espoused, King concluded that the chief problem is economic, and the solution is to restructure the whole society.

"Life, liberty, and the pursuit of happiness" was, as King and Malcolm knew, a meaningless slogan if there was no possibility of a decent education, a safe neighborhood, a job, or a living wage. King and Malcolm were also acutely aware that the permanent war economy was directly linked to the perpetuation of racism and poverty at home and abroad.

In a speech titled "Beyond Vietnam" given at Riverside Church a year before his assassination, King called America the "greatest purveyor of violence in the world today." That quote doesn't make it into many Martin Luther King Day celebrations. The *New York Times,* expressing the indignation of the liberal class, attacked King for his antiwar message. King's stance on the Vietnam War and demands for economic justice at the end of his life caused many in the liberal class, including members of his own staff, and allies within the white political power structure, to turn against him. King and Malcolm, in the final days of their lives, were solitary prophets.

"There are many ways in which Malcolm's message is more relevant today," said Cone, who also wrote *A Black Theology of Liberation*:

> King's message is almost entirely dependent on white people responding to his appeals for nonviolence, love, and integration. He depends on a positive response. Malcolm spoke to black people empowering themselves. He said to black people, "You may not be responsible for getting yourself into the situation you are in, but if want to get out, you will have to get yourself out. The people who put you in there are not going to get you out." King was appealing to whites to help black people. But King gradually began to realize that African Americans could not depend on whites as much as he had thought.

"King did not speak to black self-hate, and Malcolm did," Cone explained:

> King was a political revolutionary. He transformed the social and political life of America. You would not have Barack Obama today if

it had not been for King. Malcolm was a cultural revolutionary. He did not change the social or political structures, but he changed how black people thought about themselves. He transformed black thinking. He made blacks love themselves at a time when they hated themselves. The movement from being *Negro* and *colored* to being *black*, that's Malcolm. Black studies in the universities and black caucuses, that's Malcolm. King never would have done black studies. He taught a course at Morehouse on social and political philosophers and did not include a black person. He didn't have W.E.B. Du Bois or Frederick Douglass. None of them. He had all the white figures like Plato and Aristotle. Malcolm helped black people to love themselves.

King and Malcolm would have excoriated a nation that spends $3 trillion waging imperial wars in the Middle East and trillions more to fill the accounts of Wall Street banks while abandoning its poor. They would have denounced liberals who mouth platitudes about justice while supporting a party that slavishly serves the moneyed elite. These men spoke on behalf of people who had nothing left with which to compromise. And for this reason *they* did not compromise.

"You don't stick a knife into a man's back nine inches, pull it out six inches, and call it progress," Malcolm said.[34]

"I've decided what I'm going to do," King preached at one of his last sermons at Ebenezer Baptist Church:

I ain't going to kill nobody in Mississippi . . . [or] in Vietnam. I ain't going to study war no more. And you know what? I don't care who doesn't like what I say about it. I don't care who criticizes me in an editorial. I don't care what white person or Negro criticizes me. I'm going to stick with the best. On some positions, cowardice asks the question, "Is it safe?" Expediency asks the question, "Is it politic?" Vanity asks the question, "Is it popular?" But conscience asks the question, "Is it right?" And there comes a time when a true follower of Jesus Christ must take a stand that's neither safe nor politic nor popular but he must take that stand because it is right. Every now and then we sing about it, "If you are right, God will fight your battle." I'm going to stick by the best during these evil times.[35]

Because neither man sold out or compromised, they were killed. If King and Malcolm had lived, they, too, would have become pariahs, victims of the liberal class.

~

That liberal class is indifferent to the profound personal and economic despair sweeping through this country, still entranced with the aphrodisiac of Obama's victory. Liberals argue that offering unemployed people the right to keep their unemployed children on their nonexistent health-care policies is a step forward. They argue that passing a jobs bill that will give tax credits to corporations is a rational response to an unemployment rate that is, in real terms, close to 20 percent. They argue that the refusal to assist the estimated 2.8 million people forced out of their homes in 2009 and the estimated 2.4 million forced out of their homes in 2010 by foreclosure and bank repossessions is justified by the bloodless language of fiscal austerity.

Dean Henderson's career with FedEx ended abruptly when a reckless driver plowed into his company truck and mangled his leg. No longer able to drive, stripped of value in our commodity culture, he was tossed aside by the company. He became human refuse. Because of the swelling and the pain, he spends most of his days with his leg raised on a recliner in the tiny apartment in Fairfax, Virginia, which he shares with his stepsister. He struggles without an income and medical insurance. He fears his future.

Henderson is not alone. Workers in our corporate state earn little when they work—Henderson made $18 an hour—and they are abandoned when they can no longer contribute to corporate profits. It is the ethic of the free market. It is the cost of unfettered capitalism.

"This happened while I was wearing their uniform and driving one of their company vehicles," Henderson, a forty-year-old military veteran, told me:

> My foot is destroyed. I have a fused ankle. I have had over a dozen surgeries. It hurts to wear a sock. I was limping pretty badly, but in the spring of 2008, FedEx said I had to come back to work and sit in a chair. It saved them money on workers' compensation payments. I

worked a call center job and answered telephones. I did that for three months. I had my ankle fused in January 2009, and then FedEx fired me. I was discarded. They washed their hands of me, and none of this was my fault.[36]

Our destitute working class now understands that the cloying feel-your-pain language of the liberal class is a lie. The liberal class is not attempting to prevent wages from sinking, unemployment from mounting, foreclosures from ripping apart communities, or jobs from being exported. The gap between a stark reality and the happy illusions peddled by smarmy television news personalities, fatuous academic and financial experts, oily bureaucrats and politicians, is becoming too wide to ignore. Those cast aside are often willing to listen to anyone, no matter how buffoonish or ignorant, who promises that the parasites and courtiers who serve the corporate state will disappear. Right-wing rage is becoming synonymous with right-wing populism.

Obama, seduced by power and prestige, is more interested in courting the corporate rich than in saving the disenfranchised. Asked to name a business executive he admires, the president cited Frederick Smith of FedEx, although Smith is a union-busting Republican. Smith, who was a member of Yale's secret Skull and Bones Society along with George W. Bush and John Kerry, served as Senator John McCain's finance chair during McCain's failed run for the presidency. Smith founded FedEx in 1971, and the company had more than $35 billion in revenue in the fiscal year that ended in May 2009. Smith is rich and powerful, but there is no ethical system, religious or secular, that would hold him up as a man worthy of emulation. Such men build fortunes and little monuments to themselves off the pain and suffering of people like Henderson.

"He's an example of somebody who is thinking long-term," the president said of Smith in an interview with *Bloomberg Businessweek*, adding that he "really enjoyed talking" with him at a February 4, 2009, White House luncheon.

Smith does think in the long term. His company lavished money on many members of Congress in 1996 so they would vote for an ad hoc change in the law banning the Teamsters Union from organizing workers at FedEx. A few stalwarts in the Senate, including Edward Kennedy (in a speech reprinted in the Congressional Record on October 1, 1996) and his then-colleague Paul Simon, denounced the obvious political bribery. The company had bought its legislative exemption. Most members of Congress, then as now, had become corporate employees.

"I think we have to honestly ask ourselves, why is Federal Express being given preferential treatment in this body now?" Senator Simon said at the time. "I think the honest answer is Federal Express has been very generous in their campaign contributions."

Following the Senate vote, a company spokesman was quoted as saying, "We played political hardball, and we won."

What has happened to our historical memory? How did we forget that those who built our democracy and furthered the rights of American workers were not men like Smith, who use power and money to perpetuate the parochial and selfish interests of the elite, but the legions of embattled strikers in the coal fields, on factory floors, and in steel mills, who gave us unions, decent wages and the forty-hour work week? How was it possible to pass the Taft-Hartley Act, which, in one deft move, emasculated the labor movement? How is it possible that it remains in force? Union workers, who at times paid with their lives, halted the country's enslavement to the rich and the greedy. But now that unions have been broken, rapacious corporations like FedEx and toadies in Congress and the White House are transforming our working class into serfs.

UPS, by contrast with its competitor FedEx, is unionized. It is the largest employer of Teamsters members. Labor costs, because of the union, account for almost two-thirds of its operating expenses. But Smith of FedEx spends only a third of his costs on labor. There is something very wrong with a country that leaves a worker like Henderson in a tiny apartment in excruciating pain and fighting off depression while his former billionaire boss is fêted as a man of vision and invited to lunch at the White House. A country that stops taking care of its own, that loses the capacity for empathy and compassion, that crumples up human beings and throws them away when it is done with them, breeds dark ideological monsters that will inevitably rise to devour the body politic.

FedEx has lavished $17 million on Congress—double its 2008 total—to fight off an effort by UPS and the Teamsters to revoke Smith's tailor-made ban on unions. Smith, again thinking "long-term," plans to continue to hire thousands of full-time employees and list them as independent contractors. If his workers are listed as independent contractors, he does not have to pay Social Security, Medicare, and unemployment insurance taxes. And when they get sick or injured or old, he can push them onto the street.

Henderson says FedEx treats its equipment as shabbily as its employees. There is no difference between trucks and people to corporations that view everything as a commodity. Corporations exploit human beings and equipment, as well as natural, resources, until exhaustion or collapse.

"The trucks are a liability," Henderson said. "They are junk. The tires are bald. The engines cut out. There are a lot of mechanical problems. The roofs leak. They wobble and pull to one side or the other. The heating does not work. And the company pushes its employees in the same way. The first Christmas I was there, I worked thirteen hours without a break and without anything to eat."

VI / Rebellion

One of the only coherent philosophical positions is revolt. It is
a constant confrontation between man and his obscurity. . . .
It is not aspiration, for it is devoid of hope. That revolt is the
certainty of a crushing fate, without the resignation that
ought to accompany it.

—ALBERT CAMUS, *"An Absurd Reasoning"*[1]

ALEKSANDR HERZEN, speaking a century ago to a group of anarchists about how to overthrow the czar, reminded his listeners that it was not their job to save a dying system but to replace it: "We think we are the doctors. We are the disease." All resistance must recognize that the corporate coup d'état is complete. We must not waste our energy trying to reform or appeal to systems of power. This does not mean the end of resistance, but it does mean very different forms of resistance.

The economic devastation of global capitalism will soon be matched by ecological devastation. The liberal class's decision to abet the destruction of the global economy was matched by its tacit decision to abet the corporate destruction of the ecosystem on which human life depends. The valiant efforts of a few liberal activists, such as Bill McKibben, to organize worldwide demonstrations to pressure industrial and political leaders from the polluting nations to act swiftly at the Copenhagen Conference in December 2009, and thereby to thwart catastrophic environmental disaster, failed. The voices of the people did not register. The liberal class continued to bind itself to systems that, in theological terms, have become systems of death.

Our environment is being dramatically transformed in ways that soon will make it difficult for the human species to survive. We must direct our energies toward building sustainable, local communities to weather the coming crisis, since we will be unable to survive and resist without a cooperative effort. The liberal class, which clings to the decaying ideologies used to justify globalism and imperialism, which has refused to defy the exploitation or galvanize behind militants to halt the destruction of the ecosystem, has become a useless appendage. The decimation of our manufacturing base, the rise of the corporate state, and the contamination of our environment could have been fought by militant movements and radicals, but with these voices banished, there were no real impediments to the self-destructive forces of corporate power.

The liberal class, which sought consensus and was obedient when it should have fought back, continues to trumpet a childish faith in human progress. It continues to peddle the naïve belief that technology and science will propel us forward into greater eras of human prosperity and save us from ourselves. But Enlightenment rationality does not and will not dominate human activity. The human race is about to be abruptly reminded of the fragility of life and the danger of hubris. Those who exploit human beings and nature are bound to an irrational lust for power and money that is leading to collective suicide.

The liberal class assumed that by working with corporate power it could mitigate the worst excesses of capitalism and environmental degradation. It did not grasp, perhaps because liberals do not read enough Marx, the revolutionary and self-destructive nature of unfettered capitalism. American society, although it continues to use traditional and sentimental iconography and language to describe itself, has in fact been so radically transformed by liberal gullibility and unchecked corporatism that it bears no resemblance to its self-image. Corporate forces, whether in Copenhagen or the U.S. Congress, ignore the needs and desires of citizens. Corporate interests have seized all mechanisms of power, from government to mass propaganda. They will not be defeated through elections or influenced through popular movements. The working class has been wiped out. The economy is in ruins. The imperial expansion is teetering on collapse. The ecosystem is undergoing terrifying changes unseen in recorded human history. The death spiral, which will wipe out whole sections of the human race, demands a return to a radical militancy that asks the uncomfortable question of whether it is time to break laws that, if followed, ensure our annihilation.

The corporation state is now as cornered as the rest of us. The decimation of the working class and, increasingly, the middle class, means that corporations must employ ever greater levels of corruption and coercion to continue to increase profits. Human misery is being compounded—indeed, it is itself viewed as a source of profit. Corporations such as Bechtel are attempting to buy and control the world's supply of clean water. All essential elements for existence offer corporations the potential for profit. The demand for capitalist expansion, in a time of growing scarcity and environmental collapse, means we will endure harsher forms of abuse and repression.

By silencing those who clung to moral imperatives, the liberal class robbed itself of the language and analytical means to make sense of the destruction. Liberals assumed that the engines of capitalism could be persuaded to exercise a rational self-control and beneficence—a notion that would have gotten anyone who proposed it laughed out of old militant labor halls. The liberal class, seduced by the ridiculous dictum that the marketplace could be the arbiter of all human political and economic activity, handed away the rights of the working class and the middle class. Even after the effects of climate change became known, the liberal class permitted corporations to continue to poison and pollute the planet. The liberal class collaborated with these corporate forces and did so with a stunning gullibility. The short-term benefits of this collaboration will soon give way to a systems collapse.

The true militants of the American twentieth century, including the old communist unions, understood, in a way the liberal class does not, the dynamics of capitalism and human evil. They knew that they had to challenge every level of management. They saw themselves as political beings. They called for a sweeping social transformation that would include universal health insurance, subsidized housing, social reforms, deindustrialization, and worker-controlled factories. And for this they were destroyed. They were replaced by a pliant liberal class that spoke in the depoliticized language of narrow self-interest and pathetic "Buy American" campaigns. Our collapse, economic and environmental, might not have been thwarted by anarchists and others, but at least someone would have fought against it. The liberal class was useless.

The coup d'état we have undergone is beginning to fuel unrest and discontent. With its reformist and collaborative ethos, the liberal class lacks the capacity or the imagination to respond to this discontent. It has no ideas. Revolt, because of this, will come from the right, as it did in other eras of bankrupt liberalism in Nazi Germany, fascist Italy, and Tsarist Russia. That this revolt will be funded, organized, and manipulated by the corporate forces that caused the collapse is one of the tragic ironies of history. But the blame lies with the liberal class. Liberals, by standing for nothing, made possible the rise of inverted and perhaps soon classical totalitarianism.

As communities fragment under the weight of internal chaos and the increasingly dramatic changes caused by global warming and economic despair, they will face a difficult choice. They can retreat into a pure survivalist mode, a form of primitive tribalism, without linking themselves to the concentric circles of the wider community and the planet. This retreat will leave participants as morally and spiritually bankrupt as the corporate forces arrayed against us. It is imperative that, like the monasteries in the Middle Ages, communities nurture the intellectual and artistic traditions that make possible a civil society, humanism, and the common good. Access to parcels of agricultural land will be paramount. We will have to grasp, as the medieval monks did, that we cannot alter the larger culture around us, at least in the short term, but we may be able to retain the moral codes and culture for generations beyond ours. As those who retained their identity during slavery or the long night of twentieth-century fascism and communism discovered, resistance will be reduced to small, often imperceptible acts of defiance. Music, theatre, art, poetry, journalism, literature, dance, and the humanities, including the study of philosophy and history, will be the bulwarks that separate those who remain human from those who become savages.

We stand on the verge of one of the bleakest periods in human history, when the bright lights of civilizations will blink out and we will descend for decades, if not centuries, into barbarity. The elites, who successfully convinced us that we no longer possessed the capacity to understand the revealed truths presented before us or to fight back against the chaos caused by economic and environmental catastrophe, will use their resources to create privileged little islands where they will have access to security and goods denied to the rest of us. As long as the mass of bewildered and frightened people, fed images by the organs of mass propaganda that permit them to perpetually hallucinate, exist in this state of barbarism, they may periodically strike out with a blind fury against increased state repression, widespread poverty, and food shortages. But they will lack the ability and self-confidence to challenge in big and small ways the structures of control. The fantasy of widespread popular revolts and mass movements breaking the hegemony of the corporate state is just that—a fantasy.

Radical anarchists often grasp the extent of the rot in our cultural and political institutions. They know they must sever the tentacles of consumerism. But many also naïvely believe it can be countered with physical resistance and violence. There are debates within the anarchist movement about acceptable degrees of violent resistance. Some argue, for example, that we should limit ourselves to the destruction of property. But that is a dead end. Once you start using plastic explosives, innocent people get killed. The moment anarchic violence begins to disrupt the mechanisms of governance, the power elite will use these acts, however minor, as an excuse to employ disproportionate and ruthless force against real and suspected agitators, only fueling the fear and rage of the dispossessed.

There are times—and this moment in humane history may turn out to be one of them—when human beings are forced to respond to repression with violence. I was in Sarajevo during the war in Bosnia. We knew what the Serbian forces ringing the capital would do to us if they broke through the defenses and trench system around the besieged city. We had the examples of the Drina Valley or the city of Vukovar, where about a third of the Muslim inhabitants had been killed and the rest herded into refugee or displacement camps. The only choice, if one wanted to defend your family and community, was to pick up a weapon.

But violence has inherent problems. Those who proved most adept at defending Sarajevo came from the criminal class. When they were not shooting at Bosnian Serb forces, they were looting the apartments of ethnic Serbs in Sarajevo and often executing them, as well as terrorizing their fellow Muslims. When you ingest the poison of violence, even in a just cause, it corrupts, deforms, and perverts you.

Violence is also a drug. Those most addicted to violence are those who have access to weapons and a penchant for force. And killers rise to the surface of all armed movements, even those that could be defined as just, and contaminate them with the intoxicating and seductive power that comes with the capacity to kill and destroy. I have seen it in war after war. When you go down that road, you end up pitting your monsters against their monsters. And the sensitive, the humane, and the gentle, those with a propensity to nurture and protect life, are pushed aside and often murdered.

The romantic vision of war and violence is as prevalent among many on the radical left as it is in the mainstream culture. Those who resist with force cannot hope to defeat the corporate state. They will not sustain the cultural values that must be sustained if we are to have a future worth living. Armed resistance movements are always mutations of the violence that spawned them. I am not naïve enough to think I could have avoided these armed movements had I been a landless Salvadoran or Guatemalan peasant, a Palestinian in Gaza, or a Muslim in Sarajevo. Threatened on all sides with violence and destruction, I probably would have taken up a gun. But violent response to repression, whether it achieves its goals or not, is counterproductive. It always results in the brutal sacrifice of innocents and the destruction of the culture and traditions that make us human. Violence must be avoided, although finally not at the expense of our own survival. Nonviolent acts of disobedience and the breaking of laws to disrupt the corporate assault on human life and the ecosystem will keep us whole. Once we use violence against violence, we enter a moral void.

Democracy, a system designed to challenge the status quo, has been corrupted to serve the status quo. The abject failure of activists and the liberal class to push corporate, industrialized states toward serious environmental reform, to thwart imperial adventurism, or to build a humane policy toward the world's poor stems from an inability to face these new configurations of power.

Our passivity is due, in part, to our inability to confront the awful fact of extinction, either our own inevitable mortality or that of the human species. The emotional cost of confronting death is painful. We prefer illusion. In the wars I covered, highly educated and intelligent people, whether in the cafés in Sarajevo or later in Pristina in Kosovo, insisted that war would not break out. They, like us, failed to grasp that the paradigm of power had irrevocably altered and that the paradigm of resistance had to change as well. They, too, failed to envision the death of their society and their own mortal danger, although the edifice was also physically collapsing around them. It is a common human frailty that severs those within dying civilizations from their terminal condition.

The election of Obama was one more triumph of illusion over substance. It was a skillful manipulation and betrayal of the public by a corporate power elite. We mistook style and ethnicity—an advertising tactic pioneered by Calvin Klein and Benetton—for progressive politics and genuine change. The goal of a branded Obama, as with all brands, was to make passive consumers mistake a brand for an experience. And this is why Obama was named *Advertising Age*'s marketer of the year for 2008, beating out Apple and Zappos.

Obama had almost no experience besides two years in the Senate, where his voting record was a dismal capitulation to corporate power. But, once again, the electronic hallucinations that assault us rendered most voters incapable of thought and response. The superficial, the trivial, and the sensational mask our deep cultural, economic, political, and environmental disintegration as well as the newest political diversion approved by the corporate state. We remain hypnotized by flickering images we mistake for reality.

"Celebrity culture is a culture of faux ecstasy, since the passions it generates derive from staged authenticity rather than genuine forms of recognition and belonging," Chris Rojek writes:

> Materialism, and the revolt against materialism, are the only possible responses. Neither is capable of engineering the unifying beliefs and practices relative to sacred things that are essential to religious belief. The cult of distraction, then, is both a means of concealing the meaninglessness of modern life and of reinforcing the power of commodity culture. Celebrity culture provides monumental images of elevation and magic. The psychological consequence of this is to

enjoin us to adjust to our material circumstances and forget that life has no meaning.[2]

The belief that we can make things happen through positive thoughts, by visualizing, by wanting them, by tapping into our inner strength, or by understanding that we are truly exceptional, is peddled to us by all aspects of the culture, from Oprah to the Christian Right. It is magical thinking. We can always make more money, meet new quotas, consume more products, and advance our careers. This magical thinking, this idea that human and personal progress is somehow inevitable, leads to political passivity. It permits societies to transfer their emotional allegiance to the absurd—whether embodied in professional sports or in celebrity culture—and ignore real problems. It exacerbates despair. It keeps us in a state of mass self-delusion. Once we are drawn into this form of magical thinking, the purpose, structure and goals of the corporate state are not questioned. To question, to engage in criticism of the corporate collective, is to be seen as obstructive and negative. And these cultural illusions have grossly perverted the way we view ourselves, our nation, and the natural world. This magical thinking, coupled with its bizarre ideology of limitless progress holds out the promise of an impossible, unachievable happiness. It has turned whole nations, such as the United States, into self-consuming machines of death.

We can march in Copenhagen. We can join the International Day of Climate Action and its worldwide climate protests. We can compost in our backyards and hang our laundry out to dry. We can write letters to our elected officials. We can vote for Obama and chant, "Yes We Can," but the corporate power elite is no longer concerned with our aspirations. Appealing to their better nature, or seeking to influence the internal levers of power, will no longer work.

The rot of imperialism, which is always incompatible with democracy, militarizes domestic politics. This militarization, as Sheldon Wolin writes, combines with the cultural fantasies of hero worship and tales of individual prowess, eternal youthfulness, beauty through surgery, action measured in nanoseconds, and a dream-laden culture of ever-expanding control and possibility, to sever huge segments of the population from reality. Those who control the images control us. And while we have been entranced by the celluloid shadows on the walls of Plato's cave, these corporate forces have effectively dismantled Social Security, unions, welfare, public health services, and public housing—the institutions of social democracy. They have been permitted to pollute the planet, long after we knew the deadly consequences of global warming.

We are living through one of civilization's seismic reversals. The ideology of globalization, like all "inevitable" utopian visions, has imploded. The power elite, perplexed and confused, clings to the utopian dreams and outdated language of globalization to mask the political and economic vacuum. Massive bailouts, stimulus packages, giveaways, and short-term borrowing, along with imperial wars we can no longer afford, will leave the United States struggling with trillions in debt. Once China and the oil-rich states begin to walk away from our debt, which one day has to happen, interest rates will skyrocket. Eventually, the Federal Reserve will become the buyer of last resort. The Fed has printed perhaps as much as two trillion new dollars in the last two years. Forcing the Fed to buy this much new debt will see it, in effect, print trillions more. This is when inflation, most likely hyperinflation, will turn the dollar into junk. And at that point the entire system, beset as well by environmental chaos, breaks down.

Our mediocre and bankrupt elite, concerned with its own survival, spends its energy and our resources desperately trying to save a system that cannot be saved. Once credit dries up for the average citizen, once massive joblessness creates a permanent and enraged underclass, once the cheap manufactured goods that are the opiates of our commodity culture vanish, once water and soil become too polluted or degraded to sustain pockets of human life, we will probably evolve into a system that closely resembles classical totalitarianism, characterized by despotic fiefdoms. Cruder, more violent forms of repression will be employed as the softer mechanisms of control favored by inverted totalitarianism prove useless. And, as with collapsed civilizations in the past, the huge bureaucracy that sustained empire will cease to function as communities collapse into localized enclaves. The great monuments of capitalism, like the abandoned temples at Tikal, will stand as deserted relics of a lost age.

During its brief time on Earth, the human species has exhibited a remarkable capacity to kill itself off. The Cro-Magnons displaced or dispatched the Neanderthals. The European colonialists, with the help of smallpox and firearms, decimated the native populations in the Americas. Modern industrial warfare in the twentieth century took at least one hundred million lives, most of them civilians. And now we sit passive and dumb as corporations and the leaders of industrialized nations ensure that climate change will accelerate to levels that could mean the end of our species. *Homo sapiens*, are the "future-eaters," as the biologist Tim Flannery points out in *The Futrue Eaters: An Ecological History of the Australasian Lands and People.*

In the past, when civilizations went belly-up through greed, mismanagement, and the exhaustion of natural resources, human beings migrated somewhere else to pillage anew. But this time the game is over. There is nowhere else to go. The industrialized nations spent the last century seizing half the planet and dominating most of the other half. We giddily exhausted our natural resources, especially fossil fuel, to engage in an orgy of consumption and waste that poisoned the Earth and degraded the ecosystem on which human life depends.

Collapse this time around will be global. We will disintegrate together. The ten-thousand-year experiment of settled life is about to come to a crashing halt. And humankind, which thought it was given dominion over the Earth and all living things, will be taught a painful lesson about the necessity of balance, restraint, and humility. There is almost no human monument or city ruin more than five thousand years old. Civilization, Ronald Wright notes in *A Short History of Progress*, "occupies a mere 0.2 percent of the two and a half million years since our first ancestor sharpened a stone."[3]

We view ourselves as rational creatures. But is it rational to wait like sheep in a pen as oil and natural gas companies, coal companies, chemical industries, plastics manufacturers, the automotive industry, arms manufacturers, and the leaders of the industrial world, as they did in Copenhagen, steer us toward mass extinction? It is too late to prevent profound climate change. But why allow our ruling elite, driven by the lust for profits, to accelerate the death spiral? Why continue to obey the laws and dictates of our executioners?

The news is grim. The accelerating disintegration of Arctic Sea ice means that summer ice will probably disappear within the next decade. The dark open water will absorb more solar radiation than reflective white ice, significantly increasing the rate of global warming. The Siberian permafrost will disappear, sending up plumes of methane gas from underground. The Greenland ice sheet and the Himalayan-Tibetan glaciers will melt. Jay Zwally, a NASA climate scientist, declared in December 2007: "The Arctic is often cited as the canary in the coal mine for climate warming. Now, as a sign of climate warming, the canary has died. It is time to start getting out of the coal mines."[4]

But reality is rarely an impediment to human folly. The world's greenhouse gases have continued to grow since Zwally's statement. Global emissions of carbon dioxide (CO_2) from burning fossil fuels since 2000 have increased by three percent a year. At that rate, annual emissions will double every twenty-five years. James Hansen, the head of NASA's Goddard Institute for Space Studies and one of the world's foremost climate experts, has warned that if we keep warming the planet, it will be "a recipe for global disaster."[5] The safe level of CO_2 in the atmosphere, Hansen estimates, is no more than 350 parts per million (ppm). The current level of CO_2 is 385 ppm and climbing. This guarantees terrible consequences even if we act immediately to cut carbon emissions.

For three million years, the natural carbon cycle has ensured that the atmosphere contained less than 300 ppm of CO_2, which sustained the wide variety of life on the planet. The idea now championed by our corporate elite, at least those in contact with the reality of climate change, is that we will intentionally overshoot 350 ppm and then return to a safer climate through rapid and dramatic emission cuts. This, of course, is a theory designed to absolve the elite from doing anything now.

In his book *Requiem for a Species: Why We Resist the Truth About Climate Change*, Clive Hamilton warns that even "if carbon dioxide concentrations reach 550 ppm, after which emissions fell to zero, the global temperatures would continue to rise for at least another century. Moreover, once we reach 550 ppm a number of tipping points will have been crossed, and all efforts humans then make to cut their greenhouse gas emissions may be overwhelmed by 'natural' sources of greenhouse gases. In that case, rather than stabilizing at 550 ppm, 550 will be just another level we pass through one year on a trajectory to who knows where—1000 ppm perhaps."[6]

Copenhagen was perhaps the last chance to save ourselves. Barack Obama and the other leaders of the industrialized nations blew it. Radical climate change is certain. If annual emissions stop immediately, the past carbon emissions that remain in the atmosphere will still be enough to elevate global temperatures for centuries. It is only a question now of how bad it will become. The engines of climate change, climate scientists have warned, will soon create a domino effect that could thrust the Earth into a chaotic state for thousands of years before it regains equilibrium. "Whether human beings would still be a force on the planet, or even survive, is a moot point," Hamilton writes. "One thing is certain: there will be far fewer of us."[7]

We have fallen prey to the illusion that we can modify and control our environment, that human ingenuity ensures the inevitability of human progress, and that our secular god of science will save us. The "intoxicating belief that we can conquer all has come up against a greater force, the Earth itself," Hamilton writes. "The prospect of runaway climate change challenges our technological hubris, our Enlightenment faith in reason and the whole modernist project. The Earth may soon demonstrate that, ultimately, it cannot be tamed and that the human urge to master nature has only roused a slumbering beast."[8]

We face a terrible political truth. Those who hold power will not act with the urgency required to protect human life and the ecosystem. Decisions about the fate of the planet and human civilization are in the hands of moral and intellectual trolls such as BP's former chairman Tony Hayward. These political and corporate masters are driven by a craven desire to accumulate wealth at the expense of human life. They do this in the Gulf of Mexico. They do this in the factories in the southern Chinese province of Guangdong. The leaders of these corporations now determine our fate. They are not endowed with human decency or compassion. Yet their lobbyists make the laws. Their public relations firms craft the propaganda and trivia pumped out through systems of mass communication. Their money determines elections. Their greed turns workers into global serfs and our planet into a wasteland.

As climate change advances, we will face a choice between obeying the rules put in place by corporations, and rebellion. Those who work human beings to death in overcrowded factories in China and turn the

Gulf of Mexico into a dead zone are the enemy. They serve systems of death. They cannot be reformed or trusted.

The climate crisis is a political crisis. We will either defy the corporate elite, which will mean civil disobedience, a rejection of traditional politics for a new radicalism, and the systematic breaking of laws, or see ourselves consumed. Time is not on our side. The longer we wait, the more assured our destruction becomes. The future, if we remain passive, will be wrested from us.

If we build small, self-contained structures, ones that do as little harm as possible to the environment, we can perhaps weather the collapse. This task will be accomplished through the creation of communities with access to sustainable agriculture, able to sever themselves as much as possible from commercial culture and largely self-sufficient. These communities will have to build walls against the electronic propaganda and fear that will be pumped out over the airwaves. Canada will probably be a more hospitable place to do this than the United States, especially given America's undercurrent of violence. But in any country, those who survive will need isolated areas of farmland distant from urban areas, which will see food deserts in the inner cities, as well as savage violence, spread outward across the urban landscape as produce and goods become prohibitively expensive and state repression becomes harsher and harsher.

Acts of resistance are moral acts. They take place because people of conscience understand the moral, rather than the practical, imperative of rebellion. They should be carried out not because they are effective, but because they are right. Those who begin these acts are always few. They are dismissed by those in the liberal class, who hide their cowardice behind their cynicism. Resistance, however marginal, affirms the sanctity of individual life in a world awash in death. It is the supreme act of faith, the highest form of spirituality. Those who have carried out great acts of resistance in the past sacrificed their security and comfort, often spent time in jail, and in some cases were killed. They understood that to live in the fullest sense of the word, to exist as free and independent human beings, even under the darkest night of state repression, means to defy injustice. Any act of resistance is its own justification. It cannot be measured by its utilitarian effect. And the acts of resistance that sustain us morally are those that disrupt systems of power but do not violate the sanctity of human life—even, finally, the lives of those who enslave us.

When in April 1945 the dissident Lutheran pastor Dietrich Bonhoeffer was taken from his cell in a Nazi prison to the gallows, his last words were: "This is for me the end, but also the beginning."[9] Bonhoeffer knew that most of the citizens in Germany were complicit through their collaboration or silence in a vast enterprise of death. But however hopeless it appeared in the moment, he affirmed what we all must affirm. He did not avoid death. He did not, as a distinct individual, survive. But he understood that his resistance and even his death were acts that nurtured life. He gave, even to those who did not join him, another narrative. His defiance and his execution condemned his executioners.

Significant structural change will not occur in our lifetime. This makes resistance harder. It shifts resistance from the tangible, the immediate, and the practical, to the amorphous and the indeterminate. But to stop resisting is spiritual and intellectual death. It is to surrender to the dehumanizing ideology of totalitarian capitalism. Acts of resistance keep alive another way of being. They sustain our integrity and empower others, whom we may never meet, to stand up and carry the flame we pass to them. No act of resistance is useless, whether it is refusing to pay taxes, fighting for a Tobin tax, working to shift the neoclassical economics paradigm, revoking a corporate charter, holding global Internet votes, or using Twitter to catalyze a chain reaction of refusal against the neoliberal order. We must resist and trust that resistance is worthwhile. Our communities will sustain us, emotionally and materially. They will be the key to a life of defiance.

Those who resist, who continue to practice moral autonomy, will become members of the underclass. The remnants of traditional liberal institutions, including the media, labor, the church, the universities, the arts, and political parties will merge with the instruments of corporate oppression. As long as they collaborate with the power elite, liberal institutions will continue to offer a few collaborators positions of comfort and privilege. But all those who seek to work as artists, journalists, professors, labor organizers, dissident politicians, or clergy will increasingly struggle without adequate health insurance or reliable incomes. They will be unable to send their children to elite colleges. Their mortgages will be foreclosed. They will be denied credit cards. Their salaries, if they get any, will be miserable. They will no longer be members of the liberal class.

The death of the liberal class has been accompanied by a shift from a print-based culture to an image-based culture. The demise of newspapers—along with that of book publishing—coupled with the degradation of our educational system for all but the elites, has created a culture in which verifiable fact, which is rooted in the complexity and discipline of print, no longer forms the basis of public discourse or our collective memory. It has been supplanted by the blogosphere, the social media universe, and cable television. Print-based culture, in which fact and assertion could be traced and distinguished, has ceded to a culture of emotionally driven narratives where facts and opinions are interchangeable. This is a decline and a degeneration that has crippled the reality-based culture, in which fact was the foundation for opinion and debate, and ushered in a culture in which facts, opinions, lies, and fantasy are interchangeable. This shift has denied many citizens the intellectual tools for critical thought and civic dialogue—the discourse that creates informed citizens. Images and words defy the complex structures of print when isolated from context.

Language, as the cultural critic Neil Postman pointed out, "makes sense only when it is presented as a sequence of propositions. Meaning is distorted when a word or sentence is, as we say, taken out of context; when a reader or a listener is deprived of what was said before and after." Images, while giving the appearance of reality, distort it. The image dismembers reality. It "recreates the world in a series of idiosyncratic events." And it will be difficult to communicate with those within a culture that are fed hefty doses of emotionally charged images and words taken out of context.[10] Reality, once it is disconnected from print, is no longer placed in context. This will leave dissidents speaking in a language that will often be unintelligible to the wider society.

A populace entranced by these fragments, images, and spectacles, a populace that can no longer find the words to articulate what is happening to it, is cut off from rational discourse. It expresses reality through the use of selected and isolated facts, half-truths or lies, that do not make sense. Illusion becomes true. Artifacts from the print-based culture, such as newspapers, books, or classical drama—artifacts rooted in the complexity of print—attempt to present, examine and explain reality as something intimately related to the past. These print-based artifacts are based on the assumption that we cannot understand the present if we do not understand the past. Images and facts used to fuel a frenzy of chatter and melodrama speak in a different form. This visual language engenders confusion. It offers an endless whirlwind of emotion and cant. It fosters historical amnesia. As the culture has shifted from print to image, the old artifacts grounded in print have become as obtuse and unintelligible as hieroglyphics. Those who resist will be able to do so only as long as they wall off the new forms of communication and remain wedded to the complexity of print. But this will also result in rebels becoming foreigners in their own land.

The Internet, held out by many as a new panacea, is accelerating this cultural decline, as Matthew Hindman illustrates in his book *The Myth of Digital Democracy*. Internet traffic is dominated by a few principal corporate sites, Yahoo, Bing and Google, which aggregate and reproduce existing journalism and creative work. The goal, of course, is profit. The Web efficiently disseminates content, but it does not protect intellectual property rights. And this means financial ruin for journalists, academics, musicians, and artists. Creative work is released for free to Web providers who use it as bait for corporate advertising. And those who create reap little or nothing.

The great promise of the Internet—to open up dialogue, break down cultural barriers, promote democracy, and unleash innovation and creativity—is yet another utopian dream. The Internet is only accelerating our division into antagonistic clans, where we are sucked into virtual tribal groups that chant the same slogans and hate the same enemies. The Web, like the cable news outlets, forms anonymous crowds to vent collective rage, intolerance, and bigotry. These virtual slums do not seek communication or dialogue. They speak in the new absurdist language. They do not enrich our culture. They create a herd mentality in which those who express empathy for some perceived "enemy"—whether left or right—are denounced by their fellow travelers for their impurity. And the liberal class has become as corrupted by the Web as the right wing. Racism toward Muslims is as evil as anti-Semitism, but try to express this simple truth on a partisan Palestinian or Israeli Web site. These kinds of truths, that acknowledge human complexity, are what the liberal class once sought to protect. Social scientists have a name for this retreat into ideologically pure and intolerant ghettos: cyberbalkanization.

I spoke with Jaron Lanier, the father of virtual-reality technology. He warns of this frightening new collectivism in *You Are Not a Gadget*. He notes that the habits fostered by the Internet have further reconfigured how we relate to one another. He writes that the philosophy behind terms of art such as *Web 2.0, open culture, free software*, and the *long tail* have become enablers of this new collectivism. He sites Wikipedia, which consciously erases individual voices, and Google Wave, which permits users to edit what someone else has said in a conversation, as well as watch others as they input, as technologies that accelerate mass collective thought and mass emotions. Privacy, honesty, and self-reflection are obliterated in favor of image.

On the Internet, as in the wider society, the value and status of tastes and information are determined by the crowd, in what Lanier calls the "hive mentality." Music, books, journalism, commercials, bits of television shows and movies, along with inane YouTube videos, are thrust onto our screens and into the national consciousness based on their level of Internet traffic. Lanier says that one of the biggest mistakes he and other early computer scientists made while developing the Internet was allowing those whose works are displayed on the Internet to go unpaid. He says this decision has made it more difficult for those who create intellectual or artistic works to make a living or receive credit for their work. It has furthered the cultural rout against individual expression.

Twenty music tracks are downloaded illegally for every one bought online. It is a similar story for films and photographs. Pirated versions of newly released movies are available along with last week's *New York Times* bestsellers. Journalists, once able to sell articles to publications overseas, now see their work flash around the globe without hope of compensation. We are starving our professional critics and artists. We are turning culture and art over to part-time amateurs. And as creative artists and journalists vanish, so do the editors and producers who distill and give focus to creative and journalistic expression. The only journalism and art that will endure will be that which draws advertising. Cultural and artistic expression will be replaced by the tawdry, banal, and often idiotic distractions that draw huge numbers of YouTube hits or public-relations-created propaganda. And any work that cannot gain corporate sponsorship or attract advertising dollars will be ignored.

While disregard of intellectual property rights denies those who create the capacity to make a living from their work, aggregators such as Google make profits by collecting and distributing content to lure advertisers. Original work on the Internet, as Lanier points out, is almost always cut and mutilated. It is "copied, mashed up, anonymized, analyzed, and turned into bricks in someone else's fortress to support an advertising scheme." Lanier warns that if this trend is not halted, it will create a "formula that leaves no way for our nation to earn a living in the long term." The Internet has begun the final and perhaps the deadliest assault on the arts and intellectual inquiry.

"All of a sudden people have lost sight of the fact that people need to be paid for the work," Mark Kurlansky, who is the author of *Cod*, *Salt* and *1968*, told me:

> "I was doing a book signing in Boston for my book *The Food of a Younger Land* based on WPA food writing. I told the audience that this was the best of it, and I had discarded half of the stuff. This young guy came up to me afterwards and said, 'Why don't you take the stuff you discarded and post it on the Internet?' I was thinking, There are a couple of obvious problems, and why doesn't he see them?" First of all, if I discarded it, it was because I didn't think it was any good. And second of all, to be crude, what's in it for me? The public has this attitude that this is above money. It is not a coincidence that the only successful print medium left economically is financial journalism. It is a world that worships money. You pay your money, and you get your story.

Digital collectivism, Lanier warns, is destroying the dwindling vestiges of authentic journalism, creativity, and innovation that require time, investment, and self-reflection. The only income left for most of those who create is earned through self-promotion and the orchestration of celebrity. But, as Lanier points out, this turns all culture into a form of advertising. It fosters a social ethic in which the capacity for crowd manipulation, for the art of seduction, is valued more than truth, beauty, or intellect. Writers, musicians, artists, journalists, and filmmakers must transform themselves into celebrities to earn money, or vanish from public consciousness.

"Funding a civilization through advertising is like trying to get nutrition by connecting a tube from one's anus to one's mouth," Lanier says:

> "The body starts consuming itself. That is what we are doing online. As more and more human activity is aggregated, people huddle around the last remaining oases of revenue. Musicians today might still be able to get paid to make music for video games, for instance, because games are still played in closed consoles and haven't been collectivized as yet."[11]

Lanier is not opposed to the Internet. He is opposed to how it has evolved. He fears that if we fall into an economic tailspin, the Internet, like other innovative systems of mass communication such as television, will be used to exacerbate social enmity.

"The scenario I can see is America in some economic decline, which we seem determined to enter into because we are unable to make any adjustments, and a lot of unhappy people," Lanier said:

> The preponderance of them are [located in] rural areas and in the Red States, the former slave states. And they are all connected and get angrier and angrier. What exactly happens? Do they start converging on abortion clinics? Probably. Do they start converging on legislatures and take them over? I don't know, maybe. I shouldn't speak it. It is almost a curse to imagine these things. But any intelligent person can see the scenario I am afraid to see. There is a potential here for very bad stuff to happen.

The utopian promoters of the Internet insist that the "hive mind," the vast virtual collective, will propel us toward a brave new world. Lanier dismisses such visions as fantasies that allow many well-intentioned people to be seduced by an evolving nightmare.

"The crowd phenomenon exists, but the hive does not exist," Lanier explained:

All there is, is a crowd phenomenon, which can often be dangerous. To a true believer, which I certainly am not, the hive is like the baby at the end of *2001 Space Odyssey*. It is a supercreature that surpasses humanity. To me, it is the misinterpretation of the old crowd phenomenon with a digital vibe. It has all the same dangers. A crowd can turn into a mean mob all too easily, as it has throughout human history.

"There are some things crowds can do, such as count the jelly beans in the jar or guess the weight of the ox," Lanier said:

I acknowledge this phenomenon is real. But I propose that the line between when crowds can think effectively as a crowd and when they can't is a little different. If you read [James] Surowiecki's *The Wisdom of Crowds,* he, as well as other theorists, say that if you want a crowd to be wise, the key is to reduce the communication flow between the members so they do not influence each other, so they are truly independent and have separate sample points. It brings up an interesting paradox. The starting point for online crowd enthusiasts is that connection is good and everyone should be connected. But when they talk about what makes a crowd smart, they say people should not be talking to each other. They should be isolated. There is a contradiction there. What makes a crowd smart is the type of question you ask. If you ask a group of informed people to choose a single numeric value such as the weight of an ox, and they all have some reason to have a theory that is not entirely crazy, they will center on the answer. You can get something useful. This phenomenon is what accounts for price-fitting in capitalism. This is how markets can function. If you ask them to create anything, if you ask them to do something constructive or synthetic or engage in compound reasoning, then they will fail. Then you get something dull or an averaging-out. One danger of the crowd is violence, which is when they turn into a mob. The other is dullness or mundaneness, when you design by committee.

Humans, like many other species, Lanier says, have a cognitive switch that permits us to be individuals or members of a mob. Once we enter the confines of what Lanier calls a clan, even a virtual clan, we revert to the basest instincts within us. Technology evolves, but human nature remains constant. The twentieth century was the bloodiest in human history because human beings married the newly minted tools of efficient state bureaucracies, mass propaganda, and industrial slaughter with dark impulses that have existed since the dawn of the human species. "You become hypersensitive to the pecking order and to your sense of social status," Lanier said of these virtual clans:

> There is almost always the designated loser in your own group and the designated external enemy. There is the enemy below and the enemy afar. There become two classes of disenfranchised people. You enter into a constant obligation to defend your status, which is always being contested. It is time-consuming to become a member of one of these things. I see a lot of designs online that bring this out. There is a recognizable sequence, whether it is pianos, poodles, or jihad; you see people forming into these clans. It is playing with fire. There are plenty of examples of evil in human history that did not involve this effect, such as Jack the Ripper who worked alone. But most of the really bad examples of human behavior in history involve invoking this clan dynamic. No particular sort of person is immune to it. Geeks are no more immune to it than Germans or Russians or Japanese or Mongolians. It is part of our nature. It can be woken up without any leadership structure or politics. It happens. It is part of us. There is a switch inside of us waiting to be turned. And people can learn to manipulate the switch in others.

"The Machine Stops," a story published by E.M. Forster in 1909, paints a futuristic world where people are mesmerized by virtual reality. In Forster's dystopia, human beings live in isolated, tiny subterranean rooms, like hives, where they are captivated by instant messages and "cinematophoes"—machines that project visual images. The subterranean masses cut themselves off from the external world and are absorbed by a bizarre pseudoreality of voices, sounds, evanescent images, and abstract sensations that can be evoked by pressing a few buttons. The world of the Machine, which has replaced the real world with a virtual world, is accessed through an omniscient, impersonal voice.[12]

We are, as Forster understood, seduced and then enslaved by technology, from the combustion engine to computers to robotics. Human ingenuity is always hijacked by slave masters. They use the newest technologies to keep us impoverished, confused about our identity, and passive. The Internet, designed by defense strategists to communicate after a nuclear attack, has become the latest technological instrument of control. Technology is morally neutral. It serves the interests of those who control it. And those who control it today are destroying journalism, culture, and art while they herd the population into clans that fuel isolation, self-delusion, intolerance, and hatred.

"A common rationalization in the fledgling world of digital cultures back then was that we were entering a transitional lull before a creative storm—or were already in the eye of the storm," Lanier writes in his book. "But we were not passing through a momentary calm. We had, rather, entered a persistent somnolence, and I have come to believe that we will escape it only when we kill the hive."

The media, the arts, scholarship, and political and social movements must become conduits for unvarnished moral outrage and passion. We must defy systems, and even laws, that permit corporations to strangle our culture and the natural world. But, at the same time, all who speak in a moral voice, one tied to facts rather than illusions, will become freaks. It will be difficult to live with a conscience in an age of nihilism. Journalism will reach tiny audiences, just as the plays of Aristophanes or Racine attract small crowds in obscure theaters. Art and journalism will seek wealthy patrons who will come and go according to the dictates of their fortunes and their whims, but will not reach the larger society, which will be deluged with illusions and spectacles. A culture, once it no longer values truth and beauty, condemns its most creative and moral people to poverty and obscurity. And this is our destiny.

The French existentialist Albert Camus argued that our lives are meaningless. We cannot influence fate. We will all die, and our individual beings will be obliterated. But we have a choice in how we live.

"A living man can be enslaved and reduced to the historic condition of an object," Camus wrote. "But if he dies in refusing to be enslaved, he reaffirms the existence of another kind of human nature which refuses to be classified as an object."[13]

The rebel, for Camus, stands with the oppressed—the unemployed workers thrust into impoverishment and misery by the corporate state, the Palestinians in Gaza, the civilians in Iraq and Afghanistan, the disappeared who are held in our global black sites, the poor in our inner cities and depressed rural communities, immigrants, and those locked away in our prison system.

The elites and their courtiers in the liberal class always condemn the rebel as impractical. They dismiss the stance of the rebel as counterproductive. They chastise the rebel for being angry. The elites and their apologists call for calm, reason, and patience. They use the hypocritical language of compromise, generosity, and understanding to argue that we must accept and work with the systems of power. The rebel, however, is beholden to a moral commitment that makes it impossible to compromise. The rebel refuses to be bought off with foundation grants, invitations to the White House, television appearances, book contracts, academic appointments, or empty rhetoric. The rebel is not concerned with self-promotion or public opinion. The rebel knows that, as Augustine wrote, hope has two beautiful daughters, anger and courage—anger at the way things are and the courage to change them. The rebel knows that virtue is not rewarded. The act of rebellion justifies itself.

"You do not become a 'dissident' just because you decide one day to take up this most unusual career," Václav Havel said when he battled the communist regime in Czechoslovakia:

> You are thrown into it by your personal sense of responsibility, combined with a complex set of external circumstances. You are cast out of the existing structures and placed in a position of conflict with them. It begins as an attempt to do your work well, and ends with being branded an enemy of society. . . . The dissident does not operate in the realm of genuine power at all. He is not seeking power. He has no desire for office and does not gather votes. He does not attempt to charm the public. He offers nothing and promises nothing. He can offer, if anything, only his own skin—and he offers it solely because he has no other way of affirming the truth he stands for. His actions simply articulate his dignity as a citizen, regardless of the cost.[14]

The corporate elite does not argue that the current system is just or good, because it cannot, but it has convinced the majority of citizens that there is no alternative. But we are not slaves. We have a choice. We can refuse to be either a victim or an executioner. We have the moral capacity to say no, to refuse to cooperate. Any boycott or demonstration, any occupation or sit-in, any strike, any act of obstruction or sabotage, any refusal to pay taxes, any fast, any popular movement, and any act of civil disobedience ignites the soul of the rebel and exposes the dead hand of authority.

"There is beauty and there are the humiliated," Camus wrote. "Whatever difficulties the enterprise may present, I should like never to be unfaithful either to the second or the first."[15]

"There is a time when the operation of the machine becomes so odious, makes you so sick at heart, that you can't take part; you can't even passively take part, and you've got to put your bodies upon the gears and upon the wheels, upon the levers, upon all the apparatus, and you've got to make it stop," Mario Savio said in 1964 during the Berkeley Free Speech Movement. "And you've got to indicate to the people who run it, to the people who own it, that unless you're free, the machine will be prevented from working at all."[16]

The capacity to refuse to cooperate offers us the only route left to personal freedom and a life with meaning. Camus is right about the absurdity of existence. He is also right about finding meaning and self-worth in acts of rebellion that eschew the practical for the moral.

"Oh my soul," the ancient Greek poet Pindar wrote, "do not aspire to immortal life, but exhaust the limits of the possible."

Acts of rebellion permit us to be free and independent human beings. Rebellion chips away, however imperceptibly, at the edifice of the oppressor. Rebellion sustains the capacity for human solidarity. Rebellion, in moments of profound human despair and misery, keeps alive the capacity to be human. Rebellion is not the same as revolution. Revolution works towards the establishment of a new power structure. Rebellion is about perpetual revolt and permanent alienation from power. And it is ony in a state of rebellion that we can hold fast to moral imperatives that prevent a descent into tyranny. Empathy must be our primary attribute. Those who retreat into cynicism and despair, like Dostoyevsky's Underground Man, die spiritually and morally. If we are to be extinguished, let it be on our own terms.

The dispassionate, objective creed of the liberal class, which made them mere photographers of human reality, is useless to the rebel. It is an ideology that serves those we must defy. The cri de coeur for reason, logic, and truth, for a fact-based society, for political and social structures designed to protect the common good, will be the flag carried by forlorn and militant remnants of our dying civilization. Cicero did this in ancient Rome. But he was as despised by the crowd as he was by the power elite. When his severed head and hands were mounted on the podium in the Colosseum, and his executioner Mark Antony announced that Cicero would speak and write no more, the tens of thousands of spectators roared their approval. Tyranny in an age of chaos is often greeted with palpable relief. There often is no public outcry. The rebel must, for this reason, also expect to become the enemy, even of those he or she is attempting to protect.

The indifference to the plight of others and the cult of the self is what the corporate state seeks to instill in us. That state appeals to pleasure, as well as fear, to crush compassion. We will have to continue to fight the mechanisms of that dominant culture, if for no other reason than to preserve, through small, even tiny acts, our common humanity. We will have to resist the temptation to fold in on ourselves and to ignore the injustice visited on others, especially those we do not know. As distinct and moral beings, we will endure only through these small, sometimes imperceptible acts of defiance. This defiance, this capacity to say no, is what mass culture and mass propaganda seeks to eradicate. As long as we are willing to defy these forces, we have a chance, if not for ourselves, then at least for those who follow. As long as we defy these forces, we remain alive. And, for now, this is the only victory possible.

Notes

EPIGRAPH:

1. George Orwell, "Freedom of the Press," unprinted introduction to *Animal Farm*, first printed, ed. Bernard Crick, Times Literary Supplement, September 15, 1972: 1040.

CHAPTER 1: RESISTANCE

1. Karl Polanyi, *The Great Transformation* (Boston: Beacon Press, 2001), 76.
2. Ernest Logan Bell, interview, Norwich, New York, March 30, 2010.
3. John Gray, *Liberalism* (Minneapolis: University of Minnesota Press, 2003), 86.
4. C. Wright Mills, *The Politics of Truth: Selected Writings of C. Wright Mills* (New York: Oxford University Press, 2008), 126–128.
5. Russell Jacoby, *The End of Utopia: Politics and Culture in an Age of Apathy* (New York: Basic Books, 1999), 10–11.
6. Irving Howe, "This Age of Conformity," in *The Partisan Review Anthology*, eds. William Phillips and Philip Rahv (New York: Holt, Rinehart and Winston, New York, 1961), 148.
7. Ibid., 148–149.
8. Fyodor Dostoevsky, *Notes from Underground*, trans. Richard Pevear and Larissa Volokhonsky (New York: Everyman 1993), 7.

CHAPTER 2: PERMANENT WAR

1. Reinhold Niebuhr, *Beyond Tragedy* (New York: Charles Scribner's Sons, 1965), 39.
2. Dwight Macdonald, *The Root Is Man* (Brooklyn, NY: Autonomedia, 1995), 81.
3. Richard Rorty, *Achieving Our Country: Leftist Thought in Twentieth-Century America* (Cambridge, MA: Harvard University Press, 1998), 90.
4. "Austin Plane Crash: Full Text of Joe Stack online suicide note posted on website embeddedart.com." February 18, 2010, http:www.nydailynews.com /news/national/2010/02/18/2010-02-18_austin_plane_crash_full_text_joe_ stack_manifesto_posted_on_website_embeddedartco.html.

5. Ching Kwan Lee, *Against the Law: Labor Protests in China's Rustbelt and Sunbelt* (Berkeley: University of California Press, 2007), x.

6. Ibid., 162.

7. Ibid., 164.

8. Ibid.

9. Ibid., 264.

10. Ibid., 265.

11. Palagummi Sainath, "Series on farmers' suicides in Andhra, 2004. *India Together*, http:www.indiatogether.org/opinions/psainath/suiseries.htm.

12. P. Sainath, "Neo-Liberal Terrorism in India: The Largest Wave of Suicides in History," *Counterpunch* February 12, 2009, http:www.counter punch.org/sainath02122009.html.

13. Noam Chomsky, "The Center Cannot Hold: Rekindling the Radical Imagination," address to the Left Forum, Pace University, New York, March 21, 2010. Posted May 31, 2010, http:www.democracynow.org/2010/5/31/noam_chomsky_the_center_cannot_hold.

14. Noam Chomsky, Interview, New York, April 13, 2010.

15. Norman Finkelstein, Interview, New York, March 9, 2010.

16. Edward S. Herman and Noam Chomsky, *Manufacturing Consent: The Political Economy of Mass Media* (New York: Pantheon Books, 2002), 174.

17. Lee Feinstein and Anne-Marie Slaughter, "A Duty to Prevent," *Foreign Affairs* January/February 2004, http:www.foreignaffairs.com/articles/59540/lee-feinstein-and-anne-marie-slaughter/a-duty-to-prevent.

18. Michael Ignatieff, "Friends Disunited," *Guardian*, March 24, 2003, http:www.guardian.co.uk/politics/2003/mar/24/iraq.world.

19. *Fresh Air with Terry Gross*, National Public Radio, March 18, 2003.

20. The Academy of Motion Picture Arts and Sciences has an official YouTube channel of "important" Oscar speeches, but does not include Moore's speech. That speech appears at http:www.tagg.org/rants/mmooreoscar.html.

21. Tony Judt, "Bush's Useful Idiots," *London Review of Books* 28:18 (September 21, 2006), 3–5.

22. Jeremy Scahill, interview, Washington, DC, April 28, 2010.

23. Josh Stieber, interview, Washington, DC, April 28, 2010.

24. Malalai Joya, interview, New York, October 28, 2009.

25. Quoted in Michelle Nichols, "Afghan opium feeding Europe, Russia, Iran addicts," Reuters, October 21, 2009, http:www.reuters.com/article/idUSN20440001.

26. Matthew Hoh, Resignation letter to Ambassador Nancy J. Powell, September 10, 2009, http:www.docstoc.com/docs/13944018/Matthew-Hoh-Resignation-Letter.

27. Peter van Agtmael, *2nd Tour, Hope I Don't Die* (Portland, OR: Photolucida, 2009), 88.

28. Lori Grinker, *Afterwar: Veterans from a World in Conflict* (Milford, NY: de.MO, 2005), 58–59.

29. Ibid., 63.

30. Ibid., 96–107.

31. Ibid., 120–121.

32. Ibid., 124–125.

33. Peter van Agtmael, *2nd Tour, Hope I Don't Die*, 64–65.

CHAPTER 3: DISMANTLING THE LIBERAL CLASS

1. Randolph Bourne, *War and the Intellectuals* (Indianapolis, IN: Hackett, 1999), 3.

2. "Capper of Kansas Now Backs Wilson," *New York Times*, March 25, 1917.

3. D.S. Jordan to W. Kent, April 1, 1917, the Papers of William Kent, Yale University Library.

4. Randolph Bourne, *The War and the Intellectuals* (Indianapolis: Hackett, 1999), 3–4.

5. See Ernest Freeberg, *Democracy's Pioneer: Eugene Debs, the Great War, and the Right to Dissent* (Cambridge, MA: Harvard University Press, 2009), 136.

6. "Albert Edwards" [Arthur Bullard], "Under the White Terror," *Colliers*, April 28, 1906.

7. Ronald Steel, *Walter Lippmann and the American Century* (New York: Atlantic-Little Brown, 1980), 125.

8. Quoted in United States Committee on Public Information, *National Service Handbook*, Red, White and Blue Series, No. 2 (Washington, DC: 1917), title page.

9. George Creel, *Rebel at Large: Recollections of Fifty Crowded Years* (New York: G. P. Putnam's Sons, 1947), 157.

10. Robert Lansing, *War Memoirs of Robert Lansing, Secretary of State* (Indianapolis, IN: Bobbs-Merrill, 1935), 208.

11. "Radicals at Work for German Peace," *New York Times*, June 24, 1917, 7.

12. Stuart Ewen, *Captains of Consciousness: Advertising and the Social Roots of the Consumer Culture* (New York: Basic Books, 2001), 62.

13. John Dos Passos, *Mr. Wilson's War* (New York: Doubleday, 1962), 300.

14. Quoted in Dos Passos, *Mr. Wilson's War*, 301.

15. "Debs urges strike if nation fights," *New York Times*, March 8, 1917, 3.

16. George Sylvester Viereck, *Spreading the Germs of Hate* (New York: Horace Liveright, 1930), 178–179.

17. Dos Passos, *Mr. Wilson's War*, 302.

18. Jane Addams, *Peace and Bread in Times of War* (New York: Macmillan, 1922), 134.

19. Dos Passos, *Mr. Wilson's War*, 300.

20. Addams, *Peace and Bread in Time of War*, 182.

21. "Senators Tell What Bolshevism in America Means," *New York Times*, June 15, 1919, 40.; U.S. Senate Subcommittee on the Judiciary, Brewing and Liquor Licenses, 3:114, 123, 146–147.

22. Stewart Halsey Ross, *Propaganda for War: How the United States Was Conditioned to Fight the Great War of 1914–1918* (Jefferson, NC: McFarland and Company, 1996), 280.

23. Sidney Pollard, *The Idea of Progress: History and Society* (London: C. A. Watts, 1968), 9ff.

24. Quoted in Sidney Lens, *Labor Wars: From the Molly Maguires to the Sit-downs* (New York: Doubleday, 1973), 152.

25. Dwight Macdonald, *The Root Is Man* (Brooklyn, NY:Autonomedia, 1995), 67.

26. Ibid., 146.

27. John Houseman, *Unfinished Business* (London: Chatto and Windos, 1986), 87.

28. Mark Blitzstein, *The Cradle Will Rock*, 31, Sketch 6.

29. Ibid., 13, Sketch 3.

30. Hallie Flanagan, *Arena: The History of the Federal Theatre* (New York: Benjamin Bloom, 1940), 202–203.

31. Blitzstein, *The Cradle Will Rock*, page 15, Sketch 4.

32. Karen Malpede, interview, New York, June 6, 2010.

33. Flanagan, 364–365.

34. Ibid., 366.

35. Ibid.

36. Malpede., 367.

37. Malcom Cowley, *Exile's Return* (New York: Penguin, 1994), 58.

38. Russell Jacoby, *The Last Intellectuals* (New York: Basic Books, 1987), 67–68.

39. Ibid., 71.

40. Cowley, *Exile's Return*, 60–61.

41. Ibid., 62–63.

42. Ibid., 66–67.

43. Ibid., 149.

44. Irving Howe, *World of Our Fathers* (New York: Simon and Schuster, 1983), 501, cited in Jacoby, *The Last Intellectuals*.

45. Quoted in Victor Navasky, *Naming Names* (New York: Viking 1980), 48.

46. Walter Bernstein, *Inside Out: A Memoir of the Blacklist*, (New York: Alfred A. Knopf, 1996), 185.

47. Drama Mailbag, *New York Times*, October 16, 1955, x3.

48. Bernstein, *Inside Out*, 186.

49. Ellen Schrecker, *Many Are the Crimes: McCarthyism in America* (Boston: Little, Brown, 1998), 412.

CHAPTER 4: POLITICS AS SPECTACLE

1. Philip Roth. "On the Air," *New American Review* 10 (August 1970), 20.

2. Peter B. Levy, *The New Left and Labor in the 1960s* (Urbana, IL: University of Illinois Press, 1994), 47–48.

3. Sharon Smith, *Subterranean Fire: A History of Working-Class Radicalism in the United States* (Chicago: Haymarket Books, 2006), 216–217.

4. Murray Bookchin, *Towards an Ecological Society* (Montreal: Black Rose Books, 1980), 11–12.

5. Irving Howe, "The Age of Conformity," 151.

6. Ibid., 152.

7. Neal Gabler, *Life: The Movie: How Entertainment Conquered Reality* (New York: Vintage, 1988), 132.

8. Ibid., 135.

9. Eva Cockroft, "Abstract Expressionism, Weapon of the Cold War," in Francis Frascina, ed., *Pollock and After: The Critical Debate* (New York: Harper & Row, 1985), 132.

10. Carol Becker, *Zones of Contention: Essays on Art, Institutions, Gender and Anxiety* (Albany, NY: State University of New York Press, 1996), 9.

11. Alan Magee, interview, New York, March 30, 2010.

12. Rob Shetterly, interview, New York, July 11, 2010.

13. Ben Fulton, "Calling on artists to lead the way; Fine arts: Columbia University dean Carol Becker to speak at U," *Salt Lake Tribune*, March 27, 2010.

14. C. Wright Mills, *The Power Elite* (Oxford: Oxford University Press, 2000), 318–319.

15. C. Wright Mills, *White Collar* (New York: Oxford University Press, 1956), 130–131, 158–159.

16. Ellen Schrecker, *Many Are the Crimes: McCarthyism in America* (Boston: Little, Brown and Company, 1998), 413.

17. Ian Buchanan, *Frederick Jameson: Live Theory* (New York: Continuum, 2007), 81.

18. Russell Jacoby, *The End of Utopia: Politics and Culture in an Age of Apathy* (New York: Basic Books, 1999), 63.

19. Ibid., 63–64.

20. Zachary Karabell, *What's College For? The Struggle to Define American Higher Education* (New York: Basic Books, 1998), 94–95.

21. James W. Carey, *Communication as Culture: Essays on Media and Society* (New York: Routledge, 1992), 81.

22. Ibid., 77.

23. Ibid., 84.

24. C. Wright Mills, *The Power Elite* (New York: Oxford University Press, 1956), 314.

25. Doug McGill, interview by phone from Rochester, Minnesota, January 8, 2010.

26. Jackson J. Benson, *The True Adventures of John Steinbeck* (New York: Viking, 1984), 333.

27. Cited by Doug McGill in *The McGill Report*.

CHAPTER 5: LIBERAL DEFECTORS

1. Karl Popper, *The Open Society and Its Enemies* (Princeton, N.J.: Princeton University Press, 1971), 34–35.

2. Edward W. Said, *Representations of the Intellectual: The 1993 Reith Lectures* (New York: Vintage, 1996), 100–101.

3. Stanley Hoffman, "An American Social Science: International Relations," *Daedalus*, 106:3, "Discoveries and Interpretations: Studies in Contemporary Scholarship, Vol. I," (Summer 1977), 49–55.

4. Julien Benda, *The Treason of Intellectuals* (New Brunswick, N.J.: Transaction Publishers, 2009), 43–45.

5. "Fear and Favor at The New York Times" by Pete Hamill, *The Village Voice*, October 1, 1985.

6. Sydney Schanberg, interview, New York, January 18, 2010.

7. Norman Finkelstein, interview, New York, March 14, 2010.

8. Brian Knowlton and Michael M. Grynbaum, "Greenspan 'Shocked' that Free Markets Are Flawed," *New York Times*, October 23, 2008.

9. Tom Friedman, interview on *Charlie Rose*, Public Broadcasting System, May 30, 2003, http:video.google.com/videoplay?docid=3800770925110269 212#.

10. Martha Hennessy, interview, New York, September 24, 2008.

11. Dorthy *Day, By Little and By Little: The Selected Writings of Dorthy Day*, ed. Robert Ellsberg (New York: Alfred A. Knopf, 1983), 98.

12. Father Daniel Berrigan, interview, New York, May 7, 2009.

13. Father Daniel Berrigan, interview, New York, May 13, 2008.

14. Davidson Loehr, interview, Austin, Texas, June 19, 2010.

15. D.D. Guttenplan, *American Radical: The Life and Times of I. F. Stone* (New York: Farrar, Straus and Giroux, 2009), x.

16. Ibid.

17 Ibid., 232.

18. Ibid., 475.

19. Ibid., 473.

20. Ibid., 232.

21. Ibid., xiii.

22. Ibid., 408–409.

23. Ibid., 431.

24. Abe Peck, *Uncovering the Sixties: The Life and Times of the Underground Press* (New York: Citadel Press, 1991), 142.

25. Edward Herman and Noam Chomsky, *Manufacturing Consent*, 300.

26. Ralph Nader, interview, Washington, DC, March 30, 2010.

27. David Cay Johnston, interview, by phone from Rochester, New York, March 7, 2010.

28. Lewis F. Powell, "Attack on th eAmerican Free Enterprise System," U.S. Chamber of Commerce, August 23, 1971, http:www.reclaimdemocracy.org/ corporate_acountability/Powell_memo_lewis.html.

29. Ralph Nader, in Henriette Mantel and Steve Skrovan, *Directors, An Unreasonable Man*, Submarine Entertainment, 2006.

30. Warren P. Strobel, "Dealt a Setback, Bush Now Faces a Difficult Choice," Philadelphis Inquirer, February 15, 2003, A01.

31. James Cone, interview, Princeton, New Jersey, January, 16, 2010.

32. Malcolm X, Corey Methodist Church, Cleveland, Ohio, April 3, 1964.

33. See King's address, "Some Things We Must Do," given December 5, 1957, on the second anniversary of the Montgomery bus boycott.

34. Malcolm X, panel discussion on WNDT-TV, New York, 1963.

35. Martin Luther King, "Guidelines for a Conservative Church," Sermon given June 5, 1966, at Ebenezer Baptist Church, Atlanta.

36. Dean Henderson, interview, Fairfax, Virginia, February 20, 2010.

CHAPTER 6: REBELLION

1. Albert Camus, "The Myth of Sisyphus," in *The Plague, The Fall, Exile and the Kingdom, and Selected Essays* (New York: Everyman, 2004), 536.

2. Chris Rojek, *Celebrity* (London: Reaktion Books, 2001), 90–91.

3. Ronald Wright, *A Short History of Progress* (New York: Carroll & Graf, 2005), 55.

4. Seth Borenstein, Associated Press, "Data Show 'Arctic Is Screaming,'

Scientists Say," *New York Sun*, December 12, 2007, http:www.nysun.com/foreign/data-show-arctic-is-screaming-scientists-say/67928.

5. James Hansen, "Global Warming Twenty Years Later: Tipping Points Near," speech to the National Press Club, Washington, June, 23 2008, www.columbia.edu/~jeh1/2008/TwentyYearsLater_20080623.pdf.

6. Clive Hamilton, *Requiem for a Species: Why We Resist the Truth About Climate* Change (Washington, DC: Earthscan, 2010), 27–28.

7. Ibid., 22.

8. Clive Hamilton, "Is It Too Late to Prevent Catastrophic Climate Change?," lecture, Royal Society of the Arts, Sydney, Australia, October 21, 2009, http:www.clivehamilton.net.au/cms/index.php?page=articles.

9. Letter of October 13, 1953, from Payne Best to George Bell, in Dietrich Bonhoeffer Works, Vol. 16, *Conspiracy and Imprisonment*, 1940–1945, trans. by Lisa E. Dahill (Minneapolis, NM: Fortress Press, 2006), 468.

10. Neil Postman, *Amusing Ourselves to Death: Public Discourse in the Age of Show Business* (New York: Penguin, 1985), 73.

11. Jason Lanier, interview, San Francisco, February 12, 2010.

12. E. M. Forester, "The Machine Stops," in *Selected Stories* (New York: Penguin, 2001), 91–123.

13. Albert Camus, *The Rebel: An Essay on Man in Revolt*, trans. by Anthony Bower (New York: Vintage, 1956), 238.

14. Vaclav Havel, *The Power of the Powerless: Citizens Against State in Central Europe*, ed. John Keane (Armonk, NY: M. E. Sharpe, 1990), 63.

15. Albert Camus, "Return to Tipasa," in *Lyrical and Critical Essays*, ed. Philip Thody, trans. by Ellen Conroy Kenny (New York: Alfred A. Knopf, 1968), 169–170.

16. Mario Savio, speech on the steps of Sproul Hall, University of California, Berkeley, California, Free Speech Movement Sit-in, December 2, 1964. http:www.americanrhetoric.com/speeches/mariosaviosproulhallsitin.htm.

Acknowledgments

Eunice Wong is my most astute critic, my most important and trusted editor, and as talented a writer as she is an actor. Every idea and theme in this book was discussed, dissected, and debated with her. All that I write passes through her hands, usually a few times. Our marriage is a rare mixture of the intellectual, the emotional, the physical, and the spiritual. I want to weigh time down with boulders to prolong and hold every moment I have with her.

The *Nation* Institute, the Ford Foundation and the Lannan Foundation offered generous support. I am grateful to Hamilton Fish, Ruth Baldwin, Taya Grobow and Jonathan Schell, as well as Roane Carey and Katrina vanden Heuvel at the *Nation* magazine. Carl Bromley at Nation Books once again lifted my writing to another level. His editing is always marked by his deep intelligence, his skill as a writer, and his profound erudition. Michele Jacob, whom I have worked with on several books, again handled publicity and book events with her usual charm, patience, and efficiency. Patrick Lannan and Jo Chapman at the Lannan Foundation have for several years provided steady and invaluable support. I would find it hard to survive as a writer without them. Calvin Sims at the Ford Foundation got immediately what I was trying to do, which is not surprising, given the skill and intelligence he exhibited as reporter and foreign correspondent for the *New York Times*, and made my grant and work with Ford possible.

I run all my ideas and thoughts past the Reverend Coleman Brown, my former professor of religion and ethics at Colgate University. He has been my moral and intellectual mentor for more than three decades, and his counsel is invaluable.

John Timpane again edited the final manuscript. He has an amazing mind, an infectious love of learning, and a breadth of knowledge that is as expansive as it is intimidating. He is also endowed with a wide array of talents. He is a gifted writer, poet, and musician. It is not fair to the rest of us.

Deena Guzder did much of the research for the book. She is a great writer, a tenacious journalist, and woman with a conscience that will save her from the contamination of commercial journalism. Jake Willard-Crist assisted me with the final editing of the book. I was very fortunate to have their help. I would like to thank Robert Scheer, one of the most courageous and important jour-

nalists in the country, and Zuade Kaufmann, who together run the Web magazine *Truthdig*, where I write a weekly column. They provide the reading public
with a precious gift. I have, over the years, received encouragement, support,
and advice from Henry Giroux, who helped me with sections of this book; Dud
and Jean Hendrick, who let us stay in their cottage on Deer Isle in Maine;
Bernard Rapoport, Peter Lewis, and Jean Stein; Ralph Nader, whom I am proud
to have supported for president; Robert Jensen, Larry Joseph, Steve Kinzer,
Sami and Laila al-Arian, Peter Scheer, Ann and Walter Pincus, Maria-Christina
Keller, Lauren B. Davis, June Ballinger, Michael Goldstein, Gerald Stern, Anne
Marie Macari, Robert J. Lifton, and Tom Artin; James Cone, one of our
nation's most important theologians; Ray Close, the Reverend Michael
Granzen, the Reverend Karen Hernandez, Joe and Heidi Hough, Mark Kurlan-
sky, Margaret Maurer, Irene Brown, Sam Hynes, the great graphic novelist Joe
Sacco, Dennis Kucinich, Ernest Logan Bell, Sonali Kolhatkar, Francine Prose,
Russell Banks, Celia and Bernard Chazelle, Esther Kaplan, James Ridgeway; the
Reverend Jeremiah Wright, who became a friend when we received honorary
doctorates together at Starr King School for the Ministry; Paul Woodruff; Sheldon Wolin, our greatest living political philosopher; "Rocky" Anderson; Tom
Cornell; Noam Chomsky, who sets the intellectual gold standard for the rest of
us; Father Michael Doyle and Father Daniel Berrigan, two Catholic priests who
remind us that the church can once in a while produce prophets; Pam Dia-
mond, James Kane, the Reverend Davidson Loehr, and Karen Malpede; Stuart
Ewen, whose books proved vital to my understanding of the rise of the propa-
ganda state; Norman Finkelstein, whose moral courage I admire; John Ralston
Saul, a philosopher who gave me a vocabulary to understand much of what is
happening in contemporary culture; the uncompromising Cindy Sheehan;
Sydney Schanberg, Malalai Joya, Michael Moore, Jeremy Scahill, Sam Smith,
Rob Shatterly, Alan Magee, Doug McGill, Jaron Lanier, Mae Sakharov, Kasia
Anderson, and Charlie and Catherine Williams, as well as Dorothea von
Moltke and Cliff Simms, whom we are fortunate to have as friends and owners
of one of the nation's best independent bookstores.

Lisa Bankoff of International Creative Management, whom I have been
with since I published my first book nearly a decade ago, is a talented, smart,
and gracious agent who negotiated contracts and manages an end of this
industry that still mystifies me.

I have three deeply sensitive, inquisitive, and caring children: Thomas,
Noëlle, and Konrad. When they knock at my office door, it is not always good
for my writing, but it is very good for my life. It is with them and Eunice that I
find a joy and meaning that, after all the human suffering I have witnessed, defy
articulation.

Bibliography

Addams, Jane. *Peace and Bread in Times of War*. Urbana, IL: University of Illinois Press, 2002.

Adorno, Theodor. *The Culture Industry*. London: Routledge, 1991.

Arendt, Hannah. *On Revolution*. London: Penguin Books, 1963.

———. *The Origins of Totalitarianism*. New York: Harcourt, 1966.

Aronowitz, Stanley. *The Death and Rebirth of American Radicalism*. London: Routledge, 1996.

Aronson, James. *The Press and the Cold War*. Indianapolis: Bobbs-Merrill, 1970.

Barth, Karl. *The Epistle to the Romans*. London: Oxford University Press, 1933.

Bauman, Zygmunt. *In Search of Politics*. Stanford, CA: Stanford University Press, 1999.

Becker, Carol. *Zones of Contention: Essays on Art, Institutions, Gender, and Anxiety*. Albany, NY: SUNY Press, 1996.

Benda, Julien. *The Treason of the Intellectuals*. New Brunswick, NJ: Transaction Publishers, 2007.

Benson, Jackson J. *The True Adventures of John Steinbeck*. New York: Viking, 1984.

Bernays, Edward. *Propaganda*. New York: Ig Publishing, 1928.

Bernstein, Walter. *Inside Out: A Memoir of the Blacklist*. New York: Alfred A. Knopf, 1996.

Blitzstein, Marc. *The Cradle Will Rock*. Fairfax, VA: Library of Congress Federal Theatre Project Collection at Fenwick Library, George Mason University.

Bonhoeffer, Dietrich. Works, Vol. 16, *Conspiracy and Imprisonment, 1940–1945*, trans. by Lisa E. Dahill. Minneapolis, MN: Fortress Press, 2006.

Bookchin, Murray. *Post-Scarcity Anarchism*. Edinburgh: AK Press, 2004.

Boorstin, Daniel J. *The Image: A Guide to Pseudo-Events in America*. New York: Atheneum, 1961.

Bourne, Randolph. *The Radical Will: Selected Writings 1911–1918*. Ed. Olaf Hansen. Berkeley, CA: University of California Press, 1977.

———. *War and the Intellectuals: Collected Essays 1915–1919*. Ed. Carl Resek. Indianapolis: Hackett, 1964.

Briggs, Asa and Burke, Peter. *A Social History of the Media: From Gutenberg to the Internet*. Cambridge: Polity Press, 2005.

Camus, Albert. *The Plague, The Fall, Exile and the Kingdom, and Selected Essays*.

New York: Everyman's Library, 2004.

———. *Resistance, Rebellion, and Death.* Trans. Justin O'Brien. New York: Alfred A. Knopf, 1961.

———. *The Rebel: An Essay on Man in Revolt,* trans. by Anthony Bower. New York: Vintage, 1956.

———. "Return to Tipsa," in *Lyrical and Critical Essays,* trans. by Ellen Conroy Kenny. New York: Alfred A. Knopf, 1968.

Carey, James W. *Communication as Culture: Essays on Media and Society.* New York: Routledge, 1988.

Chomsky, Noam. *The Essential Chomsky.* Ed. Anthony Arnove. New York: New Press, 2008.

———. *Hopes and Prospects.* Chicago: Haymarket Books, 2010.

———. *Letters from Lexington: Reflections on Propaganda.* Boulder, CO: Paradigm Publishers, 2004.

Cockroft, Eva. "Abstract Expressionism, Weapon of the Cold War." In Francis Frascina, Ed., *Pollock and After: The Critical Debate.* New York: Harper & Row, 1985. 125–133.

Cowley, Malcolm. *Exile's Return: A Literary Odyssey of the 1920s.* New York: Penguin, 1994.

Creel, George. *How We Advertised America: The First Telling of the Amazing Story of the Committee on Public Information that Carried the Gospel of Americanism to Every Corner of the Globe.* New York: Harper & Brothers, 1920.

———. *Rebel at Large: Recollections of Fifty Crowded Years.* New York: G.P. Putnam's Sons, 1947.

Day, Dorthy. *By Little and By Little: The Selected Writings of Dorthy Day,* ed. Robert Ellsberg. New York: Alfred A. Knopf, 1983.

Donoghue, Frank. *The Last Professors: The Corporate University and the Fate of the Humanities.* New York: Fordham University Press, 2008.

Dos Passos, John. *Mr. Wilson's War.* New York: Doubleday, 1962.

Dostoevsky, Fyodor. *Notes from the Underground.* Trans. Richard Pevear and Larissa Volokhonsky. New York: Everyman's Library, 1993.

Ellul, Jacques. *Propaganda: The Formation of Men's Attitudes.* New York: Vintage Books, 1965.

Ewen, Stuart. *All Consuming Images: The Politics of Style in Contemporary Culture.* New York: Basic Books, 1988.

———. *Captains of Consciousness: Advertising and the Social Roots of the Consumer Culture.* New York: Basic Books, 1976.

———. *PR!: A Social History of Spin.* New York: Basic Books, 1996.

———. *Typecasting: On the Arts of Sciences of Human Inequality.* New York: Seven Stories Press, 2006.

Feinstein, Lee, and Anne Marie Slaughter. "A Duty to Prevent." *Foreign Affairs* 83:1 (January/February 2004): 136–150.

Flanagan, Hallie. *Arena: The History of Federal Theatre.* New York: Benjamin Blom, 1940.

Forester, E. M. "The Machine Stops," in *Selected Stories.* New York: Penguin, 2001.

Freeberg, Ernest. *Democracy's Pioneer: Eugene Debs, the Great War, and the Right to Dissent.* Cambridge, Mass.: Harvard University Press, 2009.

Fromm, Erich. *Escape From Freedom.* New York: Henry Holt, 1941.

Furedi, Frank. *Where Have All the Intellectuals Gone?: Confronting 21st Century Philistinism.* London: Continuum, 2004.

Gabler, Neal. *Life: The Movie: How Entertainment Conquered Reality.* New York: Vintage Books, 1998.

Giroux, Henry. *Impure Acts: The Practice of Politics of Cultural Studies.* New York: Routledge, 2000.

———. *The University in Chains: Confronting the Military-Industrial-Academic Complex.* Boulder, CO: Paradigm Publishers, 2007.

Gray, John. *Black Mass: Apocalyptic Religion and the Death of Utopia.* New York: Penguin, 2007.

———. *Enlightenment's Wake: Politics and Culture at the Close of the Modern Age.* New York: Routledge, 1995.

———. *Heresies: Against Progress and Other Illusions.* London: Granta Books, 2004.

———. *Liberalism.* Minneapolis: University of Minnesota Press, 1995.

———. *Straw Dogs: Thoughts on Humans and Other Animals.* London: Granta Books, 2002.

Greider, William. *Fortress America: The American Military and the Consequences of Peace.* New York: Public Affairs, 1998.

Grinker, Lori. *Afterwar: Veterans from a World in Conflict.* Milbrook, NY: de.MO Publisher, 2005.

Guttenplan, D. D. *American Radical: The Life and Times of I.F. Stone.* New York: Farrar, Straus and Giroux, 2009.

Hamilton, Clive. Requiem for a Species: Why We Resist the Truth About Climate Change. Washington, DC: Earthscan, 2010.

Havel, Vaclav. *The Power of the Powerless: Citizens Against State in Central Europe*, ed. John Keane. Armonk, NY, 1990.

Herman, Edward S., and Noam Chomsky. *Manufacturing Consent: The Political Economy of Mass Media.* New York: Pantheon, 1988.

Hoffmann, Stanley. "An American Social Science: International Relations." *Daedalus*, 106:3 (Summer 1977): 41–60.

Hoggart, Richard. *The Uses of Literacy.* New Brunswick: Transaction Publishers,

1998.

Houseman, John. *Run Through: A Memoir.* New York: Simon & Schuster, 1972.

Howe, Irving. "This Age of Conformity." In Phillips, William, and Philip Rahv, Eds., *The Partisan Review Anthology.* New York: Holt, Rinehart and Winston, 1955, 145–164.

Jackall, Robert, and Janice M. Hirota. *Image Makers: Advertising, Public Relations, and the Ethos of Advocacy.* Chicago: University of Chicago Press, 2000.

Jacoby, Russell. *The End of Utopia: Politics and Culture in an Age of Apathy.* New York, Basic Books, 1999.

———. *The Last Intellectuals: American Culture in the Age of Academe.* New York, Basic Books, 1992.

———. *Social Amnesia: A Critique of Conformist Psychology from Adler to Laing.* Boston: Beacon Press, 1975.

Johnson, Chalmers. *The Sorrows of Empire: Militarism, Secrecy, and the End of the Republic.* New York: Henry Holt, 2004.

Judt, Tony. "Bush's Useful Idiots." *London Review of Books*, 28:18 (September 21, 2006). http:www.lrb.co.uk/v28/n18/tony-judt/bushs-useful-idiots.

Kindleberger, Charles P. and Aliber, Robert. *Manias, Panics, and Crashes.* Hoboken, NJ: John Wiley & Sons, 1978.

Korten, David C. *When Corporations Rule the World.* San Francisco: Berrett-Koehler Publishers, 1995.

Lansing, Robert. *War Memoirs of Robert Lansing, Secretary of State.* Indianapolis: Bobbs-Merrill Company, 1935.

Lasch, Christopher. *The Culture of Narcissism: American Life in an Age of Diminishing Expectations.* New York: W. W. Norton, 1979.

———. *The New Radicalism in America 1889–1963: The Intellectual as a Social Type.* New York: W. W. Norton, 1965.

———. *The True and Only Heaven: Progress and Its Critics.* New York: W. W. Norton, 1991.

Le Bon, Gustave. *The Crowd: A Study of the Popular Mind.* Mineola, NY: Dover Publications, 2002.

Lens, Sidney. *Labor Wars: From the Molly Maguires to the Sitdowns.* New York: Doubleday, 1973.

Lippmann, Walter. *Public Opinion.* New York: Simon & Schuster, 1997.

MacDonald, Dwight. *Against the American Grain: Essays on the Effects of Mass Culture.* London: Victor Gollancz, 1963.

———. *The Memoirs of a Revolutionist: Essays in Political Criticism.* New York: Farrar, Straus and Cudahy, 1957.

———. *The Root Is Man.* Brooklyn, NY: Autonomedia, 1995.

MacKay, Charles. *Extraordinary Popular Delusions and the Madness of Crowds.*

Middletown, RI: BN Publishing, 2008.

McChesney, Robert, and John Nichols. *The Death and Life of American Journalism: The Media Revolution That Will Begin the World Again.* New York: Nation, 2009.

Mellman, Seymour. *The Permanent War Economy: American Capitalism in Decline.* New York: Simon & Schuster, 1985.

Mills, C. Wright. *The Politics of Truth: Selected Writings of C. Wright Mills.* Ed. John H. Summers. New York: Oxford University Press, 2008.

———. *The Power Elite.* New York: Oxford University Press, 1956.

Navasky, Victor. *Naming Names.* New York: Viking, 1980.

Niebuhr, Reinhold. *Beyond Tragedy: Essays on the Christian Interpretation of History.* New York: Scribner's, 1965.

Noble, David F. *America by Design: Science, Technology, and the Rise of Corporate Capitalism.* New York: Alfred A. Knopf, 1977.

Ortega y Gasset, José. *The Revolt of the Masses.* New York: W. W. Norton, 1932.

Ostertag, Bob. *People's Movements, People's Press: The Journalism of Social Justice Movements.* Boston: Beacon Press, 2006.

Peck, Abe. *Uncovering the Sixties: The Life and Times of the Underground Press.* New York: Citidel Press, 1991.

Polanyi, Karl. *The Great Transformation: The Political and Economic Origins of Our Time.* Boston: Beacon Press, 1944.

Pollard, Sidney. *The Idea of Progress: History and Society.* London: C. A. Watts, 1968.

Popper, Karl. *The Open Society and Its Enemies: The Spell of Plato.* Princeton: Princeton University Press, 1966.

Postman, Neil. *Amusing Ourselves to Death: Public Discourse in the Age of Show Business.* New York: Penguin, 1985.

Riesman, David. *The Lonely Crowd: A Study of the Changing American Character.* New Haven: Yale University Press, 1950.

Rojek, Chris. *Celebrity.* London: Reaktion Books, 2001.

Rorty, Richard. *Achieving Our Country: Leftist Thought in Twentieth-Century America.* Cambridge, MA: Harvard University Press, 1998.

Ross, Stewart Halsey. *Propaganda for War: How the United States Was Conditioned to Fight the Great War of 1914–1918.* Joshua Tree, CA: Progressive Press, 2009.

Roth, Philip. "On the Air: A Long Story." *New American Review* 10 (1970), 7–49.

Said, Edward W. *Representation of the Intellectual: The 1993 Reith Lectures.* New York: Vintage, 1996.

Saul, John Raulston. *The Unconscious Civilization.* New York: The Free Press, 1995.

Saul, John Raulston. *Voltaire's Bastards: The Dictatorship of Reason in the West.* New York: Vintage Books, 1992.

Schrecker, Ellen. *Many Are the Crimes: McCarthyism in America.* Boston: Little, Brown, 1998.

———. *No Ivory Tower: McCarthyism and the Universities.* New York: Oxford University Press, 1986.

Sennet, Richard. *The Fall of Public Man.* New York: W. W. Norton, 1974.

Smith, Sharon. *Subterranean Fire: A History of Working-Class Radicalism in the United States.* Chicago: Haymarket Books, 2006.

Snow, C. P. *The Two Cultures.* Cambridge: Cambridge University Press, 1998.

Steel, Robert. *Walter Lippmann and The American Century.* London: Bodley Head, 1980.

Theweleit, Klaus. *Male Fantasies.* Minneapolis: University of Minnesota Press, 1987.

Thompson, E. P. "Time, Work-Discipline, and Industrial Capitalism." *Past and Present* 38 (1967): 56–97.

van Agtmael, Peter. *2nd Tour, Hope I Don't Die.* Portland, OR: Photolucida, 2009.

Viereck, George Sylvester. *Spreading the Germs of Hate.* New York: Horace Liveright, 1930.

Whyte, William H. *The Organization Man.* Philadelphia: University of Pennsylvania Press, 1956.

Wolin, Sheldon S. *Democracy Incorporated: Managed Democracy and the Specter of Inverted Totalitarianism.* Princeton: Princeton University Press, 2008.

Wright, Ronald. *A Short History of Progress.* New York: Carroll & Graf Publishers, 2004.

Index

Abu Ghraib prison, 156
Accuracy in Academe, 176
Adams, Samuel Hopkins, 86
Addams, Jane, 63, 66, 78, 80–81
Afghanistan war, 54, 58, 211
   and Afghan National Army (ANA),
     48–50, 51, 53
   and corruption, 46, 47, 50, 53
   and hypermasculinity, 156
   and Kucinich, 41
   and liberals, 27, 38, 39, 43–44
   and massacres and civilian deaths,
     44, 46, 47, 53, 55
   and Obama, 28, 41, 47
   as political and social problem, 53
   and private contractors, 42–43, 51–52,
     53
   rationale for, 43
   and Soviets and British earlier, 47
   U.S. spending on, 50, 53
   and warlords and drugs, 43–44,
     45–46, 47, 53
   and women's rights, 43, 46, 58
AFL-CIO, 107, 109–110, 175
Alfaro, Saul, 56
Alterman, Eric, 178
American Business Consultants, 104
American Civil Liberties Union
   (ACLU), 107
American Federation of Labor, 87
Americans for Democratic Action
   (ADA), 103–104, 107
Amnesty International, 150
Anarchists, 15, 59, 80, 107, 158, 193, 197
Andre, Carl, 117
Annabell, Steve, 57
Anticommunism
   and Creel, 75–76
   and liberal class, 7–8, 9, 15–16
   in 1960s, 109
   post–World War I, 80, 83

   post–World War II, 16, 103–108, 153,
    158, 167
Antony, Mark, 213
Arcuri, Michael, 2
Arditi, Yossi, 55
Arnheim, Michael, 2
Arts and artists
   Angry Arts, 97
   Artists Congress, 114
   and blacklisting, 103, 106, 107
   and commercial censorship, 93
   and consumer culture, 103
   and corporations, 10, 11, 14, 113,
    119–120
   depoliticization of, 114–115
   devaluing of, 122–123
   and early modernism, 119
   and elitism, 113, 115, 116, 117, 118
   and entertainment, 98–99
   and Internet, 204, 205, 206, 207, 210
   and justice, 139–140
   and liberal class, 103, 113, 116
   and Magee and illustration, 116–119
   and mass culture, 116
   and mass propaganda, 16, 61, 68, 69,
    74, 76
   and material comfort, 10
   and media, 119–121
   and moral outrage and passion,
    214
   and permanent war, 19
   and philanthropy and patrons, 113,
    114, 147, 215
   and popular appeal, 88–89
   and religion of art, 102–103
   and resistance, 203
   and schools, 115, 116
   and self-imposed exile, 102
   and spectacle and celebrity, 113–114
   transformation from rebel to
    propagandist, 100–103

and World War I, 61, 63, 68, 69, 74, 76
Augustine, 211
al-Awlaki, Anwar, 41

Baez, Joan, 120
Bailouts, 2, 6, 27, 179, 201
Banks
    and Clinton, 12
    and Greenspan, 154
    and lending, 27
    and repossessions and foreclosures,
      12, 189
    and taxpayer subsidies, 182, 188
    and World War I, 68, 77
Bartenieff, George, 97, 99, 100
Barth, Karl, 87–88
Barthes, Roland, 124
Basshe, Emjo, 89
Bates, Blanche, 75
Beats, 101, 110, 111, 123
Beck, Julian, 96
Becker, Carol, 115, 122–123
Beinart, Peter, 38
Bell, Daniel, 114
Bell, Ernest Logan, 1–6, 13, 15, 29
Bellow, Saul, 151
Benda, Julien, 36, 144
Benitez, Horacio Javier, 57
Berkman, Alexander, 80
Bernays, Edward, 63, 81
Bernstein, Walter, 105–106
Berrigan, Daniel, 14, 111, 160–163
Berrigan, Philip, 111, 160, 161
Black Panthers, 110
Blackwater (Xe), 41
Blitzstein, Marc, 91, 92
Blix, Hans, 183
B'nai B'rith, 22
Bohemians, 101, 102, 103, 111
Bonhoeffer, Dietrich, 206
Bookchin, Murray, 111
Bosnia, 127, 197–198, 199
Bourne, Randolph, 20, 59, 63, 64–65, 66,
    78, 82
Bové, Paul, 124
Boyer, Richard O., 104
Brown, Kenneth, 96
Brubaker, Howard, 67

Bryant, William Jennings, 61
Buckley, William F., 147
Buffett, Warren, 16
Bullard, Arthur, 67–69
Burleson, Albert, 65
Burns, John, 131
Burroughs, William, 110
Bush, George W.
    and Afghanistan, 47
    and civil liberties and constitutional
      rights, 28, 178
    and evil, 21
    and Iraq, 22, 38, 39, 40, 74, 128, 178,
      183
    and judiciary, 178
    lies of, 27
    and 2000 election, 9, 178, 181
    and Yale, 190
Business Roundtable, 176

Calvin Klein, 199
Cambodia, 32, 146
Camus, Albert, 193, 215, 216, 217
Capitalism. *See* Liberal class
Capper, Arthur, 64
Carey, James W., 131
Carter, Jimmy, 180
Catholic Worker movement, 158, 161
Cato Institute, 176
Celebrity culture and promotion,
    199–200, 211
Chace, James, 37
Chaikin, Joseph, 96
Chazan, Naomi, 151
Cheney, Dick, 21
China, 30–33, 37, 106, 201, 205
Chomsky, Noam
    as critic of corporate capitalism
      reviled by liberal class, 33–34, 35–36
    and genuine intellectual inquiry and
      critical thinking, 35, 37
    and global power, 32–33
    on intellectuals, 36
    and Rosenthal, 171
    and U.S. parallels to Weimar
      Germany, 34–35
    and Watergate, 174
Christian Right, 11, 22, 159, 200

Christianity, 85, 87, 166, 178, 185
Church, 139
   and capitalism and globalization,
      10–11
   Catholic, 22, 161, 162
   decline of, 163
   and humanism and self-absorbed
      spirituality, 88
   and Iraq, 21–22
   and liberal class, 103, 163
   and permanent war, 21–22
   and radicals, 14, 111, 158–164
   and resistance, 207
   and tax-exemption and money, 10
   Unitarians, 163
   and wisdom and knowledge, 164–166
   and World War I, 64
CIA, 45, 153, 169
Cicero, 217
Citizens for a Sound Economy, 176
Civil liberties, 15
   and anticommunism, 16, 107
   assaults on, 169
   and Bush, 28
   erosion of, 6, 25
   and laws, 9
   and liberals, 27, 169
   and Obama, 27
   and terrorism, 16
Civil-rights movement, 96, 109, 111,
   120, 148, 158, 164, 169, 184
Civil War, U.S., 60, 61, 75
Climate change and global warming,
   28, 74, 154, 178, 195–205
Clinton, Bill, 12, 159, 177
Cockroft, Eva, 114
Coelho, Tony, 180
Coffin, William Sloane, 111
Cold War, 8, 19, 40, 84, 109, 114,
   115
Committee for Public Information
   (CPI), 69, 70, 74, 78, 81
Communists, 19, 24, 102, 196
   and German Nazis, 34
   and interconnectedness, 123
   and 1960s, 109, 110, 111
   and 1930s, 35
   and Palmer Raids, 80

   propaganda tying them to German
      war machine, 83
   and radical current in theater, 89,
      94–95
   silencing, banning, and blacklisting,
      15–16, 104, 106–107, 153, 158, 167
   and unions, 195
   See also Anticommunism
Cone, James, 184–187
Congress for Cultural Freedom, 153
Congress of Industrial Organizations
   (CIO), 35
Constitution, U.S.
   and Arnheim, 2
   and faith-based organizations, 178
   and inverted totalitarianism, 24
   irrelevancy of, 9
   as power's apprentice, 25
   and Sedition Act, 65
Consumer Protection Agency, 180
Consumerism and consumption, 10, 82,
   101, 102, 103, 112, 132, 197, 200, 202
Copenhagen Conference, 193, 194, 200,
   203, 204
Corporate power
   and arts, 113, 119–120
   and intellectuals, 17
   and inverted totalitarianism, 24, 26
   and laws, 8–9
   and Lewis Powell memo, 176–177
   and liberal class, 6, 8, 9–10, 14–15, 17,
      141–142, 153–154, 179, 181, 194–195
   and liberal class's death, 12–14, 15
   and mass propaganda, 17, 194
   and media, 131, 136
   and permanent war, 19–20
   and radicals, 13, 15–16
   and unions, 14
   and universities, 11
   and World War I, 7
   See also Corporations
Corporations
   assault on working class by, 181
   campaign contributions and
      lobbying of, 24–25, 173, 180, 205
   coup of, 173, 193, 196
   and crime, 24, 175
   and environment, 193–195, 201–205

hijacking of state by, 141–142
and hypermasculinity, 156
and internal security and intelligence, 41, 42, 155
and Internet, 208, 210
and Iraq and Afghanistan wars, 41–43, 51–52, 53
lack of concern with common good of, 18
and Nader, 173–176, 178
and revolt of right, 196
and taxpayer subsidies, 25, 181
and unemployment, 189
See also Arts and artists; Democratic Party; Film; Intellectuals; Journalism and journalists; Mass propaganda; Media; Obama, Barack; Republican Party; Unions; Universities
Costa, Antonio Maria, 45
Council on Foreign Relations, 143
Counterculture, 97, 101, 109, 110, 111, 123
Cowley, Malcolm, 100–103, 112
The Cradle Will Rock (musical), 91–93, 140, 175
Creel, George, 69–70, 75–78, 79, 81
Czechoslovakia, 216

Dada movement, 103, 119
Daniels, Josephus, 75
Day, Dorothy, 111, 158–160, 163, 166
Debs, Eugene, 65, 76, 78, 87
Demagogues, 13, 153
Democratic Party, 26, 29
and AFL-CIO, 107
and anticommunism, 106
betrayal of liberal principles by, 14–15
and corporations, 10, 12, 14, 178, 179, 181
impotency of, 108
and Iraq and Afghanistan wars, 43, 178
and liberal class, 103, 123–124, 157
1968 convention, 123
and Nixon's illegalities, 169
and pre–World War I reforms, 86
and Republican Party, 178

and 2000 election, 174, 177
Depression, Great, 66, 89, 97, 104, 158
Deregulation, 8, 25, 28, 180
Derrida, Jacques, 124
Dershowitz, Alan, 152
Dewey, John, 78, 81, 131
Dickens, Charles, 138
Dies, Martin, 95
Disney, Walt, 106
Dith Pran, 146
Dos Passos, John, 75, 78, 79, 89
Dostoyevsky, Fyodor, 17, 21, 153, 217
Douglass, Frederick, 187
Downes, Olin, 104
Drug companies, 25, 175, 181
Duchamp, Marcel, 118–119
Dylan, Bob, 120

Economy
and collapse and ruins, 3, 154, 155, 159, 194, 196, 197
global, 30, 32, 33, 193
and Hudson, 14
and military spending, 21
and permanent war, 15, 19, 154, 168, 185
See also Deregulation; Speculators and speculation
Education
and degradation, 207
high-quality and affordable public, 15
and Mills, 121–122
and No Child Left Behind, 178
and permanent war, 19
Edwards, John, 26
Egypt, 20
Einstein, Albert, 104
El Salvador, 56, 127, 198
Ellsberg, Daniel, 169
Elshtain, Jean Bethke, 38
Energy, 25, 177
England/Great Britain, 33, 47, 57, 61, 69, 76, 130
Entertainment industry, 11, 26, 76, 98, 104
Environment
and collapse, 154, 195–204

and degradation and devastation, 163, 193–195, 199–202
and Gore, 177
groups, 16
illusion of modifying and controlling, 204
and legislation, 174, 179
and protection, 176
and reform, 27–28, 198
See also Climate change and global warming
Environmental Protection Agency, 174, 179
Ernst, Morris, 107
Espionage Act, 65, 79
Ewen, Stuart, 74, 88
ExxonMobil, 74

Falklands War, 57
Faragoh, Francis Edward, 89
Fascists and fascism, 19, 20, 22–23, 24, 25, 26, 34, 91, 159, 196
Faulk, John Henry, 104, 106
FBI, 104, 107, 160, 167
Federal Deposit Insurance Corporation (FDIC), 27
Federal Reserve, 2, 153, 201
Federal Theatre Project, 90–96, 138
Federation of Modern Painters and Sculptors, 114
FedEx, 189–192
Field, Crystal, 97
Film
    and blacklisting, 103
    and corporations, 116
    and early modernism, 119
    and Internet, 209, 210, 211
    and war images, 55
    and World War I, 70, 76
Finkelstein, Norman, 36, 150, 151–152
Flanagan, Hallie, 90, 93, 95
Flannery, Tim, 202
Foreclosures, 12, 181, 189, 190, 207
Foreign Intelligence Surveillance Act (FISA), 27
Fornés, Maria Irene, 97
Forster, E. M., 214
France, 64, 74, 77, 123, 124

Franken, Al, 40
Freud, Sigmund, 62–63, 102
Friedan, Betty, 163
Friedman, Thomas, 143, 156
Fromkin, David, 37

Gabler, Neal, 113–114
Gardiner, John, 119
Gays and homosexuals, 23, 156, 164, 178
Gaza, 99, 127, 148–149, 198, 215
Gelb, Leslie, 143
General Motors (GM), 175, 177
Germany
    and militarized culture, 156
    Nazi, 22–23, 34, 152, 167, 196, 206
    Weimar, 13, 20, 22–23, 34, 122
    and World War I, 59–60, 61, 63, 64, 68, 69, 70, 71, 74, 78, 79, 83
Ginsberg, Allen, 110
Gitlin, Todd, 177–178
Glaspell, Susan, 89
Global warming. *See* Climate change and global warming
Globalization
    and Berrigan, 163
    and Chomsky, 34
    and churches, 10
    and Friedman, 143
    ideology of, 201
    and liberal class, 8, 13, 27, 142–143, 194
    and poor, 131, 142
    touted benefits of, 142
Gold, Mike, 89
Goldman, Emma, 78, 80
Goldstone, Richard, 148–152
Gombrich, Ernst, 117
Gompers, Samuel, 87
Goodman, Amy, 182
Goodman, Paul, 125
Goodman, Percival, 125
Google, 208–210
Gore, Al, 177, 178
Grant, Lee, 105, 106
Gray, John, 7
Greece, 30
Green Party, 181
Greenhouse gases, 203–204

Greenspan, Alan, 152
Greer, Germaine, 164
Grinker, Lori, 54, 55, 56, 57
Guantánamo Bay, 27
Gulf War, 56, 97, 127
    See also Iraq war

Hagee, John, 151
Hamas, 148, 151
Hamill, Pete, 146
Hamilton, Clive, 204
Hammett, Dashiell, 104
Harding, Warren, 65
Hartnett, Vincent, 104
Havel, Václav, 36, 216
Hayward, Tony, 204
Haywood, Bill, 86
Health care, 207
    and Bell, 2, 4, 5
    "Cadillac" plans, 14
    and Democratic Party, 14–15
    and old communist unions, 195
    reform bill, 2, 22, 25, 27
    and unemployment, 189
Hedonism and cult of self, 101, 109, 111,
    112
Hellman, Lillian, 96
Henderson, Dean, 189–192
Hennessy, Martha, 159
Heritage Foundation, 176
Herman, Edward, 169
Herzen, Aleksandr, 193
Heschel, Abraham, 163
Hesse, Herman, 111
Hibben, John Grier, 64
Hindman, Matthew, 204
Hitchens, Christopher, 35–36
Hobbes, Thomas, 7
Hoffman, Abbie, 111
Hoffman, Stanley, 145
Hoh, Matthew, 46
Hold, Hamilton, 67
Homeland Security, U.S. Department of,
    26, 27, 155
Homer, 57
Hoover, J. Edgar, 107
House Un-American Activities
    Committee (HUAC), 89, 95, 96, 106

Houseman, John, 90, 91, 92–93
Howe, Irving, 17, 103, 112, 113
Human Rights Watch, 150
Huntington, Samuel, 8
Hussein, Saddam, 22, 39, 127,
Hypermasculinity, 155–157

Ignatieff, Michael, 38–39
Im Tirtzu, 151
Image-based culture, 207–208
India, 31, 32, 33, 37, 146
Industrial Workers of the World
    (IWW), 76, 86
Inflation, 203
Intellectuals
    and Beats, 101
    Chomsky and Finkelstein on, 36
    and consumer culture, 103
    and corporations, 17, 26, 172
    Howe on, 17, 103
    Judt on, 40–41
    last generation of independent
        public, 125
    and left, 15, 40
    and mass propaganda, 16–17
    and multiculturalism, 124
    and objectivity, 114
    and popular and political passions,
        145
    and power, 17, 145
    and practical aims and material
        advantages, 145
    and self-imposed exile, 102
    and Soviet Union, 153
    and World War I, 59, 62, 63, 64–65,
        66–67
Internal Revenue Service (IRS), 28
Internet, 206–214
Iran, 20, 28, 32, 37, 150
Iraq war, 54, 58, 211
    and church, 21–22
    and Democrats, 178
    and Friedman, 143, 156
    and helicopter attack on Iraqi
        civilians, 43
    and hypermasculinity, 156
    and Kerry, 178, 181
    and liberals, 27, 38–40, 143, 183

and mass propaganda, 74
and media, 10, 55–56, 127–130, 131,
  183
and Obama, 27
and private contractors, 41–42
theater against, 97, 99
and U.N., 127, 183
and veterans, 56
Islam
  hatred for radical, 23
  and militancy, 8, 127
  Nation of, 110
  and racism, 209
  and terrorism, 16, 19
Israel, 20, 28, 42, 55, 99, 127, 129, 149–152,
  167, 209

Jacobs, Jane, 101, 125
Jacoby, Russell, 15, 101, 124, 125–126
Jameson, Frederic, 124, 125
Johnson, Lyndon, 97, 167
Johnston, David Cay, 174
Jones, LeRoi (Amiri Baraka), 96
Jones, Mary "Mother," 78
Jordan, David Starr, 64, 72
Journalism and journalists, 139, 207, 215
  and blacklisting, 103, 104
  and corporations, power, and the
    powerful, 10, 26, 133–134, 135, 136,
    146–148
  good, 132–133, 148, 169
  and impartiality and objectivity, 127,
    130, 131, 134, 136–137, 139–140,
    167–168
  and Internet, 208–211, 214
  and Iraq, 127–130, 131
  and loss of newspapers, 136, 207
  and mass culture, 167
  monitoring and controlling, 132
  and newcomers and immigrants, 148
  and schools, 115
  and Steinbeck, 137–138
  and Stone, 166–169
  and World War I, 63, 65, 69, 70–74,
    76
  See also Media; specific publications
Joya, Malalai, 44, 45–46, 46–47
Judt, Tony, 40–41

Kahn, Otto, 89
Karzai, Ahmed Wali, 45
Karzai, Hamid, 45, 46, 47, 53
Kennedy, Edward, 190
Kentridge, William, 123
Kerouac, Jack, 110
Kerry, John, 178, 181, 190
King, Martin Luther, Jr., 10, 111, 163, 164,
  183–188
King, William, 83
Komunyakaa, Yusef, 186
Korean War, 96
Kosovo, 199
Kozloff, Max, 114
Kucinich, Dennis, 2, 41, 43
Kurlansky, Mark, 210–211
Kuwait, 127

Lacan, Jacques, 124
Lanier, Jaron, 209–214
Lardner, Ring, Jr., 104
Lasswell, Harold, 81
Lawson, John Howard, 89
Le Bon, Gustave, 61
League of Nations, 66
Leary, Timothy, 110
Lebanon, 20, 99
Lee, Ching Kwan, 30–32
Left wing
  Berrigan on, 162
  and identity politics and
    multiculturalism, 123, 124
  ideological vacuum on, 16
  insignificance of, 41
  and radical current in theater, 89
  See also Communists; Marxists;
    New Left; Radicals; Socialism
    and socialists
Lenin, 41, 83
Leno, Jay, 26
Lewis, Anthony, 1565
Lewis, Sinclair, 91
Liberal class
  abandonment, purging, and death
    of, 12–14, 15, 139, 141–142, 146, 148,
    149, 152, 153, 154, 207
  and anger and sense of betrayal of
    people, 6, 28–30, 154, 178

and anticommunism, 7–8, 9, 15–16,
103–108
and capitalism, 8, 13, 16, 103, 142, 157,
194, 195
and children and education, 101–102
and Chomsky, 33–34, 35–36, 37
as conscience of nation, 13
and corporate power, 6, 8, 9–10,
12–13, 14–15, 17, 139, 141–142,
153–154, 179, 181, 194–195
and decline of religious institutions,
163
and Democratic Party, 12, 14, 103,
123–124, 157
and economic mobility and
careerism, 100, 103, 104, 142–143,
145
and environment, 193–198
and expelling apostates from liberal
institutions, 145–146
and fear, 16, 139, 140, 154
and globalization, 8, 13, 27, 142–143,
194, 201
and hollow political theater, 10
and hypermasculinity, 156
and imperialism, 8, 152, 194, 198
and indifference to economic
despair, 188–190
and inverted totalitarianism, 23–24,
196
and Iraq and Afghanistan wars,
38–40, 43–44, 143, 156–157, 183
and Islamic militancy, 8
and King, 181, 183, 184
and mass propaganda, 16–17
and material comfort, 10, 103, 104
moral bankruptcy of, 15, 27
and mythic narrative of America, 131
and Nader, 173, 177
and New Deal, 7
and Nixon's illegalities, 169
and objectivity, 139–140
and permanent war, 19–20, 21, 154,
155
and power and the state, 112, 145, 146,
169
and progress and utopia, 84–85, 103,
112, 194

and racial difference and racism, 23
and radicals, 13, 15–16, 40, 103–108,
111, 112–113, 140, 153, 169
and reform and law, 8–9, 13, 85–86,
112, 140, 141, 154
and resistance, revolt, and rebels,
196, 206, 215, 217
and self-expression and paganism,
102
and sound bites and popular appeal,
88–89
and Vietnam War, 37–38, 39
and war's brutal reality, 39–40
and World War I, 7, 66
See also Arts and artists; Church;
Liberals; Mass culture; Media;
Power elite; Unions, labor;
Universities
Liberal institutions, 6, 13, 19, 21, 29, 84,
93, 103, 107, 113, 115, 131, 133, 136,
139–140, 146, 153, 207
See also specific institutions
Liberalism
bankrupt, 192
classical, 6–7, 8, 85
collapse of, 20
and communism, 7–8, 9, 106
discarding principle tenets of,
142
and hypermasculinity, 155, 156
and Israel, 150
modern, 84–85
myth of democratic, 8
and World War I's aftermath, 80–81
Liberals
betrayal of liberal principles by, 139
and economic despair, 188–190
muzzling of, 26
policing their own, 151–152
retreat and lack of protest by, 15, 28
See also Liberal class
Limbaugh, Rush, 35, 130
Lippmann, Walter, 69, 78
Lipton, Lawrence, 101
Locke, John, 7
Loeb, Philip, 104–105
Loehr, Davidson, 163–166
London, Jack, 78

Macdonald, Dwight, 125, 166
  and entertainment, 98
  and 1960s, 111, 112
  and permanent war, 19–20
  and sound bites and easily digested
    ideas, 88–89
  and urban centers, 101
  and World War I, 87
MacLeish, Archibald, 92
Magee, Alan, 116–119
Magical thinking, 200
Malcolm X, 111, 164, 168, 184–188
Malina, Judith, 96
Malpede, Karen, 98–104
Manhattan Institute, 176
Manufacturing, 15, 21, 77, 142, 194, 202
Mao Zedong, 110
Mark, Ruben, 133
Marlowe, Christopher, 95
Marx, Karl, 17–18, 20, 157, 194
Marxists, 20, 112, 124, 126
Mass culture
  and arts, 116
  and Chomsky, 37
  consumer and commercial, 74, 82, 84
  and journalism, 167
  and left, 15
  and liberal class, 112
  rise of, 82, 87
  and World War I, 7, 62, 82
Mass propaganda, 197, 213
  and Bernays, 63, 81
  and corporations, 17, 74, 81, 82, 84,
    194, 205
  and critics, 81–82
  and defiance, 214
  and emotion, 82, 88
  and fear, 16, 82, 83–84
  first modern machine for, 69
  following World War I, 80, 81–83, 84,
    87, 88
  and Iraq, 74
  and liberal class, 16–17
  and psychology and Freud, 61–63
  and radical current in theater, 89, 90
  and Russia, 81–82
  tying communists to German war
    machine, 83

and World War I, 7, 61–63, 65, 66, 67,
    68–74, 76–78, 80, 81
Maurin, Peter, 158
McCain, John, 2, 5, 162, 181, 190
McCarthy, Eugene, 123
McCarthy, Joseph, 34, 76
McGill, Doug, 133–137
McGovern, George, 123
McKibben, Bill, 193
Meany, George, 109, 175
Media, 23, 29, 139
  alternative and underground, 145,
    169
  and art, 119–121
  and Catholic Worker, 159
  and Chomsky, 34
  and concentration and
    commercialization, 74, 82, 84
  and corporations, 10, 14, 26, 84,
    119–120, 131, 132, 135, 136, 176, 177
  and financial system, 10, 182
  and good journalism, 132–133, 169
  impact of radicals and alternative
    publications on, 169
  and impartiality and objectivity, 127,
    130, 131, 134, 136–137, 139–140
  and Iraq, 10, 55–56, 127–130, 131, 183
  and liberal class, 103
  and moral outrage and passion, 214
  and music, 120
  and Nader, 173–182
  in 1960s and 1970s, 169
  and permanent war, 19
  and public's conformity, aspirations,
    and idealized identities, 132
  and sound bites, 88, 182
  talk radio, reality television, and
    trash-talk programs, 35, 155
  and truth versus news, 131–132
  and World War I, 65, 70–74, 76,
    77–78
  See also Journalism and journalists;
    specific publications
Merton, Thomas, 161
Metropolitan Museum of Art, 147
Middle East, 16, 39, 84, 127, 129, 130, 153,
  188
Militarization, 200–201

Military spending, U.S., 21, 26, 84, 155
Mill, John Stuart, 7
Miller, Arthur, 96
Mills, C. Wright, 9, 121–122, 125, 132
Moore, Michael, 40, 148, 149
Morris, Jack, 175
Mostel, Zero, 105, 106
Moyers, Bill, 182
Muck, Carl, 79
Muir, Jean, 105
Mukasey, Michael, 162
Multiculturalism, 124, 125–126
Mumford, Lewis, 125
Museum of Modern Art (New York), 113, 118

Nader, Ralph, 173–182
National Association of Scholars, 153
National Council of Churches, 22
National Endowment for the Arts (NEA), 97
Nationalism, 10, 20, 26, 27, 64, 68, 79, 87, 151, 159
NATO, 44, 45, 46, 47, 167
Nava, John, 118
Neugebauer, Randy, 22
New Deal, 7, 90, 94, 106, 108, 140, 168
New Israel Fund (NIF), 150
New Left, 110, 111, 123, 124, 168
New York Times
    and Afghanistan, 45
    and anticommunism, 83
    and author, 127–131
    and critics of corporate state, 14
    and op-ed pieces, 143
    and Sarajevo, 57
    and World War I, 70–74, 78
Niebuhr, Reinhold, 8, 19, 129
Nixon, Richard, 34, 76, 97, 123, 169, 174, 178
North American Free Trade Agreement (NAFTA), 12, 16, 27

Oath Keepers, 28
Obama, Barack, 36, 42
    and Berrigan, 161
    and Christian fascists, 22
    and climate change, 204

and corporations, 12, 190, 199
and energy, 181
and Gulf oil spill, 16
and illusion over substance, 195
and liberal class, 188
lies and broken promises of, 27–28
and multiculturalism, 125
and wars, 27, 28, 41, 47, 58
weakness of, 21
and "Yes We Can," 200
O'Brien, Conan, 26
O'Brien, Edwin F., 21
Occultism, 110
Ochs, Phil, 120
Odetta, 120
Oil
    Gulf of Mexico spill, 16, 18, 28, 205
    and Iraq, 127
    and mass extinction, 203
    and Nader, 175
    and renewable energy, 181
    Standard, 86, 140
    and Teapot Dome scandal, 75
Olbermann, Keith, 40
O'Neil, Eugene, 89
Ortega y Gasset, José, 117
Orwell, George, 138, 168

Pacifism, 15, 22, 61, 64, 70, 76, 78, 97, 158
Pakistan, 28, 39, 45, 47, 146, 157
Palestinians, 37, 129, 149, 151, 152, 168, 198, 209, 215
Palin, Sarah, 22, 28
Patriot Act, 16, 174
Patriotism, 26, 27, 56, 70, 120, 140, 154
Paul, Ron, 2, 41
Pentagon Papers, 169
Permanent war, 140
    and Arab world, 20
    and Chomsky, 33, 36
    economy, 15, 36, 154, 168, 186
    ideology and culture of, 19–20
    and liberal class, 19–20, 21, 154
    and military spending, 21
    and patriotism, 155
    and World War I, 7, 19, 62
Peter, Paul & Mary, 120
Peters, Joan, 152

Pindar, 213
Plato, 63, 166, 188, 201
Polanyi, Karl, 1
Political action committees, 24
Pollard, Sidney, 84
Pollock, Jackson, 113–114
Poole, Ernest, 67
Pope John Paul II, 162
Populism, 2, 6, 62, 65, 80
Postman, Neil, 207
Poststructuralism, 124–125
Poverty and the poor
    and Bell's mother, 4
    and Berrigan, 163
    and Bohemia, 103
    and corporate power, 12
    and creative people, 211
    and globalization, 142
    and hypermasculinity, 156
    and King and Malcolm X, 186, 188
    and liberal class, 198
    and liberal era, 7
    long-term, 181
    and media, 10
    and radical social change and
        Catholic Worker, 157–160
    and University House writers, 67
    and utopia and progress, 84
Powell, Colin, 183
Powell, Lewis, 175–176
Power elite, 200
    and anarchic violence, 197
    and art, 113, 115, 116
    and Chomsky, 34
    and church, 21
    and Cicero, 213
    debate between two wings of, 169
    defying, 140, 143
    and environmental and economic
        collapse, 154
    and globalization, 201
    and liberal class, 9, 13, 14, 15, 37, 38,
        39, 124, 139, 141, 152, 153, 155
    and Lippmann's *Public Opinion,* 69
    and mass propaganda, 16
    and media, 146
    and multiculturalism, 125
    and mythic narrative of America, 131

and Obama, 199
and permanent war, 19, 20
and polls, 25
and protests, 109, 123
and radical current in theater, 91, 93,
    94
and resistance, 207
Prager, Robert, 79–80
Prisons, 155, 157, 186, 215
Proctor & Gamble, 133
Progressivism and progressives, 20, 62,
    63, 64, 65–66, 69
Propaganda. *See* Mass propaganda
Pure Food and Drug Act, 86
Putin, Vladimir, 128, 129

al-Qaida, 43, 45, 58, 127

Racism, 23, 183–186, 209
Radicals
    discrediting, 13
    and environment, 194, 195, 205
    impact on media of, 168
    and keeping liberal class honest, 140
    and multiculturalism, 124, 125–126
    in 1960s, 109–112, 123, 168
    and Palmer Raids, 80
    and poststructuralism, 124–125
    and psychoanalysis, 102
    rupture with liberal class of, 112–113
    silencing, banning, and blacklisting,
        15–16, 103–108, 153
    and theater, 89–96
    and University House, 67
    and utopia and progress, 84
    and vitality of liberal class, 169
    and World War I, 70–74, 87
    See also Anarchists; Communists;
        Left wing; Liberal class; Marxists;
        Socialism and socialists
Rauschenbusch, Walter, 85
Reagan, Ronald
    and anticommunism, 106
    and corporate control, 142
    and liberal class's death, 15
    and Nader, 177, 180
    and NEA grants, 97–98
Rebels, 15–16, 102, 215–219

See also Radicals; Resistance and revolt

Reform. *See* Liberal class

Religious institutions, 10–11, 14, 21–22, 163
  See also Church

Remnick, David, 38

Republican Party
  and corporations, 181
  right wing of, 34–35
  and 2000 election, 178
  and Wall Street, 2

Resistance and revolt, 193, 196–199, 205–208

Reuther, Walter, 109–110

Rice, Condoleezza, 161

Right wing, 6, 16, 22, 34–35, 40, 76, 104, 130, 159, 189, 196, 209

Robeson, Paul, 106–107

Rockefeller, John D., 76, 86

Rojek, Chris, 199–200

Roosevelt, Franklin Delano, 7, 75, 94, 104, 108, 167

Rose, Charlie, 127, 156

Rosenthal, Abe, 147, 175

Roth, Philip, 109

Russell, Bertrand, 78

Russell, Charles Edward, 63

Russia, 47, 67–68, 70, 71, 80, 81–82, 83, 196

Sainath, Palagummi, 32

Saul, John Ralston, 142

Savio, Mario, 216

Scahill, Jeremy, 41–43

Schakowsky, Jan, 42

Schanberg, Sydney, 146–148, 153

Schrecker, Ellen, 106, 107, 123

Schumann, Peter, 97

Sedition Act, 65

Seeger, Pete, 105, 106

Sennet, Richard, 87

September 11, 2001, terrorist attacks (911), 35, 41, 43, 44, 128, 129

Shange, Ntozake, 96

Sharon, Ariel, 128, 129

Sheehan, Cindy, 120

Shepard, Sam, 97

Shetterly, Rob, 119–121

Simon, Paul, 190–191

Simons, George, 83

Sinclair, Upton, 63, 75, 78, 86

Slaughter, Anne-Marie, 38

Smith, Adam, 18, 33

Smith, Frederick, 190, 191

Smith, Sharon, 110

Social Gospel movement, 85, 86, 87, 163

Socialism and socialists, 20
  and anticommunist purges, 15, 107
  and liberal era, 7
  muzzling of, 26
  pre–World War I, 62, 67, 78–79, 87
  and World War I, 62, 63, 65, 66, 67, 72, 76, 78–79, 87

Socrates, 166, 168

Somalia, 28

Soros, George, 16

South Korea, 31

Soviet Union, 20, 47, 81–82, 83, 152

Speculators and speculation, 8, 10, 12, 13, 15, 182

Spinoza, Baruch, 7

Spivak, Gayatri, 124

Stack, Joe, 28–30, 32, 33, 35

Stalin, Joseph, 110

Stanton, Olive, 92

Starnes, Joseph, 95

Steimer, Mollie, 80

Steinbeck, John, 137–138, 139

Steinem, Gloria, 163

Stern, Fritz, 22–23

Stewart, Ellen, 97

Stieber, Josh, 41, 43

Stone, I. F., 165–168

Students for a Democratic Society (SDS), 110

Stupak, Bart, 22

Sullivan, Mark, 75

Sulzberger, Arthur "Punch," 147

Supreme Court, U.S., 24, 60, 176

Surowiecki, James, 208

Surveillance, 26–27, 155

Swanson, David, 41

Syria, 20

Taft-Hartley Act, 16, 108, 191

Taliban, 44, 45, 46, 47, 48, 50, 53, 58

Tarbell, Ida, 85–86
Tarde, Gabriel, 62
Taxes, 30, 206, 216
Tea Party movement, 2, 28
Teamsters Union, 190, 191
Teer, Barbara Ann, 96
Terrorism
    domestic, 6
    and drugs, 45
    Islamic, 16, 19
    and laws, 9
    and Obama, 58
    and patriotism, 26
    war on, 41, 44, 128, 129
Theater, 215
    Bread and Puppet Theatre, 97
    and censorship, 93, 96, 98
    and civil-rights movement, 96
    and grants and commercial
        constraints, 97–98, 99–100
    Living Theatre and Open Theater,
        96–97
    radical current in 1920s and 1930s,
        89–96, 97
    as spectacle or celebrity-driven
        entertainment, 98–99
    Theater for the New City, 97
    and World War I, 70
Theweleit, Klaus, 156
Thomson, Virgil, 90
Totalitarianism
    classical, 24, 202
    and hostility toward left, 26
    inverted, 23–24, 25–26, 196, 202
    movements, 13, 24
Tracy, David, 166
Treasury, U.S., 6, 8, 12, 18, 25
Trotsky, Leon, 83, 110
Trotter, Wilfred, 61
Truman, Harry, 16, 167
Trump, Donald, 16
Truth, Sojourner, 120
Tuchman, Barbara, 152
Twain, Mark, 139
Twight, Charlotte, 25

Ulmer, Gregory, 124
Unemployment

and Bell, 1–2, 4, 5, 6
in China, 30, 31
and hypermasculinity, 156
insurance taxes, 187
and liberals, 188–190
long-term, 181
in 1930s, 35
and Obama, 12
and permanent underclass, 201
real rate of, 189
and right-wing backlash, 189, 190
Union of American Hebrew
    Congregations, 22
Unions, labor, 139
    and blacklisting, 103, 104, 107
    and Catholic Worker, 159
    and class struggle, 139
    communist, 195
    and corporations, 10, 14
    and democracy and rights of
        workers, 191
    and dignity and hope, 140
    dismantling of, 201
    and FedEx and UPS, 190–191
    as junior partners of capitalist class,
        11, 107
    and leaders' salaries, 10
    and liberal class, 103, 107
    and National Labor Relations Act,
        108
    and 1960s, 109–110
    and 1930s, 35
    percent of American workers in, 108
    public-sector, 14
    and radical leaders, 15, 108
    and Taft-Hartley Act, 108, 191
    and utopia and progress, 84, 85, 86
    and World War I, 76, 77
United Automobile Workers, 109–110
United Mine Workers, 87
United Nations (U.N.), 45, 127, 148, 183
Universities, 23, 139
    and anticommunism, 153
    and Berrigan, 162
    and children of immigrants, 140
    and collegiality, conformity, and
        tenure, 126, 143
    and common good, 139

and corporate power, 11, 14, 176
and critical thinking and
    independence of mind, 11, 122
and Finkelstein, 152
and liberal class, 103
and multiculturalism, 124
and philanthropy, 113
and poststructuralism, 124–125
and resistance, 207
and specialization, 115–116, 126
and tax-exemption and money, 10, 11
UPS, 187
U.S. Conference of Catholic Bishops, 22

Van Agtmael, Peter, 54–55, 58
Van Itallie, Jean-Claude, 97
Vietnam War, 36, 37–38, 39, 57, 99, 145,
    167, 169
    and protest, 89, 97, 109–110, 111, 120,
        123, 146, 160, 169, 187, 188
Violence, 9, 17, 22, 23, 55, 155, 156, 168, 187,
    197–198, 205

Wall Street
    bailouts, 175, 188
    and Bell, 2
    and communists, 15
    manipulation and dishonesty on, 156
    and Obama, 27
    and World War I, 64, 69, 76
Wallace, Graham, 61–62
Wallace, Henry, 103, 104, 107
Walling, William English, 63, 67
Walzer, Michael, 38
War
    brutal and savage reality of, 39–40,
        44, 54–58
    and liberal class, 183
    veterans, 28, 53, 56–57
    See also Afghanistan war; Iraq war;
        Permanent war; World War I;
        World War II
Warhol, Andy, 114
Warren, Earl, 171
Watergate, 169
Weather Underground, 110
Weavers, 105
Weber, Max, 101

Weisman, Fred, 116
Welfare, 12, 15, 201
Welles, Orson, 90, 91, 92, 93
Wellstone, Paul, 41
West Bank, 148, 150
White, Edward Douglas, 60
Whyte, William H., 125
Wicker, Ireene, 104
Wieseltier, Leon, 38
WikiLeaks, 43
Wilson, Woodrow, 59–61, 65, 66, 67,
    68–69, 70, 72, 74, 75, 76, 102
Winfrey, Oprah, 11, 200
Wolin, Sheldon, 14, 23–24, 25–26, 200
Women's rights and equality, 7, 102, 148,
    164
Woods, Tiger, 26
Works Progress Administration (WPA),
    90, 92, 96
World War I, 19, 75, 85, 89, 93, 100, 101,
    102, 141, 156
    and conscription, 74, 76
    and crumbling of antiwar
        movement, 63–64, 65, 78–79
    declaration of war, 59–61, 64, 87, 91
    end and aftermath of, 80–81, 87, 88
    and end of liberal era, 7
    and end of progressivism, 65–66
    and industrial warfare, 61, 62, 87
    and intellectuals, 59, 62, 63, 64–65,
        66–67
    and mass culture, 7, 62, 82
    and mass propaganda, 7, 61–63, 65,
        66, 67, 68–74, 76–78, 80, 81
    and nationalism, 64, 68, 79–80
    and repression of dissent, 65, 68,
        78–79, 80
World War II, 7, 16, 40, 75, 79, 84, 114, 141,
    166
Wright, Ann, 41
Wright, Ronald, 202–203

Yemen, 28, 41
YouTube, 209, 210
Yugoslavia, 13, 20, 127

Zuspann, Gary, 56
Zwally, Jay, 203